JAM BANDS

JAM BANDS

North America's
hottest live groups
PLUS how to tape and
trade their shows

DEAN BUDNICK

ECW PRESS

The publication of this book has been generously supported by the Government of Canada through the Book Publishing Industry Development Program.

CANADIAN CATALOGUING IN PUBLICATION DATA

Budnick, Dean
Jam bands: North America's hottest live groups
plus how to tape and trade their shows

ISBN 1-55022-353-4

1. Rock groups — United States. 2. Rock groups — Canada.
3. Sound — Recordings and reproducing — Amateurs' manuals.
I. Title.

ML395.B927 1998   781.66'092'27   C98-931411-1

Cover design by Guylaine Régimbald.

Design and imaging by ECW Type & Art, Oakville, Ontario.
Printed and bound by Imprimerie Interglobe, Beauceville, Québec.

Distributed in Canada by General Distribution Services,
325 Humber College Blvd., Etobicoke, Ontario M9W 7C3.

Distributed in the United States by Login Publishers Consortium,
1436 West Randolph Street, Chicago, Illinois, U.S.A. 60607.

Distributed in the United Kingdom by Turnaround Publisher Services,
Unit 3 Olympia Trading Estate, Coburg Road, Wood Green, London N2Z 6TZ.

Published by ECW PRESS,
2120 Queen Street East, Suite 200,
Toronto, Ontario M4E 1E2.

www.ecw.ca/press

PRINTED AND BOUND IN CANADA

CONTENTS

ACKNOWLEDGMENTS

As one might imagine, there are hundreds of people who contributed enormously to this project: band members, managers, record companies, fans, and numerous observers of the scene. I wish to offer them all my profuse thanks. I would also like to single out the helpful, friendly people at ECW Press who helped *Jam Bands* come to fruition: Robert Lecker, Holly Potter, Guylaine Régimbald, and Mary Williams. I am grateful, as well, for the assistance and support of my family: Alfred Budnick, Janet Budnick, Stacy Budnick (check out her handiwork at www.jambands.com), Ida Budnick, other Budnicks, and, of course, the ever-affable Leanne Barrett. Having said all that, for sundry reasons I particularly lift my coffee mug in gratitude to Randy Alexander, Sam Ankerson, Larry Bloch, Chris Brewer, Toni Brown, Roy Carter, Lynn Cingari, Darren Cohen, Lee Crumpton, Jenny Davis, Jon Dindas, Charlie Dirksen, DNA, Walter Durkacz, John Dwork, Benjy Eisen, J. Tayloe Emery, Brett Fairbrother, Peter Ferioli, Jakob Field, Curt Foehl, Canyon Foot, Andy Gadiel, Pete Gershon, Ellis Goddard, Jacob Gold, Jake Gold, Sarah Gowan, Michele Gross, Andrew Haan, Paul Hagen, Ken Hays, Jorge Hernandez, Rob "Gumby" Hillard, Sara Kelly Jones, Carrie Lombardi, John Lynskey, Neil Mandel, Lynne McGee, Zane Nashed, Brad Navin, Allen Ostroy, Paul Parietti, Chris Patras, Lisette Rioux, David Saslavsky, Doron Segal, Pete Shapiro, David Shulman, Pete Sienkiewicz, Manny Sinnegan, Thomas Smith, Andrew Stahl, Jake Szufarowski, Ben Tanen, Jon Topper, Howard Turkenkopf, Rob Turner, Joe Urtz, John Wanzung, Kirk West, Carol Wade, Jeff Waful, Andrew Wagner, Jim Walsh, Rebecca Yudenfreund, Chris Zahn, Jon Zazula, Marsha Zazula, and Gina Z.

INTRODUCTION

JAMBOREE

Something is in the air. I've been enjoying live improvisational music for many years now, but it seems that today, more than at any other time I can recall, we are awash in accomplished bands incorporating a range of genres and unified by a commitment to improvisation. Jon Zazula (impresario of Crazed Management who guides Disco Biscuits, Juggling Suns, and Ominous Sea-pods with his wife and partner, Marsha), has described it to me as a New Renaissance, and I think he's right. What's more, I can see by the swelling audiences at many of these shows that people are eager to experience this music. Nowadays, individuals are drawn to those bands that vest every performance with vigor and creativity, that are not merely playing the same songs note for note night after night. These groups are stretching, allowing their inspiration to lead them into some fascinating realms. All of the bands collected in this book have the courage and artistry to do this, and there are plenty of them out there for you to discover and enjoy.

The impetus for this book was supplied by the jazz and blues encyclopedias that line my bookshelves. Over the years, I've acquired a large but in many cases sketchy knowledge of many notable jazz and blues performers. So, when one of these artists comes to town or when someone recommends a particular recording to me, I'll often consult one of my books in order to learn a little more about the performer in question. Similarly, I had come to realize that there were many jam bands whose names I recognized without knowing much more about them. So I wrote this book to fill my own need — and, I hope, yours as well. My aim was to provide a resource: when a group comes through your town or someone mentions a band, you can pick up this book and enlighten yourself. If one of the jam bands listed is playing near you, I hope you'll decide to check it out, as I believe that every band I've included is well worth seeing; that's why they're here. Still, of course, everyone has his or her own taste.

I have to confess that an additional goal I had in putting this book together was to spread the good word about bands that you may not know (and that may not be heading to your local venues — at least not yet). There are a number of captivating groups out there that just tear it up night after night but are not yet national names. Also, go out and support your local heroes to keep their momentum building. Ensure that they keep playing so that we will all be able to enjoy them for years to come.

Each entry in this book introduces you to a different band. I have tried to evoke their aims and accomplishments in a few paragraphs. In almost every case, I have highlighted their most recent recordings to give you a better idea of their artistry and intent. I hope that the web information I have provided will allow you to acquaint yourself further with many of these groups.

The appendices are intended to complement your experience and provide a more expansive overview of recent developments. Appendix A, "How to Tape and Trade Live Shows," will be most helpful to those of you who do not yet have a massive tape collection or are debating whether to purchase your first portable deck and mikes. Appendix B, "Wetlands: Ten Years of Grooves," will introduce some readers to a unique and wonderful venue and will serve to enhance the memories of other readers. The information in Appendix C, "Additional Resources: Magazines and Music," tips you to organizations, publications, and other resources devoted to the thriving jam-band scene. Finally, Appendix D, "Zero Degrees of Separation," outlines a game that I hope will entertain you while you're riding to a show or during a set break.

All in all, I hope my efforts lead you to appreciate the many wonderful bands that are currently performing across the country on a daily basis. Purchase their recordings, collect their tapes, but above all go out and see them play live. Join in the jamboree (and please feel free to contact me via the Web site www.jambands.com).

AGENT PORRIDGE

- **BRIAN BISKY:** *piano, keyboards, vocals*
- **BRIAN CHAPADOS:** *tenor saxophone*
- **MIKE GOEBEL:** *bass*
- **SAM MARTINA:** *alto saxophone, vocals*
- **BRETT ROTHENHAUS:** *drums*
- **ALEX WEINSTEIN:** *guitar, banjo, vocals*

Agent Porridge may be the quintessential American band in that the group's music is an amalgamation of the country's indigenous musical forms, from jazz and funk to bluegrass. The group formed at the State University of New York's Fredonia campus in 1995, and the only thing more diverse than its members' musical tastes may be their academic majors: these range from English education to speech pathology to recombinant-gene technology. Speaking about the band's musical eclecticism, guitarist Alex Weinstein (the lone music major) states: "We've followed the examples of the bands out there that we're really into, and we've tried to cover as much ground as we can."

The members of Agent Porridge believe that the group's live performances, which draw on so many genres, achieve unity through a collective enthusiasm. Weinstein adds, "we try to put a ton of energy into it, we try to have fun with the crowd. As we've been growing, though, we've turned more to the funk side of things. The horns are very Maceo Parker influenced." When asked how the horn players occupy themselves when they are not being utilized in a particular song, Weinstein answers, "Well they certainly don't dance. Actually, one of them [Sam Martina] sings, and the other [Brian Chapados] does some freestyle rapping when we give him the nod."

Another of the band's strengths is its core of capable songwriters. Although keyboardist Brian Bisky composed the bulk of the songs on Agent Porridge's first release, other band members also contribute.

Weinstein notes, "the rule is that once you bring an idea to the band it becomes a communal thing." This last phrase seems to capture the spirit of Agent Porridge, which is starting to build a following of devoted listeners who anticipate that the group will provide music, energy, and humor for some time to come.

DISCOGRAPHY

The Territory Shall Be the Universe (1997). This release presents the band's diverse offerings. Within the first cut, "Push Me Over," jangly guitar gives way to an unexpected, funky horn break. "Where You Are," the bluegrass number that follows, tiptoes a fascinating line between enthusiasm and caricature (Weinstein's brief turn on the jawharp, Snoopy's instrument of choice in *Snoopy, Come Home*, enhances the mystery). "Broadway Joe," which comes up next, is an extended instrumental that veers off to explore new sonic avenues in a manner similar to the elaborate orchestrations of Trey Anastasio. Moreover, "Detune" evokes images of chanting monks who have been offered some swinging sax assistance, while a steady reggae backbeat defines "Ziggy." Finally, with its lively cover of James Brown's "Pass the Peas," the band demonstrates yet another affinity.

WEB SITE

www.watchtowerent.com\agentporridge

AGENTS OF GOOD ROOTS

- **BRIAN JONES:** *drums, vocals*
- **J.C. KUHL:** *saxophone*
- **STEWART MYERS:** *bass, vocals*
- **ANDREW WINN:** *guitar, vocals*

Richmond, Virginia's, Agents of Good Roots is a band that seeks to craft strong compositions yet chooses to transform these creations in the live setting. The quartet will often use its well-designed songs as a starting point for some agile improvisation.

For instance, J.C. Kuhl might interject a vivid saxophone soliloquy. Andrew Winn may then counter with a guitar solo that reflects his classical training. Meanwhile, bassist Stewart Myers and drummer Brian Jones will lock in on their own animated grooves.

The band has honed its performance skills through an intensive touring schedule. Beginning as a trio — guitar, bass, and drums — Agents of Good Roots first performed at an open-mike night in the fall of 1992, garnering immediate recognition for its engaging songs and Winn's distinctive, gruff vocals (the product of an operation to rebuild his larynx after a skiing accident rendered him speechless for a few months). Three years later, the band decided to draw in a saxophone player, working with a few before inviting Kuhl to join. Myers recalls, "We were excited by what J.C. offered. He added a heavy jazz element, along with his strong musical sense and ability." The band was soon averaging more than two hundred dates a year.

As a result, Agents of Good Roots has emerged at the fore of a new generation of jam bands. Nonetheless, Myers expresses some discomfort with the appellation: "I'm not altogether comfortable with the term 'jam band,' because we're definitely song-oriented. There is a stigma that a jam band can't write a song and that's why they rely so heavily on jamming. Then again, when you see us live, we definitely expand on things and really take it to another level. In part, I think, that's why things are starting to build. We are really starting to crank."

DISCOGRAPHY

Where'd You Get That Vibe? (1996)

Straightaround (1997)

One by One (1998). Agents of Good Roots cuts a wide swath on this release. "Come On" is an edgier offering with some gutsy guitar riffs. "Upspin" seems at the outset to be an entrancing shuffle but soon transforms into a vibrant slice of soul, abetted by strident background vocals. "Miss Misbelieving" introduces some country twang. "Smiling Up the Frown" is mellow, jazzier fare enriched by Winn's piano and Kuhl's saxophone accents. Finally, "Time Bomb" is an aptly titled fulmination.

WEB SITE

www.agentsofgoodroots.com

ALLMAN BROTHERS BAND

- **GREGG ALLMAN:** *vocals, organ, and piano*
- **DICKEY BETTS:** *vocals, electric and acoustic guitar*
- **OTEIL BURBRIDGE:** *bass*
- **JAIMOE JOHNSON:** *drums and percussion*
- **JACK PEARSON:** *electric and acoustic guitar*
- **BUTCH TRUCKS:** *drums and percussion*
- **MARC QUINONES:** *percussion*

The Allman Brothers Band remains one of the most riveting groups committed to the live-concert experience. The band crafts a sound that has been road tested for over twenty-five years while remaining fresh, free, and engrossed in the moment. At times, the band's guitars may command attention, whether it be Dickey Betts's passionate phrasings, Jack Pearson's stinging slide, or their rousing twin leads. On other occasions, the absorbing, soulful vocals of Gregg Allman hold sway. The bass lines of barefooted Oteil Burbridge prove by turns both rock steady and harmonically inventive. Situated above these players on the stage is the trio that fashions a spellbinding percussive collage comprised of Butch Trucks's thunderous drive, Jaimoe Johnson's crackling counterpoints, and Marc Quinones's lucid flurry. There's a lot happening here.

The band's origins can be traced back to Daytona Beach, Florida, in the early 1960s. It was there that Gregg Allman bought his first guitar, which was soon appropriated and eventually mastered by his older brother, Duane. The pair formed a number of bands while Gregg attended high school, and after his graduation they took one such outfit on the road under the name Allman Joys. Although that group soon disbanded, in 1967 the duo traveled to Los Angeles, where they formed a new band, Hour Glass, and began to record. Although this group broke up too, perhaps the most notable aspect of the Allmans West Coast tenure was that Duane committed himself to the slide guitar. In fact, he taught himself the art while in bed with a cold – he would stroke the guitar with a glass Coricidin container, which soon became the trademark of his bottleneck playing.

Duane returned home a year later and was invited to Muscle Shoals, Alabama, to participate in a Wilson Pickett session. The young guitarist quickly distinguished himself. While there, he met drummer Jaimoe Johnson, who had backed such luminaries as Otis Redding. Duane also befriended members of the band Second Coming and started to sit in with them. That group featured bass player Berry Oakley and a guitarist named Dickey Betts (the band also included Larry Reinhardt, who would later play with Iron Butterfly). Anxious to form a new group of his own, Duane recruited his pal Butch Trucks (who had met the Allmans while in Jacksonville with his band the Bitter Ind). Finally, Duane encouraged Gregg to return from Los Angeles, and the Allman Brothers Band was born.

This lineup accomplished more over the next two and a half years than many have done in five times that amount of time. After a number of intensive practice sessions, the elder Allman and Betts began to develop their signature dual leads. Meanwhile, Johnson and Trucks began to craft their own complementary styles. Oakley's bass supplied crisp yet lively polyphony. Above all, the band wrote songs that have become standards, which the group continues to reconsider today with ferocity and vitality: "Whipping Post," "Dreams," "In Memory of Elizabeth Reed," "Midnight Rider," and "Blue Sky" all emerged from this fruitful era. The Allman Brothers Band swiftly distinguished itself by performing more than five hundred epic live shows that explored its originals along with a selection of blues classics.

However, twin tragedies soon struck the band. In October of 1971, Duane died following a motorcycle crash. He was twenty-four. A little more than a year later, Oakley also passed away when his cycle crashed into a bus. The band eventually regrouped, drafting able bassist Lamar Williams and keyboardist Chuck Leavell (who would later perform with Sea Level, Eric Clapton, and the Rolling Stones). In the wake of these losses, the band still managed to produce such noteworthy songs as "Rambling Man," "Melissa," "Jessica," and "Southbound." The group's popularity escalated, and in the summer of 1973 the band performed two memorable shows with the Grateful Dead, including one at Watkins Glen, New York, that drew more than half a million people. By the end of the decade, feeling burnt out, the band dissolved.

In 1989, however, it reformed with a roster of musicians that would remain intact for more than eight years. Warren Haynes came aboard to challenge Betts with his own muscular turns on guitar. Allen Woody added his thunderous bass. The group was further invigorated by the arrival of percussionist Marc Quinones. As the band gelled, so did its songwriting: to the Allman Brothers Band canon were added "End of the Line," "True Gravity," "No One to Run With," "Back Where It All Begins," and "Seven Turns." The latter two songs describe the events of early 1997, when Haynes and Woody left to put their energies into the band Gov't Mule, leading the Brothers to invite Pearson and Burbridge into the fold. The resulting tours have affirmed the vitality of this new incarnation. The circle remains.

SELECTED DISCOGRAPHY

The Allman Brothers Band (1969)

Idlewild South (1970)

The Allman Brothers at Fillmore East (1971)

Eat a Peach (1972)

Brothers and Sisters (1973)

Dreams (1989). This four-CD set with accompanying booklet includes demos, live cuts, and classic tracks that collectively sum up much of the band's prehistory and first twenty years.

Seven Turns (1990)

Shades of Two Worlds (1991)

An Evening with the Allman Brothers Band (1992)

Where It All Begins (1994). Old friend and longtime producer Tom Dowd was behind the board for this release, which many feel ranks as one of the band's classic albums. The standout track may be Betts's soaring composition "Back Where It All Begins." Other notable songs include "No One to Run With," which has a Bo Diddley feel, Haynes's powerful "Soulshine," and the slide-friendly "Sailin' 'Cross the Devils' Sea," which future Brother Jack Pearson helped to compose.

Second Set (1995)

Fillmore East February 1970 (1997). This is a companion piece to the classic *At Fillmore East*, which was recorded a year later. Offerings include an inchoate "In Memory of Elizabeth Reed," "Hootchie Cootchie Man" (which features Oakley's strong vocals), a stinging "Statesboro Blues," an earlier, gripping arrangement of

"Mountain Jam," and a stellar version of Ray Charles's "Outskirts of Town."

Mycology: An Anthology (1998)

AQUARIUM RESCUE UNIT

- **KOFI BURBRIDGE:** *flute, keyboards*
- **OTEIL BURBRIDGE:** *bass, vocals*
- **PAUL HENSON:** *vocals*
- **JIMMY HERRING:** *guitar*
- **LEE VENTERS:** *drums and percussion*

Ever since Aquarium Rescue Unit emerged from a series of 1990 Georgia jam sessions, the band has boasted an all-star roster of players. Original guiding force Colonel Bruce Hampton has taken his chazoid and poetry on to Fiji Mariners (but don't miss his appearance in the film *Sling Blade*, and in *Getting It On*, for that matter). Oteil Burbridge is currently slinging his six-string bass in both ARU and the Allman Brothers Band — actually, one measure of his talent is that he switches to picking a four string with the Allman Brothers Band (in the movie realm, don't overlook Burbridge's performance with Peter Sellers in *Being There*). Jimmy Herring has tantalized audiences with his ferocious guitar as a member of Frogwings and Jazz Is Dead; he has also taken the stage with a number of bands, including the Allman Brothers Band and Phish. Former band member the seemingly six-armed Apt. Q258 (a.k.a. Jeff Sipe) recently performed some surreal gigs with Jonas Hellborg and appears these days with Leftover

Salmon. Matt Mundy has moved on to lend his estimable mandolin talents to a number of performers, including Bela Fleck. Multi-instrumentalist Kofi Burbridge joined ARU after stints with Stevie Wonder and Whitney Houston. The band's present membership is completed by Paul Henson, who lends his soulful, rough-hewn vocals to the mix.

The original incarnation of the group, with front man Hampton, offered a southern musical fricassee heavily seasoned with spontaneity and a twisted sense of humor. The group found itself with a legion of devoted listeners that included numerous fellow musicians. In 1992, Aquarium Rescue Unit was one of six bands to appear on the original HORDE tour (along with Blues Traveler, Bela Fleck and the Flecktones, Phish, Spin Doctors, and Widespread Panic). One of that tour's standout moments was the transition from ARU's set to Widespread Panic's slot, which occurred in mid-musical stream: Widespread Panic's players slowly wandered onstage to jam with ARU's musicians, who gradually departed.

The members of Aquarium Rescue Unit had to make a difficult decision in the spring of 1994. The rigors of touring had led Bruce Hampton to quit the group less than a year after Mundy had left. The remaining members finally reached a decision: they would keep playing together. Oteil Burbridge recalls, "We didn't try to repeat what we had with Bruce because it would have been too contrived. It didn't happen that way in the first place. It was always just a motley crew: me and Matt and Jimmy and Sipe and Bruce — that was it. No one could pull that together but Bruce. Everything with Bruce happens out of it happening. It's all spontaneous." Initially, Burbridge stepped in for Hampton, performing double duty on bass and vocals. Eventually, however, the band brought in Henson, a fan of long standing whose deep, rich vocal tones belie his years. The band also expanded its instrumentation by recruiting Kofi Burbridge, Oteil's older brother, to play both flute and keyboards. Oteil notes that this changed the band's sound: "It probably came out a lot funkier because of Kofi. I was dying for that anyway because I thought we do jazz, blues, bluegrass, Latin, rock. We had one funky tune, which was 'Working on a Building,' and that was it. I really felt that to be covering all this ground we needed to be hitting some more hard-core funk, because that really was a place I was coming from growing up. So when Kofi got in, we definitely hopped on that. Now, it's practically a funk band, but it's still got elements of jazz and rock and Latin. Not as much bluegrass because without a banjo or a mandolin it's just pointless."

The band remains committed to its musical legacy. Recently, it has scaled back its dates because its members are involved in other projects. Nonetheless, Aquarium Rescue Unit remains an ongoing entity comprised of five technically gifted players who are always ready to emerge and share their spellbinding mosaic of sound.

DISCOGRAPHY

Col. Bruce Hampton and the Aquarium Rescue Unit (1992)

Mirrors of Embarrassment (1993)

In a Perfect World (1994). The level of musicianship is quite high on this disc. Apt. Q258 lends zest throughout. Oteil Burbridge is also creative and compelling, particularly on songs such as "Stand Up People" and the jazzy instrumental "Plain or Peanut." Guitarist Herring distinguishes himself on a number of tunes, including "Search Yourself" and "Satisfaction Guaranteed." Henson's gruff vocals are consistently solid but particularly rise to the fore on the smoky "Turn It On." The funky tones of "How Tight's Yer Drawers" are notable not merely for Herring's phrasings but also for Kofi Burbridge's bluesy flute solo.

WEB SITE

www.netspace.org/aru/

BAABA SETH

- **DEREK BOND:** *bass*
- **MIKE CHANG:** *guitar, vocals, percussion*
- **HOPE CLAYBURN:** *alto and baritone saxophone, flute, vocals, percussion*
- **TIM LETT:** *trumpet, percussion*
- **DIRK LIND:** *vocals, guitar, percussion*
- **MARK MAYNARD:** *trombone, percussion*
- **JIM RALSTON:** *drums*
- **LEN WISHART:** *percussion*

Charlottesville, Virginia's, Baaba Seth describes its music as "hometown world groove." This tag is inadequate because it fails to reflect the full scope of the band's sound, which weaves elements of jazz, rock, and funk into a tapestry of African rhythms. However, this succinct description is also apt because Baaba Seth's music celebrates the diverse sounds of the globe while being very much a product of its local music scene.

Baaba Seth began in 1991 with a revolving cast of musicians kicking back on friend Kevin Lynch's porch. The results persuaded singer Dirk Lind to assemble a formal collective ("baaba" is a word that reflects the band's cross-cultural influences, as in a number of languages it designates a spiritual teacher/guru; Seth is the name of Lind's son). This initial incarnation of the group rapidly won local acclaim: for instance, it finished second in a competition at Charlottesville's Trax music club, losing out to the Dave Matthews Band while placing ahead of the Boyd Tinsley Band (Tinsley, who was playing with his own group as well as DMB, also participated in some of the original Baaba Seth porch jams). In 1995, as the band's notoriety increased and touring became a bit more rigorous, some members withdrew, leaving only Lind and percussionist Len Wishart (the recipient of formal training under master Mohammed Dacosta). The pair decided to reform the group and include horns; they ultimately recruited a number of players from the University of Virginia's jazz ensemble. This infusion of new talent contributed new tonalities and textures to the group's euphony.

Baaba Seth's marathon live performances often seem to glorify sound itself, as extended collective grooves spiral from one instrument to another. The band's percussionists (which at any given moment can include every member of the group plus guests) captivate with a range of polyrhythms. Meanwhile, Hope Clayburn bounds about, lending a playful stage presence and contributing saxophone, flute, and vocals. Lead guitarist Mike Chang adds to the tableau, at times restrained, at times dexterous and splashy. Principal songwriter Lind supplies phrasings in the tradition of such passionate vocalists as Bob Marley. The results are carrying Baaba Seth and its "African-soaked rock-jazz dance music" to new hometowns nationwide.

DISCOGRAPHY

Crazy Wheel (1997). This lively release presents the band's aims and energies rather effectively. For example, the opener, "Delhi," fuses propulsive beats, jazzy horns, and engrossing vocals. The moving "Poor Man" is enlivened by aggressive, entrancing drumming and a taste of didgeridoo. In "Troubled World," jubilant guitar answers insistent brass. Noted jazz trumpeter John D'earth appears on "When You Hear Our Song." *Crazy Wheel* also presents the sparer, primal percussive expressions "Traveler's Song" and "Joili."

WEB SITE

www.baabaseth.com

BAREFEET AND COMPANY

■ **ADAM ALEXANDER:** *drums*
■ **DENISE BRABANT:** *vocals*
■ **BENSON HARDESTY:** *cello, vocals*
■ **MATT MCGUIRE:** *guitar*
■ **RUS REPPERT:** *bass*
■ **JOSH WEIDNER:** *keyboards*

Barefeet and Company's bass player, Rus Reppert, believes that "the band sounds the way West Virginia feels." Reppert, who was raised in the state, began his relationship with Appalachian folk and bluegrass at the age of three. His comments, however, not only encompass West Virginia's indigenous music but also that state's natural, untrammeled beauty, which he thinks is evoked by the band's "free, organic grooves."

Over the past year, the group's sound has evolved. Originally, Barefeet and Company performed with two guitarists who played off each other in a manner familiar to audiences of the Allman Brothers Band. The departure of one of these players cleared room for cellist Benson Hardesty. Until that point, the group had used the cello as a rhythm instrument, comping the guitar phrases; but Hardesty, a former member of the West Virginia University Symphony Orchestra, now takes a much more active role, adding to the band's other strengths, which include Denise Brabant's powerful voice and Matt McGuire's fluid guitar. The group's songs draw on regional music, jazz, and Chicago blues. Reppert characterizes the mélange as "mountain rock."

Barefeet and Company takes particular pride in its penchant for improvisation. Drummer Adam Alexander often initiates the action by simply changing the key of a song, leading other band members to introduce ideas extracted from their personal musical influences and passions. Many of these jams are elevated by the band's sense of dynamics. Reppert observes that "it becomes a roller coaster. We take our audience on a ride that leads them from melancholy to bliss." Pianist Josh Weidner adds, "We produce some sounds that I never thought possible."

DISCOGRAPHY

In the Company of Friends (1996)

Working for the Sun (1997). Although a studio release, *Working for the Sun* effectively captures the intensity and improvisation of a live set. This recording was made by a slightly earlier incarnation of the band; it features second guitarist Chris Wilson, who placed more emphasis on the blues. Still, *Working for the Sun* offers a taste of those aspects of Barefeet and Company sound that make the group a live-concert draw. Standout tracks include the driving "Sister Serene," the rich tapestry "Left Hand Jimmy," the powerful "Nutshell," and the acoustic coda "Duska."

WEB SITE

www.imagixx.net/~action/

BEATROOTS

- ■ **MIKE BENNETT:** *percussion, vocals*
- ■ **MIRIAM BROADY:** *guitar, violin, vocals*
- ■ **BRUCE MACQUAID:** *bass*
- ■ **TOM RUSH:** *drums, vocals*
- ■ **BOWEN SWERSEY:** *guitar, flute, vocals*

Bar Harbor, Maine's, the Beatroots have spanned the globe to perform music that earns the designation "world beat." In the 1980s, Miriam Broady and Bowen Swersey met in India, where Broady was involved in a formal study of the country's music and Swersey was busking on the streets. The two traveled across Europe, Asia, and Africa together, soaking up indigenous sounds. The pair eventually married, and with the Beatroots they have formalized their musical connection as well.

In 1993, when drummer Tom Rush and bassist Bruce MacQuaid came aboard, the band began to produce original compositions in addition to songs that its members had absorbed in the course of their journeys (MacQuaid's father had been in the military, and Bruce had circled the globe as a child). Later, Mike Bennett joined the group to add percussive force to the mix. MacQuaid reveals, "We wish to take those foreign musical languages and express them in a rock fashion. I think we particularly challenge audiences in terms of our rhythms. We often move away from 4/4 timing – in many instances, we do 11/8, 7/8, and 5/4."

The Beatroots achieved additional notoriety in the summer of 1997 when Phish selected the band to perform on site at its Great Went festival. This event helped expose the group to new fans. MacQuaid remarks, "The band is only half the story. The audience energy is the other half, and these are the type of people who provide it. I'll see someone out there doing some crazy dance, and it feeds what I'm doing. Sometimes, I'll even throw in a beat for that guy, because he'll be onto something." In describing the Beatroots, he also somewhat jokingly laments, "My wife keeps telling me now that there's finally a band out here that we could show up and dance to, it turns out that I'm in it." Recently, many like-minded individuals have started to catch on, and they're coming out to dig the beat.

DISCOGRAPHY

Dig the Beat (1997). This release reveals the Beatroots's enthusiasm for the music of other cultures. The group performs a series of traditional songs from Hungary, Macedonia, Gambia, and Jamaica. Original Beatroots songs also demonstrate the pervasive influence of such sounds; this is literally manifested in "Love Song for Saint Lucia," a tune written by Swersey for a school carnival on the Caribbean island of St. Lucia and sung in Spanish.

Secret Door (1998). This recording demonstrates that the band's sound continues to evolve. While the group has not abandoned its roots (Bulgarian and Romanian folk songs are covered), it has worked up the grooves with a bit more vigor. Also, electric guitar often comes to the forefront to supplement the group's effective use of flutes, violins, and congas. The result yields such notable tracks as "Timber Jack" (which also includes some pleasing vocal harmonies), "Human Condition," and "A Person Is."

WEB SITE

www.beatroots.com

BIG HEAD TODD AND THE MONSTERS

- **TODD PARK MOHR:** *guitar, vocals*
- **BRIAN NEVIN:** *drums*
- **ROB SQUIRES:** *bass*

Big Head Todd and the Monsters's distinctive blend of blues, soul, and rock has been road tested since 1986. It was in that year that Colorado College student Todd Park Mohr joined forces with two students of the University of Colorado, Boulder – Brian Nevin and Rob Squires – to form a band. Over the ensuing years, the group has crisscrossed the United States to perform more than 1,500 live dates. Before they were forced to retire their van, the creaking "Colonel," the trio logged more than 400,000 miles in it. The group slowly expanded its ambit, eventually exposing its music to many new listeners through its participation in the 1993 HORDE. It has maintained a steady tour docket that has included a notable 1995 coheadlining bill with the Dave Matthews Band. The trio has been able to remain tightly knit through all of this because Mohr, Nevin, and Squires were high school friends long before they became a musical group.

The group's sound represents a union of styles. For instance, the name Big Head Todd pays homage to blues legend Eddie "Clean Head" Vinson, a stellar vocalist and saxophone player. However, the band also incorporates elements of rhythm and blues and even country – during early gigs, the trio would often juxtapose a Johnny Cash cover with an offering from Sly and the Family Stone. Mohr's compositions are often vivid, melodic portraits of relationships; one interesting twist is offered on *Strategem*, where many of Mohr's verses are attempts at Buddhist koans. All of these songs are elevated and enhanced during the band's dynamic live shows. In particular, Mohr's quicksilver guitar exclamations often excite listeners. Yet many fans are also drawn to his more measured tones and his emotive vocals. Nevin's exuberant drumming supplies an additional charge, and Squires holds things together with his incisive basslines. In short, the trio's vitality and its stalwart execution fuel its reputation as an outstanding live band.

DISCOGRAPHY

Another Mayberry (1989)

Midnight Radio (1990). This disc was originally released on the band's own Big Records label and remains a favorite of many. All of the tracks are drawn from live performances and are presented without overdubs. Although many songs are taken from club gigs, some, such as the six-minute version of "Bittersweet" (which later appeared on *Sister Sweetly*), were recorded in the group's basement. The band's vivid, galvanic concert presentation (albeit at an earlier stage of its career) is well represented on this offering.

Sister Sweetly (1993)

Strategem (1994)

Beautiful World (1997). Former Talking Heads guitarist Jerry Harrison produced this release, which effectively expands on the trio's sound without diluting its essence. For instance, the title track brings in P-Funk alumnus Bernie Worrell and some backup vocalists for a funky foray. "Caroline" introduces a violin as an atmospheric counterpoint to some crunching guitar work from Mohr. Other notable songs include "Resignation Superman," the soulful, grooving "If You Can't Slow Down" (featuring a strong vocal turn by Hazel Miller), and the driving older offering "True Lady." An added treat is the voice of John Lee Hooker as the band tears through his classic 1962 boogie "Boom Boom."

WEB SITE

www.bigheadtodd.com

BIG SUGAR

- **PAUL BRENNAN:** *drums*
- **KELLY HOPPE:** *saxophone, harmonica*
- **GORDIE JOHNSON:** *acoustic and electric guitar*
- **GARRY LOWE:** *bass*

Toronto's Big Sugar creates a correspondingly big sound out of multiple music genres. The seeds of the group took root in Windsor, Ontario, when harmonica player Kelly Hoppe met bass player Gordie Johnson and persuaded him to play guitar in his blues band, the Windsor Dukes. Hoppe gave Johnson a blues primer, starting him out with Freddie King's instrumental releases, moving next to John Lee Hooker, and then on through the pantheon. Johnson, who had grown up with a particular taste for the sounds of AC/DC and Kiss, nonetheless proved a quick study, adeptly acquiring a blues vocabulary.

Johnson gigged with the Dukes for a number of years before moving on to Toronto. There he formed his own group after spending some time in the Pine Trio, a backing band for a range of jazz, blues, and even country artists. Johnson carried elements of these forms into his new outfit, along with an affection for harder music. Big Sugar's distinctive sound really emerged, however, when Johnson asked Canada's renowned reggae bass player Garry Lowe to join. The group was completed when Johnson expanded his guitar/drums/bass trio into a foursome by adding his old friend Hoppe on saxophone and harmonica.

The disparate influences and styles of Big Sugar's players yield uncommon results. For instance, while in concert Johnson will often come out blasting (at times in a manner reminiscent of Jimmy Page), he is anchored by Lowe's steady reggae tones. Hoppe lends his own stylings. Big Sugar has been characterized as a blues band, but this misses the mark: few blues bands incorporate fuzztone guitars, dub breaks, and reggae riffs. These elements also yield some intriguing improvisations during Big Sugar's live shows, many of which approach three hours in length.

DISCOGRAPHY

Big Sugar (1992)
El Seven Niteclub Featuring Big Sugar (1994)
500 Pounds (1994)
Dear M.F. (1995)
Hemi-Vision (1996). Big Sugar's musical tableaux are well represented here. Johnson crunches throughout the opener, "Diggin' a Hole."

"Joe Louis/ Judgement Day" layers some spacier arrangements onto Lowe's prominent reggae bass. A nod to the Mississippi Delta is delivered with the porch blues "Tired All the Time." The disc closes with "Tobacco Hand," nine minutes of entrancing textures enriched by Ashley MacIsaac's fiddle.

WEB SITE

www.citw.com/bigsugar/

THE BIG WU

- **CHRIS CASTINO:** *guitar, vocals*
- **JASON FLADAGER:** *guitar, vocals*
- **ANDY MILLER:** *bass*
- **AL OIKARI:** *keyboards*
- **TERRY VANDEWALKER:** *drums, percussion, vocals*

The Big Wu is rapidly defining itself as a Twin Cities institution. Since 1996, whenever the band is in town, it performs regular Wednesday-night gigs at Minneapolis nightclub the Cabooze. The band's loyal fan base turns out week after week to hear the group work through two sets of material, pleased to take in its original tunes but especially anticipating its massive, exploratory jams.

The group formed in 1991 in Northfield, Minnesota, where guitarist Chris Castino, guitarist Jason Fladager, and drummer Terry VanDewalker were attending St. Olaf College. Bassist Andy Miller joined them a few years later (in 1992, the callow Miller ran for mayor of Northfield and took thirteen percent of the vote). Local keyboardist Al Oikari, who'd gained experience playing with a number of other local bands, completed the lineup when he joined the Big Wu in 1996.

The Big Wu truly enjoys interpreting its music before a live audience. The band's release *Tracking Buffalo through the Bathtub* contains the credit "All songs written (and rewritten every show) by the Big Wu." The group thrives on this reinvention, which guitarist Castino insists "is the beauty of our Cabooze gigs." He also notes, "The people there hear us week after week, so they keep us on our toes. They don't want to hear us play the same show any more than we do." The band constantly reconfigures its original tunes through improvisation, and it is particularly gifted at creating focused yet impromptu segues — occasionally, these will drift into one of its potent Grateful Dead covers. Although Castino writes many of the Big Wu's songs, the band's harmony-rich compositions are ultimately created collectively, both within the band and through audience response. Once again, Castino emphasizes the role of fans: "We bring our new song arrangements to them, and they offer criticism; we trust them because they're really in touch with our music. Usually, over a number of weeks, they're able to watch us bring songs to fruition."

The band's name is taken from the 1990 Tom Hanks film *Joe versus the Volcano* — the volcano in question was called the Big Wu. The choice proves apt: when the group is onstage working through a twenty-minute version of "Red Sky," explosive adjectives come to mind.

DISCOGRAPHY

Tracking Buffalo through the Bathtub (1997). The songs that serve as bookends for this release demonstrate two sides of the Big Wu. "Silkanturnitova" kicks things off in a funky vein, yielding a chorus that is a catchy mouthful. By contrast, "Red Sky" is a nine-minute opus powered by Fladager's guitar leads and VanDewalker's energetic drumming, concluding with some inviting vocal harmonies. "Bloodhound" demonstrates the lively bluegrass side of the Big Wu, while the epic "Take the World by Storm" is a Big Wu original that mirrors the composition-style, vocal intonations and guitar tonalities of early-1970s Jerry Garcia (with a hint of Bob Weir). An interesting effort.

WEB SITE

www.thebigwu.com

BLACK CROWES

- **STEVE GORMAN:** *drums*
- **EDDIE HARSCH:** *keyboards*
- **SVEN PIPIEN:** *bass*
- **CHRIS ROBINSON:** *vocals, harmonica*
- **RICH ROBINSON:** *guitar*

Chris and Rich Robinson grew up in a musical household. Their father, Stan, was a performer in the 1950s and early 1960s; he once appeared on *Dick Clark's American Bandstand*, and his song "Boom-a-Dip-Dip" climbed the 1959 Billboard charts. So it should not have surprised anyone that the brothers were eager to start their own musical group. They first did so, as teenagers, in 1984, forming the loose Mr. Crowe's Garden, which began gigging in the Atlanta area. By 1988, the project had evolved into a committed band that toured up and down the East Coast performing original music influenced by the rock and soul of the 1960s and early 1970s. At about this time, the group's moniker mutated, and Mr. Crowe's Garden became the Black Crowes.

The group quickly earned renown for the intensity of its live shows. Chris Robinson, the point man, frantically exercises his agile vocal chords while executing an array of equally lithe physical movements. His bandmates feed him with a steady supply of rhythm that often trails into dank, psychedelic realms. However, the group has also demonstrated its ability to craft some memorable melodies, as evidenced by songs such as "She Talks to Angels," "Twice as Hard," "Remedy," "Sting Me," and "She Gave Good Sunflower." Invited to join the 1994 and 1995 HORDE tours, the group has also been welcomed to the stage by the Allman Brothers Band for some notable versions of "Southbound." The Black Crowes opened for the Grateful Dead during the summer of 1995. Due to its positive reception on the latter occasion, the group headlined the 1997 Further Festival, where it delivered some spirited sets (even though, if truth be told, some older Dead Heads found them a tad loud) and remained on stage for most of the climactic intraband jams that concluded the shows.

The group has further distinguished itself by maintaining a strong relationship with its fan base. During the fall of 1994, it premiered new material at a number of small venues under a series of pseud-onyms, tipping off its supporters in advance to these appellations, which included Blessed Chloroform and the OD Jubilee Band. Further evidence of the band's kind spirit is the fact that it performed a benefit for the victims of the Oklahoma City Bombing. Finally, the Black Crowes has helped to foster a fan-band liaison organization that supplies newsletters, musical gifts from the group, mail-order ticket-ing, and a tape-trading network.

DISCOGRAPHY

Shake Your Money Maker (1990)

Southern Harmony and Musical Companion (1992)

Amorica (1994)

Three Snakes and One Charm (1996). The Crowes are joined by several guests on this eclectic release. Such tracks as "Good Friday" and "Blackberry" testify to the group's piquant southern soul. The Dirty Dozen horn players appear to add some kick to "Let Me Share the Ride." Parliament vocalists Gary "Mudbone" Cooper and Gary Shider join Robinson for the funky "(Only) Half-way to Everywhere," which recalls Sly and the Family Stone. The disc closes with the psychedelic-flavored "Evil Eye."

By Your Side (1998)

WEB SITE

www.tallest.com

BLEW WILLIE

- ■ **RYAN CHESIRE:** *percussion*
- ■ **DUSTIN HENDERSON:** *guitar, vocals*
- ■ **KEN KELLNER:** *bass*
- ■ **DYLAN MCINTOSH:** *drums*
- ■ **JOSH MCINTOSH:** *vocals, guitar*
- ■ **DAVID RICE:** *percussion, mandolin, vocals*

San Francisco sextet Blew Willie produces exuberant, extended acoustic jams. The band's starting point is its catalog of concise, original songs, which are rooted in the folk tradition and often provide biting social commentary. However, when the group performs these compositions live, the synergy of the band and the ingenuity of its players keep the music aloft. Evidence of the compelling nature of the results is the fact that Blew Willie's "Rainwalk" will be presented in its seven-and-a-half-minute entirety on the soundtrack of the film *Around the Fire*, a fictional account of the Grateful Dead tour scene.

The group originated near San Francisco's North Beach in 1994. Josh McIntosh and David Rice were busking in the street when an older man stopped by, watched their performance, introduced himself as Willie, and joined them for an evening of impromptu music. As a tribute to this man's spirit and enthusiasm, the pair named themselves Blew Willie. However, after playing in the acoustic duo for a period, Rice decided to step away and focus on his studies.

In July of 1995, McIntosh joined with best friend and fellow song-writer Dustin Henderson to form a fuller but still acoustic version of Blew Willie. The present lineup includes McIntosh's younger brother Dylan on drums, Ryan Chesire on percussion, and Ken Kellner on bass. Josh McIntosh plays lead guitar, and Henderson adds some subtle rhythm accents through amplifiers that sharpen and deepen the sound. Rice has returned to supply harmony vocals and mandolin accents; he also serves as a third percussionist. The band entertains a swelling group of supporters at its live shows – these include performances during the 1998 HORDE tour and the High Sierra Music Festival. Fans also keep up with Blew Willie by perusing the band's quarterly magazine, *From the Belly*.

DISCOGRAPHY

Sound Whole (1998). This studio recording captures the group's live facility (although the band roster was not complete at the time of the sessions). Many of the songs demonstrate Blew Willie's improvisational capabilities, beginning with the ten-minute "All My Promises" and continuing with "The Garden." However, this release also establishes that the group can compose meaningful, melodious compositions, albeit ones that the band still loves to jam. Other notable offerings include "Rainwalk," the spirited "Me and Lucy," and the scampering "World Apart."

WEB SITE

www.blewwillie.com

BLUE DOGS

- **HANK FUTCH:** *electric upright bass, vocals*
- **JASON HAWTHORN:** *electric and acoustic guitar*
- **BOBBY HOUCK:** *vocals, acoustic guitar, harmonica*
- **GREG WALKER:** *drums and percussion*
- **DOUG WANAMAKER:** *Hammond organ*

The Charleston, South Carolina, *Post and Courier* declared 1997 "The Year of the Blue Dog." Although the band had been performing together professionally since 1988, this was its first year as a full-time touring outfit. During the summer, the band released its first disc comprised entirely of its own compositions. One of these selections, "I'd Give Anything," was chosen to appear on the *AWARE 5* compilation. The Blue Dogs were then invited to play a number of high-profile gigs, including the opening of Charleston's Riverdogs Stadium along with Widespread Panic, Fiji Mariners, and G. Love and Special Sauce.

Childhood friends Bobby Houck and Hank Futch had performed together as an acoustic duo while they were growing up. In 1988, they started gigging with Futch's college roommate, Phillip Lammonds, on lead guitar. Five years later, they took on drummer Greg Walker and began playing acoustic-based shows with a strong bluegrass flavor – the Blue Dogs even traveled west to perform at the Telluride Bluegrass Festival. One important step in the band's evolution occurred late in 1996, when Lammonds decided to retire from active touring and the remaining band members invited their friend Jason Hawthorn to join them (Lammonds continues to write songs for the group and participates in its studio recording sessions). At about this time, the Blue Dogs also began to expand its sound into the realm of more rootsy, countrified rock. Most recently, the group has welcomed the full-time participation of longtime associate and keyboard player Doug Wanamaker (who has played with Gibb Droll, the Dave Matthews Band, and his own, Virginia-based group, Indecision).

Particularly since Wanamaker's arrival, the band's live performances have taken on a zest and ardor. Houck notes, "we're certainly not what I would call a traditional jam band. Now, Doug Wanamaker, his old band, Indecision – they went up there and just tore things up for twenty minutes at a stretch. We don't do that. Although now that we have Doug with us, we're starting to do a bit more of that." In fact, the band has always done this, albeit in a manner drawn from its bluegrass roots whereby it works up a collective improvisation, tosses it around for a solo or two, and then returns to the song. However, with Wanamaker's addition these efforts have become more spirited and inviting.

DISCOGRAPHY

Music for Dog People (1991)

Soul Dogfood (1993)

Live at Dock Street Theatre (1995). This live recording presents the band in a predominantly acoustic setting with a strong bluegrass feel. It balances some original compositions with covers of, among others, "Muleskinner Blues," "Dark Hollow," "Brown-Eyed Women," and Counting Crows's "Rain King."

Blue Dogs (1997). Although the instrumentation here is top-notch, many of the songs succeed due to Houck's warm vocals and Futch's harmonies. The opener, "Walter," is a rollicking toe tapper with some dandy mandolin from Lammonds. Additional pleasures are offered by the gentle "Long Gone Goodbye," the bluesier "Riverside," and the endearing "Hope She Falls in Love." This release also features some stellar guest appearances by Gibb Droll, Son Volt pedal-steel player Eric Heywood, Blue Miracle's Jon Gillespie, and coproducers John Alagia and Doug Derryberry.

WEB SITE

www.bluedogs.com

BLUE HONEY

- **MATT DEMARINIS:** *vocals*
- **TY DOWNING:** *drums*
- **ALAN GLICKENHAUS:** *guitar, fiddle, banjo, pedal steel, mandolin*
- **TOM NIEDER:** *bass*
- **MITCH WILLET:** *guitar*

Since its formation in 1995, Portland, Oregon's, Blue Honey has attracted new audiences with its riveting live performances and spirited, sparkling grooves. Matt Demarinis's urgent vocals and the collective proficiency of Blue Honey's players produce an enthusiastic amalgam of blues, country, rock, and bluegrass. Bassist Tom Nieder comments that "anyone who comes out to see us can expect to see us play our asses off. We are really energetic up there. I mean we're not doing cartwheels or anything – we're just very intense about our music. Anytime we go out there it feels like the first time we ever played. Sometimes it feels like we can't play hard enough." He adds, "we don't just noodle up there. We're not a jazz odyssey band." Still, the group leaves lots of space within its arrangements for animated interplay and exploration.

In 1998, Blue Honey added some new textures by recruiting Alan Glickenhaus of Portland's jam-band heroes Higher Ground. Says Glickenhaus, "[Blue Honey] had played with Higher Ground a few times, and one day I went out and saw their set. Matt has that big, rich voice – he's like a male Janis Joplin, he just wows people. And their instrumentation impressed me. So the next time they played, I sat in. It turns out they were huge Higher Ground fans. Some time afterwards, they asked me if I might like to play with them permanently, and I think I may have surprised them when eventually I said yes." Nieder remarks, "The amazing thing about adding Alan was we didn't have to change our sound. The very first time we asked him to come on stage with us he knew how to play in the holes." As a result, the band's music has taken on a new vibrancy. Glickenhaus hauls a collection of instruments to the stage for every gig, moving back and forth from guitar to dobro to mandolin to banjo to pedal steel. He complements guitarist Mitch Willett's sweeping expressions, while Nieder and drummer Ty Downing supply a steady, vigorous backbone. "A lot of people really seem to enjoy this lineup," observes Glickenhaus. "What they don't realize is that we're still in that early phase, we're only starting to figure out what we can do."

DISCOGRAPHY

Blue Honey (1997)

Remember the Future (1998). This recording reflects the group's current live vigor. The opening track, "Wapiti," demonstrates the sway of Demarinis's deep, soulful vocals. Glickenhaus animates "Pisa" (which appears sans fiddle on the band's debut). "Fiddy" allows the group to walk convincingly through some blues progressions. Other strong offerings include "Live Here," where Willett takes it up a notch, "Eeyore's Blunder," and "Augusta," a magnificent jam enlivened by the entire quintet.

WEB SITE

www.thebluehoney.com

BLUE MIRACLE

- **JOHN ARTHUR:** *guitar*
- **JUNIOR BRYCE:** *alto and tenor saxophone, flute*
- **STEVE CYPHERS:** *percussion, vocals*
- **JON GILLESPIE:** *keyboards, vocals*
- **KEVIN O'BRIEN:** *bass, vocals*
- **RYAN WICK:** *drums*

Blue Miracle is a band that practically dares its audiences not to arise and express themselves physically on the dance floor. Percussionist and singer Steve Cyphers is up front projecting, pounding, and pattering. Guitarist John Arthur notes, "We definitely encourage people to get up, go nuts, and let themselves go. Steve will often tell people that they don't need to sit there, that this isn't *Seinfeld* or *Friends*. They should come on up and get a groove on." The band's music is seemingly designed to this end, as it is built on a core of funk, driving rock, and some thundering percussion. Recently, Blue Miracle has grown to include Junior Bryce on saxophone, and his explosive contributions only further the boogying impulse. Arthur observes: "At our shows, people can expect a lot of variety. We draw on funk, rock, soul, southern stuff, Latin. Our bass player even likes to work in some hillbilly music every now and then." Although the bulk of the band's sets is comprised of original tunes, one way to glimpse this versatility is through the range of covers Blue Miracle performs. On any given evening, it might offer selections from James Brown, Edgar Winter, Santana, the Marshall Tucker Band, Brand New Heavies, and — most recently, since the arrival of Junior Bryce — the Greyboy Allstars.

Blue Miracle also likes to work up a jam. Each member of the sextet, which has been performing together since 1990, can become assertive during these navigations. Jon Gillespie will often lead the group off in one direction with a flurry of keystrokes. This may generate a thunderous response from Cyphers and drummer Ryan Wick. In turn, Arthur and bass player Kevin O'Brien may interject their own sparkling touches. Bryce contributes his own vocabulary, which is particularly rich in the idioms of jazz. The incendiary results have carried the Maryland-based band on tour across the United States and all the way to Alaska, where Blue Miracle contributed to the big thaw at Alaska's Girdstock Festival.

DISCOGRAPHY

Blue Miracle (1994)

Stick It Out (1997). This release has a full sound that evokes the band's live presence. It also features a number of percolating rhythms, percussive accents, and keyboard flourishes. "Stir It Around" opens with funky guitar that quickly yields to an infusion of horns and drums. "Little Dog" creates a thick groove enlivened by the band's deep bottom. The instrumental track "The Grill" demonstrates Blue Miracle's affinity for Latin beats. Finally, "Every Hour" develops a laid-back vibe with some jazzier keyboard touches.

WEB SITE

www.vfan.com

BLUE YARD GARDEN

- **RANDY BALL:** *bass*
- **JOHN NATALE:** *electric and lap steel guitar, mandolin, and vocals*
- **TED NATALE:** *drums*
- **WILLIAM OLSON:** *acoustic and electric guitar*
- **JEFF ZUTANT:** *lead vocals*

Blue Yard Garden distinguishes itself from the legion of roots-based rock bands on the strength of Jeff Zutant's compelling lead vocals. Zutant's resounding voice invites comparisons with those of Eddie Vedder and Van Morrison. But while Zutant represents the front line of Blue Yard Garden, he is quick to hail the virtues of his bandmates: "They're the ones who are creating the groove. I just lay a little candy on top of it."

The band is winning throngs of new admirers with its live shows. Zutant describes the defining element of those performances as "Passion. I let it all out up there. When I'm done, I'm drained. I have to sit down for a while. And I know it's the same way for every member of the band." Bass player Randy Ball — one of the many emerging disciples of Victor Wooten — Zutant describes as "the backbone of the band. It drives me nuts how good he is." Ball holds the bottom with drummer Ted Natale, who "loves the heavy rhythms." Natale supplies those rhythms behind his father, John, who plays lead guitar. Zutant remarks: "I would imagine we're one of the few bands where you'll hear the drummer yelling at the guitarist, 'Shut up, dad.' No, seriously — you know what, though, they get along great. I would think they're brothers. But, much more importantly, John is a player. He really knows what to place in the empty spaces." Zutant also marvels at rhythm guitarist William Olson, whose "wrists don't stop. I want everyone to recognize what he's contributing to the sound. He keeps it lively."

Blue Yard Garden is a commanding live act that remains focused on song craft. In the concert setting, the group's jams often turn inward, exploring the nuances of individual compositions. The band is particularly sensitive to the new ideas that emerge in this context. Zutant notes, "Sometimes when we kick back after a show and listen to the tapes, we realize that we can get a couple of songs out of it. And that's what's important to us, we're always trying to write the next best song."

DISCOGRAPHY

Table for One (1995)

On the Galaxy (1996). This release effectively showcases the band's earnest compositions and tight performances. Notable tracks include "Shade," which features a subdued, catchy chorus; "Morning's Over," in which Zutant's gritty vocals are sweetened with some mandolin fills; "React to Me," which simmers in a manner reminiscent of the Black Crowes; and "Step Out Lady," a song reminiscent of an early 1970s Van Morrison soul raveup.

No Good Sundays (1998)

WEB SITE

www.blueyardgarden.com

BLUES TRAVELER

- **BRENDAN HILL:** *drums and percussion*
- **CHAN KINCHLA:** *guitar*
- **JOHN POPPER:** *vocals, harmonica, guitar*
- **BOB SHEEHAN:** *bass*

In 1983, Princeton, New Jersey, was home to a group of young musicians who dubbed themselves the Blues Band. They had come together through the collaboration of harmonica player John Popper and drummer Brendan Hill. The pair burned through a series of lead guitarists and then finally, three years later, invited high school jock

Chan Kinchla to join the band. After experiencing similar difficulty latching onto a bass player, they brought Bob Sheehan on board. The resulting synergy soon became apparent, as jams would often extend for more than three hours (it was during one such instance, and the smoke break that followed, that the quartet first encountered the black cat that would become its muse and mascot). Soon afterward – due, in part, to Kinchla's observation that during their intense improvisations it often felt as if there were a fifth entity in the room – the band changed its name. Popper suggested "entity" be translated into "traveler" (via Gozer the Traveler from *Ghostbusters*), and Blues Traveler was born.

By the summer of 1988, Blues Traveler had relocated to New York, where it became a fixture on the downtown music scene. The quartet initially rented an apartment in Brooklyn along with another hometown friend, Chris Barron, who would often perform on guitar between the band's sets (Barron eventually joined forces with Eric Shenckman, whom Popper had met at the New School of Social Research, to form Spin Doctors). The Blues Traveler circle during this period also included Joan Osborne, who occasionally lent her explosive vocals to the group's performances. Blues Traveler soon found itself spear-heading a burgeoning music scene while doing shows at clubs such as Mondo Perso and Nightingale; it was at the latter venue that Blues Traveler was taken under the wing of the inimitable, personable Gina Z., who still works with the group and is referenced in Traveler's song "Gina." In 1989, with the opening of the Wetlands Preserve, the band found a new home, playing regular gigs at the club. Wetlands founder/visionary Larry Bloch recalls: "They were the first band that took that scene to another level. I have fond memories of dancing away the night in the club when they were playing."

As the band expanded its geographic ambit, it befriended a number of musicians who shared its commitment to improvised music. In 1992, a summit took place with representatives of many of these groups, including all four members of Blues Traveler, all four members of Phish, Eric Shenckman, Widespread Panic's John Bell, and Colonel Bruce Hampton of Aquarium Rescue Unit fame. This skull session led to the inception of the original eight-date HORDE tour of July 1992, which featured all of these bands (although Phish had other commit-ments and yielded its place to Bela Fleck and the Flecktones after the first four shows). The tour has rapidly become a summer tradition, and Blues Traveler has joined the HORDE every year, although in 1997 it limited its participation.

Through its commitment to vital live performance, Blues Traveler has fostered a dedicated fan base. By the end of 1995, the group had achieved Popper's goal of saturating the country and becoming a steady concert draw in each of the fifty states (the evolution of the map on which Popper colored in each new conquest can be seen in the booklet that accompanies *Live from the Fall*). The group has continued to refine and expand its sound – the harmonica-clad Popper, in particular, has started to pick up his guitar more frequently. Meanwhile, Blues Traveler has maintained a high profile, opening nine stadium dates for the Rolling Stones, appearing in the movie *Kingpin*, contributing music to *Roseanne*, and often enlivening *The Howard Stern Show*.

Perhaps the one question that fans pose most frequently about the quartet's future is what will happen at its annual New Year's Eve show on December 31, 1999. In 1990, the band inaugurated a tradition of symbolically exterminating its black cat at midnight. No one is quite sure what will happen on December 31, 1999, when the unfortunate feline runs out of lives. It is, however, abundantly clear that Blues Traveler will not exhaust its groove.

DISCOGRAPHY

Blues Traveler (1990)

Travelers and Thieves (1991)

Save Our Soul (1993)

Four (1994)

Live from the Fall (1996). This two-CD release captures the band's live prowess and vigor rather effectively. Notable tracks include a sterling twenty-one-minute run from "Mulling It Over" to "Closing Down the Park," a gripping "Mountain Cry," a standout version of "Alone" with Popper on guitar, and another finely segued sequence from "Go" to "Low Rider" back into "Go" and then into "Runaround."

Straight on till Morning (1997). Here Blues Traveler creates some varied textures. The disc opens with the infectious boogie "Carolina Blues," which is animated by Popper's vocals. "Felicia" features some salsa rhythms. "Justify the Thrill" supplies a harder edge, with some bristling accents from Kinchla. The band changes pace with the intriguing ballad "Yours," which incorporates a twenty-six-piece orchestra. Finally, John Medeski guests on "Make My Way," which closes the release with some absorbing improvisation.

WEB SITE

www.bluestraveler.com

BOUD DEUN

- **MATT EILAND:** *bass*
- **ROCKY CANCELOSE:** *drums*
- **GREG HISER:** *violin*
- **SHAWN PERSINGER:** *guitar*

Boud Deun is currently crafting some intriguing, innovative instrumental groove music. One initial reference point for the Virginia-based band is John McLaughlin's innovative Mahavishnu Orchestra of the early 1970s. However, at times there is also a darker, progressive-rock-based sound that calls to mind King Crimson. Yet these comparisons alone are inadequate, as the band incorporates other elements to create a music that can best be described as punk fusion or heavy-metal bluegrass, with some flavors of funk and Middle Eastern as well.

The group first assembled in 1994 to piece together a sound of its own from the musical predilections of its members. Guitarist Shawn Persinger, who also composes many of the group's songs, is certainly a McLaughlin disciple, but he also affirms his affection for the piercing guitar of AC/DC's Angus Young. Fellow songwriter and bassist Matt Eiland enjoys the fusion of the late 1960s and early 1970s as well as the punk of the 1980s. Boud Deun's sound, however, takes another turn due to the contributions of violinist Greg Hiser. A traditional bluegrass player who has performed with a number of area groups, Hiser adds some zesty fiddle to the mix. Drummer Rocky Cancelose is equally adept at providing jazz fills or throbbing exclamations. All of these elements coalesce in the live setting, where the band builds on the structures of its original compositions with some fierce jams that often seem to flirt with anarchy while never losing their intensity or focus.

DISCOGRAPHY

Fiction and Several Days (1995)
Astronomy Made Easy (1998)

WEB SITE

www.clark.net/pub/nicklin/bouddeun.html

BOX SET

- **MARK ABBOTT:** *drums*
- **JIM BRUNBERG:** *vocals, acoustic and electric guitar, pedal steel, mandolin, banjo*
- **CHAD HEISE:** *bass*
- **SAM JOHNSTON:** *keyboards, harmonica*
- **JEFF PEHRSON:** *vocals, acoustic guitar*

In 1991, singer/songwriters Jim Brunberg and Jeff Pehrson met in a San Francisco coffeehouse. They immediately acquired an appreciation for each other's music and recognized that they shared a devotion to their craft. Brunberg and Pehrson also realized that they had complementary voices with which they could create soaring harmonies. The pair began performing together as an acoustic duo throughout California, steadily gaining repute. They then decided to hold their breath, quit their jobs, and take off for Europe to immerse themselves in performing. A few months later, having done this, they returned home, and the experience enriched their song craft and collaborative skills.

The pair soon discovered that the number of ears eager to hear their musical stories and vibrant harmonies had increased. Critics began comparing them to Simon and Garfunkel and – due to a dearth of male folk duos – started labeling them "the Indigo Boys." However, in 1993, the pair decided to diversify their sound. With the addition of keyboardist Sam Johnston, drummer Mark Abbott, and bass player Chad Heise, Box Set took the form it has today, although, on occasion, the band's founders will still gig as an acoustic tandem.

Although Brunberg and Pehrson's compositions remain at the group's core when Box Set performs live, it unabashedly opens up these songs to explore their nuances and textures. Brunberg steps up on electric guitar, mandolin, or pedal steel. Pehrson contributes some accents on his acoustic guitar. Johnston elevates a number of jams with his keyboards. The versatile rhythm section (which has at times performed with Shelley Doty) keeps it all aloft. So Box Set draws on two strengths, as manifested by the fact that in 1995 the National Academy of Songwriters named it group of the year, and in 1997 the quintet earned a Bay Area Music Award for being the best club band.

DISCOGRAPHY

Box Set (1994)
Twenty-Seven (1995)

Mean Time (1996)

Thread (1997). On this, the band's Capricorn debut, Box Set both reinterprets some older favorites and commits some original compositions to disc for the first time. The opener, "Back to You," introduces the group's dulcet harmonies and bright instrumentation. "Train" pulses with an intriguing amalgam of folk and funk. Other standout tracks include the winsome, longtime fan favorite "Amsterdam," the ethereal "One Step," the violin-accented "Valentine," and the evocative "Eighteen Days of Rain."

WEB SITE

www.boxset.com

TONI BROWN BAND

- **MARTY BOSTOFF:** *bass*
- **TONI BROWN:** *vocals*
- **GARY KROMAN:** *guitar*
- **MIKE NICITA:** *drums*
- **JEFF PEARLMAN:** *keyboards*
- **ROB WOLFSON:** *guitar*

Although Brooklyn-based Toni Brown may be better known for her publishing ventures than her musical ones, the times just might be a-changin'. Brown's prose skills and her love for improvisational music led her to join Les Kippel's *Relix Magazine* in 1979. A few years later, when Kippel decided to focus his energies on a record label, Brown became the magazine's publisher, and she has nurtured that enterprise ever since. Yet Brown had performed in a band as a teenager, and she now acknowledges, "After being around this music for so long, how could I not play?" So, when Robert Hunter gave her one of his guitars and encouraged her to start making music once again, she happily complied.

Brown's eventual emergence as a performer resulted from her friendship with members of the David Nelson Band. Over the years, Brown had used Hunter's gift to compose a number of songs but still had no steady vehicle with which to express them. Then, in April 1995, she joined the DNB in the studio to work through a number of her tunes. She was pleased with the results, which led her to assemble a band of her own. The group currently includes guitarists Rob

Wolfson of Illuminati and Gary Kroman. Tiberius bassist Marty Bostoff and drummer Mike Nicita anchor the Toni Brown Band, and Jeff Pearlman contributes on keyboards. The sextet performs her compositions in the spirit of the music that she savors, replete with improvisation. As a result, her tour docket has become full. She has been booked for a number of club shows and festival performances, including an April 1998 Japan run that reunited her on stage with the David Nelson Band.

DISCOGRAPHY

Blue Morning (1996). On Brown's debut release, she is backed by a stellar group of musicians. The David Nelson Band appears on many of these cuts. Jorma Kaukonen and Michael Falzarano lend support as well – Falzarano also produced the disc. Due, in part, to the nature of the players on *Blue Morning*, there is a country feel to many of the songs that often evokes the Flying Burrito Brothers or the New Riders of the Purple Sage (the latter is certainly attributable in part to the players on this recording). Brown's warm vocals express her evocative metaphors on tracks such as the reggae-tinged "Walk on Water" and the shuffling "Last Row of the Balcony." Other notable offerings include "Double Shot of Tequila" and the ten-minute exploration "Stars."

WEB SITE

www.relix.com/records/tonibrown.html

BURLAP TO CASHMERE

- **SCOTT BARKSDALE:** *percussion*
- **STEVEN DELOPOULOS:** *vocals, guitar*
- **MICHAEL ERNEST:** *guitar, percussion, vocals*
- **ROBY GUARNERA:** *bass, vocals*
- **THEODORE PAGANO:** *drums*
- **JOHNNY PHILIPPIDES:** *guitar, vocals*
- **JOSH ZANDMAN:** *keyboards*

Burlap to Cashmere began when cousins Steven Delopoulos and Johnny Philippides took to playing together in New Jersey coffeehouses. However, in 1995, due to the encouragement of one avid fan who would go on to become their manager, the pair decided to bring their compositions to a full band. In time, they expanded it into a seven-piece outfit partially fueled by the Afro-Cuban rhythms of Scott Barksdale's congas, Theodore Pagano's full drum kit, and Michael Ernest's guitar and djembes. Roby Guarnera's bass and Josh Zandman's keyboards complete the band's multifaceted sound. The results lift the cousins' compositions to a new level, inscribing them with a fervor that has swiftly earned the band raves from a wide spectrum of listeners.

During its live show, the septet displays a range of intriguing elements. The foundation is laid by the robust songs, which Delopoulos drafts; these often have a strong spiritual component. Additionally, Philippides, who arranges the music, contributes uplifting vocal harmonies. Another distinctive aspect of Burlap to Cashmere's sound is the flamenco-style guitar that colors many of its tunes. Also, the band will often work up a percussive flurry with Barksdale, Ernest, and Pagano leading an extended session. The results have elicited comparisons to performers such as Rusted Root, Simon and Garfunkel, and the Gipsy Kings. However, as the diversity of these artists suggests, Burlap to Cashmere's sound is distinct.

DISCOGRAPHY

Live at the Bitter End (1997). This five-song release highlights the group's notable features. Vocal harmonies abound on songs such as "Anybody Out There?" and "Chop Chop." The band's guitar stylings are well showcased on "Anybody Out There?" and "Divorce." Finally, "Basic Instructions" supplies a taste of the group's interlocked percussion.

WEB SITE

www.burlaptocashmere.com

CALOBO

- **DAVID ANDREWS:** *acoustic guitar, vocals*
- **BRIAN BUCOLO:** *drums*
- **JENNY CONLEE:** *piano, organ*
- **KENNY ERLICK:** *electric guitar*
- **CALEB KLAUDER:** *acoustic guitar, mandolin, vocals*
- **NATE QUERY:** *bass*
- **MICHELE VAN KLEEF:** *vocals*

Calobo began as a coffeehouse duo comprised of boyhood friends David Andrews and Caleb Klauder, who began gigging under this moniker while attending college in Oregon. After two years in this formation, the pair decided to augment their music with a female vocal counterpoint. The band then slowly expanded as both Andrews and Klauder worked in additional players to see how the sound might change. Klauder recalls that, "as kids growing up in a small town [Orcas Island, Washington], we'd always wanted to form a band. Although as we got older we began to have our own ideas as to what that band might be like. Calobo is very much a fusion of those ideas." Eventually, Calobo expanded to include electric guitar, bass, drums, and keyboards.

The seven personalities who comprise Calobo have coalesced to create one of the most popular touring and recording acts in the Northwest. Michele Van Kleef's warm vocals invite listeners into the mix, both when she sings lead and, perhaps more importantly, when her harmonies soar. Gifted electric guitarist Kenny Erlick is adept at knowing when not to play, so that when he does step up the results are often sublime. Also, after some collective Calobo-goosing, Erlick has recently agreed to assume some vocal duties. Jenny Conlee, a classically trained keyboardist, layers the band's sound with rich textures. Nate Query assumes an important role on bass, serving as the nexus between the various approaches and feels the group puts forth. Drummer Brian Bucolo is equally proficient at negotiating the passages within the acoustic and electric realms. Of course, although they often downplay it, Andrews and Klauder remain the heart of Calobo, bringing to the group a spirit and an enthusiasm along with their acoustic guitars. These longtime friends compose and sing most of Calobo's songs, which offer winsome melodies while conveying evocative stories and social themes, often with a bit of humor.

Calobo's live sound has been described as "acoustic groove music." Indeed, despite the group's expansion, Andrews and Klauder have remained true to their early commitment to acoustic instrumentation (albeit in a bed of sound enhanced by electric bass and guitar). The band's spirited jams frequently begin with Klauder and Andrews building textures; the other players will both comp and then step forward themselves. The results are both exhilarating and entrancing. Klauder remarks: "It's amazing how this has worked out. I feel lucky to have hooked up with everyone. The individual members bring so much talent that we've had to work hard to figure out how to best harness it. But now that we are better able to harness and direct it, I feel that our shows are only getting better."

DISCOGRAPHY

Calobo (1992)

Runnin' in the River (1993). The band attempted to capture its live feel with these fourteen offerings. The disc was recorded over two days, without overdubs, in the basement of a house Calobo had rented for the occasion. The songs present the band's friskier side – some lyrics were created on the fly, and there is the improvised jam "Flipside." Standout offerings include the gentle "Down the Line," the sweet, catchy "When My Love Grows," "Dishwater Blues" with its raucous turns, the joyous "Put down Your Pipe Baby," and the subtle closer "Let It Roll."

Ya Dum Di Dum (1995)

Stomp (1997). This recording suggests that the members of Calobo have reached a new creative apex, as four members of the band contribute songs (with Andrews and Klauder the most prolific). Conlee's piano, in particular, stands out: it provides a number of subtle counterpoints and flourishes that enrich many of these compositions. Query's "What Is Real" opens the disc as Klauder's mandolin phrasings give way to Van Kleef's glowing vocal expressions. "Stitched in Wool" is a finely crafted story song that presents the band's trademark harmonies enhanced by some well-arranged acoustic and electric guitar. Other notable tracks include the aptly named "Bright Day," "Slow Train," in which Calobo transforms Mississippi Delta blues into its own métier, and "Could've Been," a moving ballad drenched in gorgeous harmonies.

WEB SITE
www.calobo.com

CHIEF BROOM

- **BRUCE BELL:** *electric and acoustic guitar, dobro*
- **DAVE CIERI:** *vocals, piano*
- **JESSICA GOODKIN:** *vocals*
- **BAPTISTE IVAR:** *bass*
- **PUTNAM MURDOCK:** *vocals, acoustic guitar, mandolin*
- **BRIAN RAVITSKY:** *drums*

A product of Boulder, Colorado, Chief Broom, like its literary namesake from *One Flew over the Cuckoo's Nest*, is poised to bust out. The group's live shows are epic affairs, drawing heavily on the improvisational gifts of its members. Keyboardist Dave "D-Train" Cieri often takes the lead, bobbing his head as he carries the group off in unanticipated directions. Guitarist Bruce Bell typically responds with passionate phrases, and Putnam Murdock might at any given moment contribute on mandolin. These players are supported by an in-the-pocket bottom led by Brian Ravitsky on drums. Jessica Goodkin, who completes Chief Broom, is equally capable of supplying rich vocal tones or striking ululations.

The band formed at a University of Colorado dormitory floor inhabited by Bell, Murdock, and Ravitsky. The three friends enlisted Cieri and began performing as an acoustic quartet with the keyboardist supplying bass lines with his left hand. Chief Broom was completed by vocalist Goodkin, whom Bell recalls as "the first person I met at school. We were both in the music department. Once we got the band together, I went looking for her."

Chief Broom's powerful live presentations are anchored by its original compositions, which meld jazz, funk, bluegrass, and rock. Additionally, as Bell notes, the band has "three awesome vocalists, which I think sets us apart from a lot of other jam bands." Bell also pinpoints the contributions of Cieri: "He surprises me every time I play with him. He was classically trained, but he pulls together a lot of other influences, such as Ramsey Lewis, and bronzes them." The guitarist concludes by identifying a key strength of the band as "the diversity, both within our music and from show to show. In fact, when we play the same place or area from night to night, we'll totally mix it up and try to freak everyone out by making them think it's another band."

DISCOGRAPHY

Chief Broom (1997). The band's eponymous debut is brimming with propulsive keyboards, three-part harmonies, acoustic interludes, and electric-guitar fury. Many of these characteristics are manifested in tracks such as "Ride" and "Stills." Other worthy offerings include the instrumental "Colossus," which shows off a jazzier side of the band (in particular, Cieri's swinging keys); "There You Go," a rollicking acoustic number; and "101 Knights," in which the band lies low, taking a backseat to Goodkin's plaintive vocals.

WEB SITE

www.chiefbroom.com

CONEHEAD BUDDHA

- ■ **PETE BENCINI:** *drums*
- ■ **CHRISTIAN DE FRANCQUEVILLE:** *bass, vocals*
- ■ **CHRIS FISHER:** *vocals, percussion, guitar*
- ■ **CHRIS KENNEDY:** *guitar*
- ■ **SHANNON LYNCH:** *tenor saxophone, vocals*
- ■ **TERRY LYNCH:** *trumpet, vocals*

Chris Fisher, lead singer and principal songwriter of Conehead Buddha, describes his band as a cross-training sneaker: "The idea is you can use us for a number of different purposes. We offer a bunch of different styles to fill your musical needs." The band's music does, in fact, contain elements of ska, Latin, funk, and rock. The footwear metaphor is also appropriate because this is a band that strives to kick the audience in its collective rear to get everyone up and dancing.

Fisher assembled the group in his hometown of Climax, New York, in 1993. "When I put the band together, the intention was to create a Latin salsa band, but once we started playing together we just went off in other directions." The one common theme in the group's music is infectious, driving beats. Working without a setlist, the sextet (insert Climax, New York, joke here) will often assess the moment and then select a song (or engage in a good-natured dispute about what its next offering will be, to the amusement of many). At times, the brassy brother-sister combination of Terry and Shannon Lynch on trumpet and saxophone will fuel a raveup. On other occasions, some players will switch over to percussion instruments for a frenzied exchange. Fisher himself moves from acoustic to electric guitar to percussion as required by a given tune. Conehead Buddha's songs often juxtapose wry observations or dark musings with catchy melodies and bright instrumentation. Fisher further notes that "our focus is on the songs, so that when we jam, we take it out within that context."

Conehead Buddha thrives in the live setting, where its kinetic shows typically extend beyond the two-hour mark. The band also distinguished itself during three days of marathon performances at Phish's 1997 Great Went: it played in the lots between Phish's sets and then long into the morning. "We're musicians," Fisher affirms, "because we love to play. There have been times on tour when we've had nights off and we hustled to find a gig just to play."

DISCOGRAPHY

Easter Island Vacation (1993)

Put It On (1993)

I Wanna Be like . . . You (1995)

The Man with the Hat Gives and Takes with Ease (1998). The diversity of Conehead Buddha's offerings is reflected on this vibrant live release. "S.W.M." is a splashy ska tune. "Unspeakable" showcases the band's Latin flair as well as its commitment to address serious issues through engaging melodies: this song is told from the perspective of a boy who witnesses another child being molested. "Johnny and the Fighting Boys" contains a vigorous vocal jam with a bonus Men at Work quote. The disc concludes with "Sights," which features some rousing guest guitar from Max Verna of Ominous Seapods.

WEB SITE

www.coneheadbuddha.com

COOL WATER CANYON

- **DREW ALLEN:** *vocals, guitar*
- **CARTER BEIM:** *bass*
- **MATT GROVER:** *drums, vocals*
- **BRIAN STONE:** *keyboards, vocals*
- **JESSE TYRE-KARP:** *vocals, guitar*

Cool Water Canyon has emerged as one of southern California's notable jam bands. Ever since 1995, when the band's three founders – Drew Allen, Jesse Tyre-Karp, and Carter Beim – arrived in Santa Barbara, they have been building a devoted fan base eager to see the group create its enticing, blues-flavored grooves. Cool Water Canyon's live vigor has become widely recognized: in 1998, it was named best area band by students of the University of California, Santa Barbara, placing ahead of several national touring acts, including Big Bad Voodoo Daddy.

Cool Water Canyon presents melodious songs, strong vocal harmonies, and a penchant for inventive improvisation. Allen and Tyre-Karp are the group's two principal songwriters, and each assumes lead vocals on his respective offerings. Allen also provides piercing guitar leads, and Tyre-Karp adds some inventive rhythm accents. The two are well complemented by the sonic structures Beim creates on bass. Drummer Matt Grover has proven himself quite skilled at adding his own ideas to the band's improvisations. In 1997, the group's sound was augmented by keyboard player Brian Stone. Tyre-Karp sums it all up: "I'm proud of what we've accomplished from a musical perspective, and I think we'll all remain energized as long as we continue to make progress. We haven't stalled yet."

Cool Water Canyon (1998). The band's debut offers solid song craft and a number of tight jams. "Sunday Morning" is a bluesy power-house featuring some euphonious vocal harmonies. Other strong tracks include the soulful "Cannonball"; "Diamond in the AshTray," which is colored by jazzier guitar expressions; the powerful ballad "Kings and Queens"; and the saxophone-abetted "Cadillac."

WEB SITE

www.coolwatercanyon.com

CROSSEYED

- **PAUL BENOIT:** *electric and acoustic guitar, vocals*
- **TIGE DECOSTER:** *bass*
- **DOUG SCHOOLCRAFT:** *electric and acoustic guitar, vocals*
- **DAN WEBER:** *percussion*

Seattle's Crosseyed is named after a Muddy Waters song. Actually, the song is titled "Crosseyed Cat," but another band was already using that moniker, so the group went with Crosseyed (but called its first release *Crosseyed Cat*). The blues sensibility suggested by this association with the Chicago master informs many of the quartet's compositions as well as its performances. But Crosseyed is not bound to any one style, and the band itself characterizes its songs as, alternatively, "spooky desert jazz," "ethereal groove," "spaghetti-western rocker," "psycho ragtime blues," and "Latin groove."

Crosseyed typically plays without set lists. Instead, band members call out the next tune in midflight; or, just as often, they work up a jam and wait until an appropriate segue presents itself. These improvised interludes are generally most compelling when the band performs in an acoustic setting. Paul Benoit and Doug Schoolcraft – the group's two guitarists, vocalists, and songwriters – often lead the barrage, buttressed by Tige DeCoster's supple bass and Dan Weber's steady percussion.

The band's current lineup reflects, to some degree, the incestuous nature of the Seattle music scene. Crosseyed features two members of the band Hanuman (Benoit and DeCoster), which in turn had been formed by two members of the group Trillian Green when cellist Christine Gunn was off in Europe gigging with the band the Walkabouts.

DISCOGRAPHY

Crosseyed Cat (1996). The band's debut displays its musical diversity and showcases the tight, well-paced compositions of Benoit and Schoolcraft. A number of tracks distinguish themselves, including "Feet on the Fire," the "spooky desert jazz" piece "We're Not Alone," and the galloping rocker "Bend." "Circus Freak" simmers, built on Benoit's vocal phrasings and guitar flashes and embellished by the contribution of cellist Christine Gunn.

It's a Shame (1997). This is an all-acoustic offering with some particularly tasty slide guitar that enhances the spare, moody atmosphere. *It's a Shame* celebrates the band's affection for Mississippi Delta blues (which is somewhat ironic, as the group is named after a song by the Chicago electric king). The songs are by no means traditional blues, however: some numbers are country-inflected, while others are built on folk picking. DeCoster's double bass adds stealth wizardry, supplying subtle yet poignant phrases and support. Zesty offerings include the title track; "Together Again," which presents a taste of Benoit and Schoolcraft's guitar interplay; and "Tear," a haunting song enriched by Dan Weber's percussion and Marc Olson's guest appearance on pedal steel.

WEB SITE

www.omnivine.com/crosseyed/index.html

DAY BY THE RIVER

- **WALT AUSTIN:** *keyboards, vocals*
- **DAVE BROCKWAY:** *drums and percussion*
- **TED LAHEY:** *vocals, guitar*
- **PATRICK MCDONNELL:** *acoustic and electric bass, vocals*
- **JASON RABINEAU:** *guitar, vocals*

The members of Athens, Georgia's, Day By The River have been performing together since their high school days, when they would often take their guitars and head off to play beside the nearby Oconoee Waterway. This led to the creation of a cover band, Cherubic Creatures, which disbanded in 1989 when keyboardist Walt Austin left to study music at the University of Miami. However, a few years later, Austin was joined there by former Creatures Dave Brockway, Ted Lahey, and Patrick McDonnell. In 1992, the group reformed as Day By The River and began to build a following. The band's fans were enticed by its dense and captivating dual guitar work, Lahey's thick, resonant baritone, McDonnell's rubbery bass lines, Austin's vibrant, jazz-inflected keyboards, and Brockway's crackling drums. The group soon released *Shimmy*, which captured these components of its sound.

A turning point came in the summer of 1995 when guitarist Buck Pryor departed the group. Says Austin: "That really threw us. To some degree, we had to start all over again and rethink exactly what we were doing in every song." Uncertain how to proceed, band members convinced Aquarium Rescue Unit guitarist Jimmy Herring to join them on lead guitar for eight shows. Herring, who had met the band when Day By The River opened for ARU, revitalized the group. Austin explains, "He brought it all back together for us. And his playing –

I just cannot say enough amazing things about the guy." Soon afterward, guitarist Jason Rabineau, who had studied with Herring, came aboard, and the band built a new momentum.

Day By The River's live performances are now attracting repeat listeners on the strength of the band's affinity for cooperative, organic improvisation as well as its original compositions. Austin insists that both are important to the band: "At some point during the set, we definitely drop all form and jam. For instance, a song like 'Taking Over' is never close to the same from show to show. But it's important to us that it all happens within the context of a song. We're really into songwriting, because if that's not there, everything else falls apart. " Day By The River's live shows frequently offer even more: an entertaining story rap that changes from night to night. Austin says: "We try to make our shows different because we see many of the same faces out there and because we have tapers as well." Occasionally, to celebrate its song "Naked," the band encourages collective nudity, with Lahey occasionally leading by example. All of this has created a growing cadre of Day By The River fans that has taken to attending multiple shows, often with taping gear in hand; these fans appropriately dub themselves River Rats.

DISCOGRAPHY

Shimmy (1993)

Fly (1997). This release presents the band's rich sounds and memorable melodies. The opener, "Naked," is a fine example, as are "River Road" and "Japanese Motel." The title track, which initially captivates through its bass lines, yields additional gratification with each listen. Finally, the lively "Puddin'" is further elevated by Jimmy Herring's guest appearance on guitar.

WEB SITE

www.daybytheriver.com

DEEP BANANA BLACKOUT

- **BENJY CARR:** *bass*
- **JEN DURKIN:** *vocals*
- **JOHN DURKIN:** *percussion*
- **FUZZY:** *guitar, vocals*
- **ERIK KALB:** *bass*
- **CYRUS MADAN:** *keyboards*
- **ROB SOMERVILLE:** *tenor and soprano saxophone, vocals*
- **ROB VOLO:** *trombone, guitar, vocals*

Deep Banana Blackout appeared to Jen Durkin in a dream. Actually, not the entire band, just Fuzzy the guitarist, and at that time the fledgling group was named Back to Funk. In the dream, Fuzzy approached her and decreed that the band's name should be changed to Deep Banana Blackout. The force of her ensuing laughter actually woke Durkin. However, soon afterward, all this became a reality, demonstrating the power of dreams, or at least this band's appreciation of really goofy ones (which says a lot about the humor and spirit of Deep Banana Blackout).

The group came into being in the summer of 1995. Vocalist Durkin, drummer Erik Kalb, and bass player Benjy Carr had all performed in the popular northeast-based funk band Tongue and Groove. Soon after that outfit split up in 1994, guitarist Fuzzy began working with Durkin and Kalb to assemble a new group. Carr soon joined, followed by horn players Rob Somerville and Rob Volo, who had been roommates in Baltimore. All shared an enthusiasm for the sounds of Parliament Funkadelic, and James Brown, with individual affinities for Stevie Wonder, Jimi Hendrix, Little Milton, and even classical music. Carr emphasizes that the underlying factor linking all of these performers and genres is passion: "A lot of the stuff that we like was really built on feel."

Deep Banana Blackout soon began to create its own adrenaline-laced grooves for appreciative audiences throughout the northeast. Says Carr, "Our live show is where it's at. When we play and people hear us throw down, they come right back at us with their own energy, and the level of intensity and excitement goes through the roof." The band performs its own compositions along with a few choice covers (of tunes by those artists who inspired its members). Above all, Deep Banana Blackout strives to keep people on the dance floor. A number of devotees further revel in the fact that the band varies its show from night to night, as many tunes become the starting points for blistering collective jams. At any Deep Banana Blackout gig, there is the possibility that something novel will occur: during a show that the group performed after returning from New Orleans, it led the audience outside for a spontaneous late-night parade. Perhaps the best testimonial to the vigor and dynamism of the group comes from funk saxophone master Maceo Parker, who was so taken with the band when it opened for him that he emerged from the wings to lead the crowd in chanting "Deep Banana Blackout! Deep Banana Blackout!"

DISCOGRAPHY

Live in the Thousand Islands (1997). This recording opens with the declaration "What we know as funk has been attained." This statement certainly is realized, although it is unduly limiting as the band also works through songs with a more traditional rock feel (the shuffling "Here My Song" and the ballad "Ballade"), a Latin/jazz number ("El Sol esta en Fuego"), some Dixieland ("Anesthetic Highway"), and even a brief blues offering at the end of the disc. This release is brimming with ideas and sounds (many textures are contained within the veritable musical suite "Mama's Boy"). Of course, there's plenty of horn-abetted, rumbling-bassed funk here as well, perhaps best represented by the opening instrumental "Brandy Wrecker," which segues into the hyperkinetic "Get'Chall in the Mood."

WEB SITE

www.deepbananablackout.com

DEXTER GROVE

- ■ **STEVE DRIZOS:** *percussion*
- ■ **CHARLEY ORLANDO:** *acoustic guitar, vocals*

Despite the fact that Dexter Grove is comprised of only two musicians, both of whom perform on acoustic instruments, it is a jam band. Ever since guitarist Charley Orlando and percussionist Steve Drizos linked up in January 1995, they have demonstrated their joint affinity for vigorous improvisation. Each performer interjects his own ideas, which are then entwined to produce some distinctive sounds. The duo has shared the results with audiences nationwide, performing more than two hundred nights a year. Many more listeners have begun to enjoy Dexter Grove's efforts through its involvement in the Home Grown Music Network.

The tandem's sound is clearly folk inspired, but it often incorporates psychedelic grooves as well. Orlando's six-string is equipped with a number of effects that enable him to produce some mesmerizing tones. Drizos works primarily with a set of congas, but he also uses a series of other implements that add intriguing textures. The pair share songwriting duties, building compositions that utilize elements of blues and country and even have a Middle Eastern feel. Yet all of Dexter Grove's songs are transformed in the live setting, where Orlando and Drizos perpetually introduce new ideas, explore novel realms, and create varied moods in order to keep their music fresh and spirited.

DISCOGRAPHY

420 (1995)

Alive and Well at the Gates of Eden (1997). This disc captures the duo's invigorating, entrancing live show. The opener, "Flowers," starts out as a traditional acoustic offering, but it soon charges into spacier environs. Particularly notable is the third track, a twenty-four-minute journey that moves seemlessly through four separate songs, including the appealing "Pictures."

WEB SITE

www.goodnet.com/~gsche/dextergrove/

THE DISCO BISCUITS

- ■ **SAM ALTMAN:** *drums, percussion*
- ■ **MARC BROWNSTEIN:** *bass*
- ■ **JON GUTWILLIG:** *guitar, vocals*
- ■ **ARON MAGNER:** *keyboards, vocals*

The Disco Biscuits have finally started to live up to their name. For a long while, the group's moniker seemed deceptive or even off-putting to a number of people who weren't quite sure what to expect. In fact, prior to adding keyboard player Aron Magner, the Philadelphia quartet called itself Zex Sea, part of an elaborate mythology that band members had created surrounding a fictional body of water near the Aegean Islands. "It didn't quite work," explains bassist Marc Brownstein. When Magner joined, the group recognized that a similarly epic change in chemistry had occurred. Brownstein remarks that "Aron had grown up playing jazz piano. He was doing really well backing people in Philadelphia when he met us. Then after he caught us playing one evening, he approached us and, as nicely as possible, suggested that we were one man away from really doing something amazing. So we brought him in, and it was clear that if we could harness him that we would have something." They could and did. That accomplished, the band decided to select a new name. When the four became fixated on the two words, which they had overheard someone use in conversation, the selection process was complete.

However, until recently disco has been far from the band's sound. Instead, the group had become known for its propensity to embrace complex orchestration, which is why Frank Zappa's "Pygmy Twylyte" had become a live staple. As of late, though, the band has started to make some forays into techno. Says Brownstein: "Whatever you hear all the time is bound to seep into your music. If you hear Phish, you'll sound like Phish. Ten years ago, a lot of bands were listening to the Dead, so they sounded like the Dead. But our drummer had been in his room playing with a techno synthesizer through his computer. That's what we'd been hearing, and that's what's coming through in our music. We're really crafting our own sound. It has really freed us up to do whatever we want. We work the drums and bass into a loop, the guitar melody does the same, and then the keyboard lays down on top of that. Then we just let things evolve from there."

While drawing on this technique, the band's live performances continue to offer those elements that have become the Disco Biscuits hallmarks. The band's compositions often feature rapid melodic transitions and tempo shifts. When interpreting the songs, the Biscuits will expand on these ideas with elaborate improvisations. Guitarist Jon Gutwillig and keyboardist Magner trigger musical departures with searing runs on their instruments while Brownstein and Altman fuel them with complementary ideas. More and more people are attending the group's shows and taping the proceedings; this Brownstein attributes to the force of the group's live shows: "You put your game face on and rap a solid one. It helps." The Disco Biscuits are taking it deep.

DISCOGRAPHY

Encephalous Crime (1996). The opener, "Mr. Don," initiates the Biscuits's distinctive aural assault with charges led by Magner's swirling keys and Gutwillig's responsive guitar. The band also uses the studio to good effect as guest Elliot Levin contributes saxophone to the maniacal "Stone" and flute to the macabre "Devil's Waltz." The release concludes with two live songs: the band's impressive reading of Zappa's "Pygmy Twylyte" and its own, labyrinthine "Basis for a Day."

Uncivilized Area (1998). Band members demonstrate their ongoing development as songwriters and performers on this splashy release, which is brimming with ideas. All of the songs are performed live in the studio without overdubs, showcasing the group's improvisations offerings such as the jazz-flavored "Aceetobee" and "Morph Dusseldorf." However, the disc's cornerstone is the fifteen-minute techno-odyssey "Little Betty Boop." The quartet also shows that it can swing on the blithe closer "Awol's Blues."

WEB SITE

www.discobiscuits.com

DOMESTIC PROBLEMS

- ■ **JOB GROTSKY:** *alto and tenor saxophone, flute, clarinet*
- ■ **ANDY HOLTGREIVE:** *vocals, guitar*
- ■ **BILLY KENNY:** *trumpet, flügelhorn, mandolin*
- ■ **JASON MOODY:** *bass*
- ■ **JOHN NIEDZIELSKI:** *guitar, vocals*
- ■ **CHRISTIAN STANKEE:** *drums*

Grand Rapids, Michigan's, Domestic Problems injects its frenetic live shows with a healthy dose of humor. Thus, while the band continues to gain recognition for its vigorous performances, it also pens songs with lines such as "Where have you gone Mr. Snuffeleaupagaus?" (in "Ernie's Tragic Love Triangle"). Such lyrics might be expected from a band that drew its name from a line in the film *The Blues Brothers*. Moreover, although front man Andy Holtgreive doesn't do backflips across the stage like Jake Blues, the group does provide a high-octane spectacle.

The band's music reflects its affinities for funk, ska, soul, bluegrass, and rock. Billy Kenny, who cofounded the band with Holtgreive after they appeared as a duo in an Aquinas College talent show, moves from mandolin to trumpet to flügelhorn. Job Grotsky is similarly versatile, switching from brass to woodwinds. Guitarist John Niedzielski lays down some trenchant guitar lines. Holtgreive contributes bright vocals. These vivid grooves are supported by bassist Jason Moody and drummer Christian Stankee. Although the sextet imbues all of its songs with spirited, interlaced instrumentation, it maintains an emphasis on its entertaining, original compositions. All of this earned Domestic Problems several dates on the 1997 HORDE tour. In describing the group, Holtgreive explains: "We do not have extended jams in all of our songs, but that spirit of improvisation is always there, and it certainly comes out through our humor and our energy. We put on a different show every night."

DISCOGRAPHY

Scattered Pieces (1996)

Play (1997). This disc presents some varied and entertaining offerings. The title song is a splashy, horn-abetted introduction to the group's roster. "Ernie's Tragic Love Triangle" is an upbeat account of several *Sesame Street* characters that is built around Kenny's mandolin. "Just Let Go" starts off with a bluegrass feel and ends with some blustery scatting from Holtgreive. "Hob Nob" demonstrates the band's funkier side. Finally, the band shows that it can also play it straight with the gentle "My Only Love."

WEB SITE

www.domesticproblems.com

DONNA THE BUFFALO

- ■ **TOM GILBERT:** *drums*
- ■ **JED GREENBERG:** *bass, vocals*
- ■ **JIM MILLER:** *electric and acoustic guitar, vocals*
- ■ **TARA NEVINS:** *vocals, fiddle, accordion, acoustic guitar, tambourine*
- ■ **JEB PURYEAR:** *vocals, electric guitar*
- ■ **JOE THRIFT:** *keyboards, vocals*

Donna the Buffalo's origins can be traced to fiddle conventions. Guitarist Jim Miller notes, "We came to rock and roll through traditional music. We've been playing fiddle music together since the early 1980s. This genre, which is the precursor to bluegrass, has its own devoted subculture. We would often sit around in a circle and play a single tune for half an hour. In that situation, you play for yourself because you're the only audience. You play yourself into a trance, and you try to achieve a higher plane." Despite these beginnings, however, Donna the Buffalo explores different genres and sounds – particularly zydeco, reggae, Cajun, and rock. Furthermore, Tara Nevins is the only band member who performs on fiddle, and even she will often pick up an accordion, an acoustic guitar, or a washboard.

Always vibrant and meaningful, Donna the Buffalo's music can also be life affirming. Many of its lyrics convey a social message, whether issuing a moral challenge or sharing a life lesson. The group's principal songwriters, Nevins and Jeb Puryear, also pen evocative love songs. The band's instrumentation draws together electric guitars, Lowrey organs, and Nevins's sundry musical tools to produce warm, spirited sounds that in the live setting often instigate ardent dancing. "When everything's going," remarks Miller, "and we get a good vibe, and the space feels right, some songs just seem to take on a life of their own, and sometimes they don't seem to want to stop."

The band also hosts its own music festival. The Fingerlakes Grassroots Music Festival has been held annually near the band's home of Ithaca, New York, since 1991. The group donates receipts from the event to area charities. Miller jokingly insists that the festival came about because "Nobody was inviting us to play any festivals, so we decided that we better start our own so that we can play at one." The band has, in fact, graced a number of notable festivals, including the Merle Watson Festival, Birmingham's City Stages Festival, the Big Easy Bash, and the Berkshire Mountain Music Festival. However, Miller also comments that "There are some weekends that we still won't commit to anything else. Those are the times we get together and head out to the fiddle conventions."

DISCOGRAPHY

Donna the Buffalo (1993)

The Ones You Love (1996)

Rockin' in the Weary Land (1998). This release features a number of playful, uplifting compositions. "Tides of Time" is a pleasing opener, enriched by accordion and some well-placed guitar phrasings. "Funky Side" lives up to its name, but in true Donna the Buffalo fashion it also incorporates some fiddle. "Mr. King" is a paean and a promise to the slain civil-rights leader. "All the Time" is elevated by Nevins's rich vocalization of an engaging melody. "Conscious Evolution" is a pulsing, hook-filled song that is reminiscent of Bob Dylan. The disc closes with nearly eleven minutes of the hypnotic "Let Love Move Me."

WEB SITE

www.donnathebuffalo.com

SHELLEY DOTY

■ **SHELLEY DOTY:** *guitar, vocals*

Shelley Doty first captured the attention of many through her work with the band Jambay. For more than seven years, that group was renowned for its urgent, enthralling live performances. During that time, Jambay also recorded three releases and toured the United States. When the quartet finally disbanded in the fall of 1996, guitarist, songwriter, and vocalist Doty commenced a solo career. She currently performs both by herself and with her band, the Shelley Doty X-Tet. This group's roster of performers tends to fluctuate, but due to the great respect a number of area players have for Doty it often includes members of Box Set, the Living Daylights, and Pele Juju, along with some former Jambay bandmates.

Any given Doty performance promises a triple treat. Her songs are brimming with evocative lyrics and her gift for melody. Doty is also a distinctive singer whose rich vocals often incorporate some terser intonations, which add emphasis and verve. Finally, although her guitar supplies gentle folk expressions and incorporates some jazzier vocabulary, Doty can also crunch. Particularly when performing with a group, she is also willing to lead some excursions on the instrument. This has prompted a number of bands to invite Doty to appear with them on lead guitar, most notably Pele Juju. In any context, Doty is an emotive, compelling performer.

DISCOGRAPHY

Opportunity (1997). This five-song release showcases Doty's voice, her songs, and her acoustic guitar as she performs with the sole assistance of former Jambay bandmate Matt Butler on traps and percussion. "Sparrow Song" is elevated by Doty's passionate singing. The title track looks back on a missed chance by means of some playful musings. "Teeth" is a vibrant proclamation with a hint of snarling guitar.

WEB SITE

home.earthlink.net/~pietr/shelleydoty

DRIFTING THROUGH

- ■ **EVERETT BOLTON:** *bass, vocals*
- ■ **JAY DOYLE:** *guitar*
- ■ **RANDALL KIRSCH:** *vocals, guitar, percussion*
- ■ **PAUL MADIGAN:** *drums*
- ■ **BRIAN WERNER:** *keyboards*

Drifting Through's name reflects the Raleigh, North Carolina, group's professional aspirations (and echoes a line from a Jim Morrison poem). Bass player Everett Bolton elaborates: "What we really want to do is be a touring band. Playing live music is what gives us the most enjoyment. We want to go out and explore the country, town by town, state by state, just playing a show and then moving on." So far, the band's travels have taken it throughout the southeastern United States, but its peregrinations may soon carry it farther. The group has recently expanded into a quintet – the addition of Brian Werner on keyboards has thickened its grooves.

Vocalist/guitarist Randall Kirsch and bassist Bolton first assembled the group at Wake Forest University in 1995. They soon drew in guitarist Jay Doyle, and the band's dynamic sound emerged from the interplay of these three players. Kirsch and Bolton churn around one another to build a jam while Bolton pushes the duo. At present, steady drummer Paul Madigan and Werner also mesh on the group's original songs. Drifting Through also offers piquant arrangements of other artists' music, including an entertaining, extended take on Men at Work's "Down Under," which it breaks down and then slowly reconstructs. Bolton notes, "we try to bring the audience to an emotional high along with us, and we get there when we produce an uplifting improvisational jam."

DISCOGRAPHY

Extended Play (1996). On this six-song release, Kirsch's rich, buoyant vocals and the band's enthusiastic jams stand out. "The Ride" opens the disc and carries the listener for more than seven minutes. "Hatteras" builds from a funk riff, achieving explosive guitar textures. "Prophecy" presents some lively, acoustic-driven, percussive grooves.

GIBB DROLL BAND

- **BOB BOWEN:** *bass*
- **GIBB DROLL:** *guitar, vocals*
- **PETE MATHIS:** *keyboard, vocals*
- **MIKE WILLIAMS:** *drums*

Gibb Droll is one of the most passionate performers touring today. His assertive vocals partially account for this, but Droll has achieved particular renown for his volcanic guitar artistry. On any given evening, Droll will produce some stunning blues-based riffs and runs that affirm his command of the instrument. He is also an animated showman, at times drawing his guitar behind his head for a rapid-fire solo. One of his performance aims is to elicit from the audience what he describes as "a warm, friendly, exciting feeling. Hopefully, we will make people smile for a few hours." The Virginia-based musician realizes this goal most every evening, and, as a result, he is frequently compared with some of his own heroes and influences, including Albert King, Albert Collins, and Stevie Ray Vaughan.

In the years since the Gibb Droll Band's initial performance in 1991, the group has incorporated many other sounds and styles. In particular, Droll and his bandmates have drifted toward jazz. The quartet produces, for example, an intriguing transposition of Miles Davis's "All Blues." Droll will also occasionally offer a nod to a rock-guitar hero of yesteryear with a rapid-fire version of "Machine Gun." Still, the core of the band's live show consists of Droll's original music, which melds a number of these traditions. Observes Droll: "When we first started, the band was rooted firmly in the blues. Now it's more of a jazz-blues-rock fusion thing. But still I'd have to say that the blues will always provide an undercurrent to everything I do. It gives me a thrill to play a song before some people who might not have a deep knowledge of the blues and tell them that it was based on a version of Albert Collins's 'Frosty.'"

The guitarist has been able to hone his sound with the aid of the three musicians who join him on stage. Pete Mathis has been with the band since 1994, performing on a Fender Rhodes. Droll notes, "He contributes dark melodic structures. His melodic ear is wonderful, but because it's applied on the Rhodes it comes across that way. It's a big component of our sound." Droll also praises drummer Mike Williams, commenting, "He's the backbone. He has this loud, aggressive kick drum, which is essential to push anything along." The most recent addition to the band is upright bass player Bob Bowen. Remarks Droll: "He's not flashy. For him, it's all about laying behind the kick drum or pushing the kick drum. I'd have to say that in looking back when we were younger, a lot of times we'd really push it and try to play as many notes as possible. But I think Bob has supplied many lessons by example, and as a result he's really furthered our sound. He's taught us that space is a beautiful thing."

DISCOGRAPHY

Dharma (1994)

Narrow Mouth Jar (1995). The quartet performs nine of Droll's compositions on this release. The band's affinity for jazz is most apparent in the swinging "Ducky," which showcases each band member. The group's bluesier side is manifested in "Drop Dee." Other strong offerings include the funk-laced opener, "Time," the soulful "Fade Away," and the more atmospheric "A Dobro of Adam's." Finally, Droll offers homage to bluesman Albert King, welcoming the Gingerbread horn section for King's "You're Gonna Need Me."

WEB SITE

www.gibbdroll.com

DUDE OF LIFE

- **STEVE "DUDE OF LIFE" POLLAK:** *vocals*
- **GREAT RED SHARK**
- **PAUL GASSMAN:** *bass*
- **CLIFF MAYS:** *electric and acoustic guitar, vocals*
- **MARC THORS:** *keyboards*
- **JIM WEINGAST:** *drums, vocals*

Dude of Life was born at Connecticut's Taft School in the early 1980s. Steve Pollak was partying there one evening with Trey Anastasio and some other friends when the transformation occurred. Pollak recalls, "I entered the room clad in a tapestry, goggles, and a hat. Then I started spewing out utterings the nature of which remain shrouded in mystery. The next thing I knew, I was knighted the 'Dude of Life.'" In the days that followed, the Dude would reappear from time to time to lend vocals to Anastasio's high school group, Space Antelope. The pair maintained their friendship over the years, and Pollak later contributed lyrics and songs to Anastasio's band, Phish, including "Run like an Antelope" and "Suzie Greenberg." Pollak has also appeared on stage with Phish dressed in full Dude of Life regalia.

All the while, Pollak continued to compose songs of his own. These tunes graft his own delightfully skewed observations onto melodies and arrangements influenced by his idols: Iggy Pop, David Bowie, and the Beatles (his "Lucy in the Subway" riffs on "Lucy in the Sky with Diamonds"). "I had been working on these songs over an eight-year period," recalls Pollak, "so one day I just said to Trey, 'Why don't we go into the studio?' So we practiced for a few weeks, and then we recorded the tunes. It was a blast." When the disc was released in 1994, Pollak assembled the first Dude of Life band and mounted a tour. Over the ensuing years, the group has had a number of incarnations as various players have stepped in to lend a hand (including a number of Burlington luminaries and alumni of the group Shockra). While on the road, Pollak won a number of new supporters; one result of this was the Dude's appearance with moe. at that group's 1996 Wetlands New Year's Eve show, during which they performed Pollak's composition "Pete Rose."

In 1997, Pollak undertook a collaboration with the band Great Red Shark (one indication that these performers were kindred spirits was the fact that the group was named after the car in Hunter S. Thompson's *Fear and Loathing in Las Vegas*). Great Red Shark, which features the spirited guitar work of Cliff Mays, has built its own reputation as an improvisational outfit. Through all of this, Pollak has continued to don the same set of goggles that he wore on that fateful day at Taft. "I've always been true to my own heart," he says. "If I'm entertained by it, then my hope is that other people will be too. I think there should be a sense of fun and celebration involved, or what's the freaking point?"

DISCOGRAPHY

Crimes of the Mind (1994). This collection of Pollak's compositions features arrangements and performances by Phish. The eccentric imagery of "Dahlia," the opening tune, is melded to a catchy chorus. Other notable songs include the pulsing title track, the amusing ballad "Ordinary Day," and the vigorous "Self" (which not-too-coincidentally sounds like Phish's "Chalkdust Torture").

WEB SITE

www.dudeoflife.com

EKOOSTIK HOOKAH

- **DAVE KATZ:** *vocals, keyboards, acoustic guitar*
- **ERIC LANESE:** *drums, vocals*
- **ED MCGEE:** *guitar, vocals*
- **CLIFF STARBUCK:** *bass, vocals*
- **STEVE SWEENEY:** *guitar, vocals*

Ekoostik Hookah has distinguished itself in a variety of realms. First, and perhaps most importantly, the band creates rousing improvisational music, routinely delivering three hours of diverse, absorbing sounds without a set list. Drummer Eric Lanese remarks that "The only time I can remember we used a set list was one night opening for

Widespread Panic when we had a pretty tight time limit. Otherwise we might have spent twenty-five minutes on 'Viper' and then had time for one more song." Additionally, the group hosts its own biannual grassroots music festival, which brings thousands of fans to central Ohio. Finally, Ekoostik Hookah has the dubious honor of being the band with the most frequently misspelled name — in fact, it's even printed incorrectly here, as the first letter is not technically an E but rather a *schwa*, which looks like a backward E.

The Columbus-based band came together in 1991, playing purely for the fun of it. At the time, keyboardist Dave Katz, guitarist Steve Sweeney, and bassist Cliff Starbuck all had full-time gigs with other bands. However, the trio joined up with some more players for appearances at various local venues just for the fun of playing. Things took a turn when a friend who enjoyed the collaboration decided to produce a studio recording for them. The results convinced all of the players that the band should become their first priority. Ekoostik Hookah's original roster also included drummer Steve Frye — who was replaced by Lanese in 1993 — and rhythm guitarist John Mullins; during the summer of 1996, Mullins, who had contributed a number of memorable tunes to the group's repertoire, departed and was replaced by fellow songwriter Ed McGee.

The band's music builds on a blues-based rock core but also incorporates folk, jazz, and psychedelia. When asked to identify the band's influences, Sweeney states, "We're influenced by everything we've ever heard and everything we've yet to hear." Sweeney's piercing lead guitar is a commanding presence. McGee adds his own accents through the undervalued art of rhythm guitar playing. Primary vocalist and songwriter Katz contributes some swirling keys and occasionally straps on an acoustic. Cofounder Starbuck supplies some particularly tangy bass lines. Lanese proves particularly adept at presenting the band's atypical rhythms and time signatures.

The band is also known for its Hookaville Music Festival, which takes place on Memorial Day and Labor Day weekends. Hookaville debuted in 1993; despite having been advertised for only a few weeks, the event drew eight hundred people. Says Lanese: "Originally, we just wanted to play outside, invite some friends, and cook out. Now we like it because these are the two shows a year where we are totally in control. We can make sure that we have the best lights and the best sound." In recent years, the festival has grown steadily: now ten thousand revelers come to spend the weekend. The band has hosted a number of fine acts at Hookaville, including Merle Saunders, Leftover Salmon, Max Creek, Hypnotic Clambake, the David Nelson Band, and Zero. Of course, for many concertgoers, the climax of the festivities is the appearance of Ohio's own riveting jam band.

DISCOGRAPHY

Under Full Sail (1992)

Dubbah Buddah (1994)

Double Live (1996). This release presents two and a half hours of live Hookah. McGee is not heard on any of these tracks, which are drawn from a series of early-1995 performances. The band is in fine form as it works through a number of melodious compositions and creates a series of galvanic jams. It particularly stretches out on songs such as the seventeen-minute "Viper." Other solid offerings include "Brighter Days," "Ol' Montana Red Dog," and "Somewhere down the Line."

Where the Fields Grow Green (1998)

WEB SITE

www.ekoostik.com

ELECTRIC CIRCUS

- **GARY DUTRA:** *guitars, vocals*
- **CHRIS HENDERSON:** *bass*
- **MIKE WALTZ:** *drums, vocals*
- **DERRICK ZANE:** *guitar, vocals*

Electric Circus is a dynamic member of the thriving Chico, California, music scene. The band has earned plaudits for the diversity of its live performances. Some of this eclecticism is musical, as the group explores rock, funk, country, and psychedelia. However, on any given night the band also welcomes additional players to the stage to add zest to the fricassee – from a guest vocalist to a horn section to a pedal steel player. Moreover, drummer Mike Waltz explains, the members of Electric Circus "used to dress up in costumes for every show. But we cut back on that once we started playing three or four times a week. What are you supposed to do when your chrome-crotch pants fall apart?"

The group first performed together in 1990. Waltz had come to California to attend Chico State University, and there he'd hooked up with childhood friends Gary Dutra, Chris Henderson, and Saul Henson. The band soon gained notoriety while hosting several late-night events. Recalls Waltz, "We had a number of shows at the Love Barn. There everyone parked out back in the orchard, and unless you knew what was going on, there was no sign of any earthly pleasures." As a result of one particularly exhilarating show in Tahoe, the band was invited to contribute to the soundtrack of the snowboarding film *Carpe Diem* alongside Leftover Salmon and Metallica.

In 1997, local legend Henson left Electric Circus, and this loss prompted the group to reevaluate its musical aims. After working with a series of players, the remaining band members chose Derrick Zane to replace Henson; Zane now contributes some assertive guitar and vocals. Says Waltz: "The audiences are still coming out and responding to what we're doing. That's the important thing, because we thrive on that. They're the conductors."

DISCOGRAPHY

Magic Mountain (1994)

Argus Dreams (1997). Here Electric Circus is joined by some guest players who help the band work through varied grooves. "What You Take" features some crunching guitar and solid vocal harmonies. "Machine" is a swampy offering reminiscent of ZZ Top, "Argula" presents the group's funkier side, and "Grease Monkey" incorporates tenor sax for some swinging blues. The disc closes with the epic "Gloryhole Revisited," which layers Hammond organ and pedal steel to create a more complex sonic environment.

WEB SITE

www.electriccircus.com

EMMA GIBBS BAND

- **BRENT BUCKNER:** *harmonica*
- **DREW CANNON:** *guitar*
- **ANDREW LEVASSEUR:** *drums and percussion*
- **JEFF REMSBURG:** *bass*
- **WILL STRAUGHAN:** *mandolin, trumpet, vocals*
- **RICHARD UPCHURCH:** *vocals, guitar*

The Emma Gibbs Band features nary an Emma nor a Gibbs, but the Winston-Salem, North Carolina, sextet does provide some upbeat, jaunty grooves. The group builds on blues and bluegrass traditions to create a sound that it describes as "a sweet blend of corn-fried okra and Miller High Life." This combination is further flavored by the enthusiasm and spirit of the band's players, many of whom have been performing together in various formations and incarnations since they were in grade school. Along with its original music, the Emma Gibbs Band presents some covers that reflect its background and intent — from Sam Bush's "Same Ol' River" to Stevie Ray Vaughan's "Tight-rope" to a few songs by the erstwhile southern jam band Indecision: "Engine 49" and "Walk the Corner."

The consistently creative contributions of all six members are the source of the band's strength. Richard Upchurch introduces most songs with his vivid vocal tones, which some have likened to those of Strangefolk's Reid Genauer. Guitarist Drew Cannon varies his tangy leads to enrich the sound. Will Straughan supplies flat picking on mandolin and occasionally adds trumpet flourishes. Brent Buckner carefully selects the spaces to interject his harmonica soliloquies. Bass player Jeff Remsburg lends a range of assertive tones. Finally, Andrew LeVasseur contributes a crackling backbeat that is heavily informed by the language of jazz. All of these players step forward in the live setting, and it is their collaborative ethos that defines and elevates the Emma Gibbs Band.

Emma Gibbs Band (1996). The band's debut is comprised of eleven solid, original tunes (one of which was written by LeVasseur's brother Jason). "Skinny Legs," the disc's bright opener, is laced with ebullient harmonica. "New England," the pleasing song that follows, has some solid fills on mandolin. Other strong offerings include the rollicking "Ain't Going Nowhere," the catchy "Circles," and the spirited jam "Golden Dream."

THE EMPTYS

- ■ **DOUG DERRYBERRY:** *electric guitar, vocals*
- ■ **PETER FRAIZE:** *saxophone*
- ■ **LELAND NAKAMURA:** *drums*
- ■ **JEFF REICH:** *bass*
- ■ **MITCH TREGER:** *vocals, acoustic guitar*

Doug Derryberry, guitarist for the Emptys, may be best known for his production work. His career started in the 1980s when he performed in the duo Derryberry and Alagia. Although that act developed a following, particularly in the southeast, Derryberry and musical partner John Alagia were cast into the national spotlight when they produced and engineered the first two Dave Matthews Band releases. Since then, Derryberry has worked with a number of other groups, including the Gibb Droll Band, Fighting Gravity, Everything, Blue Miracle, the Emma Gibbs Band, and Blue Dogs. It was one such session with the members of the Emptys that led to his greater involvement with the group.

In February 1992, the band approached him to produce a demo. Derryberry recalls, "at that time, it was clear that Mitch [Treger] had great songs, but I was not altogether sold on the band." However, when the Emptys returned to work with him a year later, its lineup had changed considerably. Soon afterward, when the band started playing out, it invited Derryberry to join in on electric guitar, and within a few months he was a full-fledged member. "We never really decided that," he remembers. "It just kind of happened." In 1994, the group issued an invitation to noted jazz saxophonist Peter Fraize, and he has been with the Emptys ever since.

The band performs rock music with a jazz sensibility. Fraize has served as coordinator of jazz studies in the Department of Music at George Washington University. Drummer Leland Nakamura is similarly trained in the genre. Derryberry heaps praise upon Treger for his songwriting abilities: "He has a singularly unique approach to writing. It is within the accepted parameters of pop song craft, but he makes up songs and phrases that are unique yet still resonate within a large number of people's sensibilities." In the live setting, the band often draws on the improvisational talents of its players to create some inviting grooves, although it also maintains its focus on Treger's compositions. Derryberry affirms, "It's all about the songs. There are a lot of styles embodied in our repertoire, and hopefully some good playing."

DISCOGRAPHY

Bridge across the Ocean (1994)

Pick Your Ears Up (1995). This release collects a number of mellisonant, literate offerings. Treger's writing is particularly engrossing on tracks such as "Destination Non-Action" and "Sipping from the Fountain." "Shadows in the Sand" presents the band's jazz-inflected expressions along with Treger's smooth vocals. Saxophonist Fraize animates a few tracks, including "Born to Live." Derryberry steps up on guitar throughout the disc — during "TV," for instance.

WEB SITE

www.emptys.com

ENTRAIN

- **BRIAN ALEX:** *guitar, vocals*
- **SAM HOLMSTOCK:** *percussion, trombone, keyboards, vocals*
- **TOM MAJOR:** *drums and percussion*
- **ROB SOLTZ:** *percussion, didgeridoo*
- **STEVE TULLY:** *tenor, baritone and soprano saxophone, keyboards, vocals*

Entrain first came together on Martha's Vineyard in 1993. Founding member Tom Major, a veteran of world tours with Bo Diddley and Southside Johnny, designed the group as a percussion-oriented project. Sam Holmstock joined after his own popular polyrhythmic ensemble, the Ululators, dissolved. Holmstock notes, "The group's name refers to synchronization. Our band provides a marriage of rhythms. Of course, if you look in a dictionary the first definition you'll see is getting on a train, which is appropriate in a metaphoric sense as well."

Attending an Entrain show can be like boarding a train. The combustive engine is undoubtedly represented by the group's drummers, whose zesty, boisterous rhythms keep the music rolling. Additional energy is generated by the band's thunderous improvisations: as Holmstock remarks, "Almost every song has some moment of release where a player or combination of players has a chance to open things up." However, the band also retains an emphasis on its original compositions, crafting an expanding catalog of music that incorporates funk, ska, Latin, and rock. The results have earned Entrain such plaudits as a Boston Music Award for outstanding live performance.

In September of 1994, Entrain was invited to perform for the White House press corps, which was stationed on Martha's Vineyard while President Clinton vacationed there. Carly Simon joined the band during its set and then encouraged the president to do the same. Clinton took the stage and jammed with the group for nearly an hour, performing on rock standards as well as on some Entrain originals. Entrain's visibility is increasing: the band is referenced on the television program *Buffy the Vampire Slayer* – an Entrain bumper sticker appears on the locker next to Buffy's (and in the girls' bathroom next to the towel dispenser).

DISCOGRAPHY

Entrain (1994)
Can You Get It (1996)

No Matter What (1997). The group's varied offerings are well represented on this, its third recording for its own Dolphin Safe Records
label. The opener, "Colorblind," is marked by bright vocals and a
winsome melody. The title track supplies some splashy funk. The
entertaining "Bathtub Jesus" is built on a ska beat. Also, the
group's arrangement of the traditional "Che-Che Kore" provides
a compelling vehicle for Entrain's flexible rhythms.

WEB SITE

www.tiac.net/users/entrain

EVERYTHING

- **RICH BRADLEY:** *tenor saxophone, guitar, vocals*
- **NATE BROWN:** *percussion, vocals*
- **CRAIG HONEYCUTT:** *vocals, guitar*
- **WOLFE QUINN:** *keyboards, trombone*
- **DAVID SLANKARD:** *bass*
- **STEVE VAN DAM:** *guitar, alto saxophone, clarinet, vocals*

Everything's moniker is not a misnomer. The Virginia sextet crafts
songs that playfully blend genres, including funk, ska, soul, reggae,
rock, and jazz. In particular, band members single out their regard for
Washington, DC's, indigenous go-go music, a style that melds hip-hop
rhythms and strident horns. The group puts forth these sounds during
its kinetic live frolics, which feature both burnished arrangements and
spontaneity.

The band came together at James Madison University in 1989. Its members initially practiced in the dorms and gigged regularly at local clubs and colleges. In 1992, however, they decided to commit collectively to their music on a full-time basis. So they moved into the remote renovated farmhouse that still serves as their rehearsal space, recording studio, and communal environment in which to explore and hone creative impulses. Soon afterward, Everything embarked on a relentless tour schedule and currently plays more than two hundred dates a year.

The band has achieved renown for its entertaining live performances. They are powered by the group's euphonious compositions channeled, in part, through Craig Honeycutt's engaging vocals. Additionally, Everything's versatile players provide varied instrumentation, at times within the context of a single song. For instance, Rich Bradley, Wolfe Quinn, and Steve Van Dam can put down their respective instruments and reconstitute themselves as a brash horn trio. Meanwhile, the group strives to augment the concertgoing experience even further, bringing liquid lights and computer-graphics presentations to a variety of venues that rarely witness such enhancements. The band's members have a penchant for creative costuming as well: they've been known to don dresses and other female finery, although this practice has abated in recent years. All in all, these many aspects of the band's show, along with Everything's affinity for improvisation, have given rise to a dynamic, vivacious concert environment, where anything (and everything) seem possible.

DISCOGRAPHY

Sol*id (1993)

Labrador (1994)

Everything (1996)

Super Natural (1998). On this release, Everything's canvas is brushed with a variety of vivid sounds. The title track boasts buoyant keys and brass with some hip-hop flavorings. "Hooch" is a contagious, entrancing offering that displays the band's honeyed vocal harmonies. In "Good Thing (St. Lucia)," the horns transport festive New Orleans street sounds to the Caribbean. "Ladybug" is also noteworthy, because it introduces some jazzy guitar expressions.

WEB SITE

www.ecolon.com

FAT CATS

- **JEFF COWELL:** *drums and percussion*
- **CHRIS GATCHENE:** *vocals, guitar*
- **TYLER GIBSON:** *keyboards, vocals*
- **TODD GILLES:** *vocals, guitar*
- **DAVE HILL:** *bass*
- **JOEL STOUFFER:** *drums and percussion*

The core members of the Fat Cats have known each other since high school. The solid friendships between guitarists/vocalists Chris Gatchene and Todd Gilles and keyboardist Tyler Gibson have both facilitated the band's musical communication and enabled the band to endure. When the Fat Cats came into being in the Canadian province of Ontario in 1992, these players were joined by three other musicians, including another vocalist. But although the original trio eventually parted ways with these players, they remained committed to their music. For a period during 1997, the band actually performed a number of gigs without a drummer. Recently, however, the Fat Cats has been twice blessed in the percussion department, and the revitalized group now gigs as a sextet once again.

The Fat Cats is one of Canada's preeminent jam bands. Gatchene and Gilles provide bluesy, spiraling guitar leads, and Gibson contributes his own swirling, resonant expressions on a Hammond organ. Bass player Dave Hill has worked with the trio for some time now, and he is skilled at anchoring the band. Drummers Jeff Cowell and Joel Stouffer have injected new vigor into the group's sets. Band members are skilled at negotiating the space around one another to produce some absorbing sounds. Because the group encourages both audio and video recording of its shows, it continues to gain supporters as Fat Cats tapes make the rounds.

DISCOGRAPHY

Cruelty's Cure (1994). Although this release features an older lineup (a new disc is imminent), it still demonstrates the allure of the band. Gatchene, Gibson, and Gilles all make substantial contributions to the music presented here through their performances and their songwriting. In particular, tunes such as "Too Many Choices" and "As Much as This" highlight the talents of these players. Additionally, former vocalist Deanna Knight appears on several tracks, including "Might Have Been Something" and "Weary."

FAT MAMA

- **ERIK DEUTSCH:** *keyboards*
- **MARVIN GARRETT:** *bass*
- **JONATHAN GOLDBERGER:** *guitar*
- **JON GRAY:** *trumpet, trombone*
- **BRETT JOSEPH:** *tenor saxophone*
- **MIKE RHODE:** *didgeridoo, percussion*
- **JOE RUSSO:** *drums*

Fat Mama is another tantalizing constituent of Boulder, Colorado's, rich improvisational-music scene. However, unlike many of the region's bands, this octet's sound is not grounded in bluegrass or rock. Instead, Fat Mama incorporates some intriguing instrumentation, including a Moog synthesizer and a didgeridoo, to produce an amalgam of jazz and funk that yields some thick, majestic grooves.

The group developed at the University of Colorado, where a few of the players met in the dorms. Bassist Marvin Garrett and saxophonist Brett Joseph had been playing with a reggae band that had dissolved. As other players came aboard, including keyboardist Erik Deutsch, the band developed a more funk-flavored sound. However, with the addition of trumpeter Jon Gray and guitarist Jonathan Goldberger, the group turned toward jazz. Its music now proves distinctive, drawing together resonant keyboards, delicate guitar, brash horns, two entwined drummers, and, of course, the didgeridoo.

Fat Mama is particularly vital live, when its adventuresome players revel in unfettered extemporization. But Fat Mama does not simply walk into a room and jam — this is a band with a plan. Percussionist/didgeridooer Mike Rhode explains: "Before we play a show, we'll always spend quite a bit of time talking about the last show, analyzing what worked, what didn't, and why. The best nights are when we really stretch out and do something new, particularly when we think through concepts and manifest them." The group's compositions serve as structures from which its players may introduce perilous runs, articulate expressions, and more contemplative musings. Fat Mama also works through several covers, including a version of Miles Davis's "What I Say" that sometimes approaches the thirty-minute mark. Rhode expresses the spirit of the band by observing, "You can only say so much in words. The reason we play music is because that is how we express ourselves. Especially live, because that is where the creation is happening."

DISCOGRAPHY

Mamatus (1997). This release documents the band's ingenuity, inviting the listener to sit in as Fat Mama fashions its spellbinding improvisations. "Pimp Slap" bounds out of the box with some charismatic horns layered over a funky bottom. In "Gefilteluv," the band's percussion moves to the fore, while "Alpha Zulu" features some fluid guitar declarations. "Blue Monte" contains some strident horn work, while "Cameljob/When the Machine Breaks Down" proves more ethereal.

WEB SITE

www.fatmama.com

FIGHTING GRAVITY

- **MIKE BOYD:** *drums and percussion*
- **SCHIAVONE MCGEE:** *vocals*
- **DAVID PETERSON:** *bass, vocals*
- **DAVID TRIANO:** *guitar, vocals*

In 1986, while they were still Richmond, Virginia, college students, guitarist David "Tree" Triano and bass player David Peterson decided to put together a band that could perform the music that they appreciated — in particular, ska. They set out to enlist like-minded bandmates. Drummer Mike Boyd soon joined the pair (a move that would alter his educational path: the former Virginia Tech student subsequently earned a music degree from Virginia Commonwealth University). After recruiting a horn section, the group solidified with the addition of singer Schiavone McGee, a former vocal major at Virginia Commonwealth University who was invited to join the band after Triano heard him singing along to an English Beat song in the record store where he worked. With this lineup in place, the group soon earned a number of gigs under the name Boy O Boy.

Boy O Boy swiftly earned acclaim as one of the area's premier ska outfits. It was particularly noted for its high-octane live performances. Beginning in 1991, the group produced recordings on an annual basis through its own BOB Records label (which is an acronym for the band's name and a configuration that worked its way into the titles of these releases). By 1994, however, although the group retained its affection for ska and solidified its grounding in the genre, its members had decided that, in order to keep their performances and their songwriting fresh and animated, they would have to expand their musical offerings. They resolved to keep exploring world beat while turning up the rock knob a bit. This evolution — and a name conflict with another group — ultimately led to the creation of the grassroots musical dynamo that is Fighting Gravity. The quartet has toured relentlessly (playing in excess of two hundred dates a year) while refining its music. The band's renown as a committed touring collective led to a 1996 *Rolling Stone* feature article on its road ethic.

Regardless of the crowd or venue size (although both are certainly on the rise), Fighting Gravity supplies athletic stage feats and musical dynamism. McGee's smooth vocals and affable presence are an additional source of acclaim, as is Triano's guitar work, a series of concise exclamations and extended declarations. Spirited horn arrangements are interspersed throughout. The band's zeal and dedication to its live shows are perhaps best evinced by the time when Boyd literally dented his head a few hours prior to a gig; he had an emergency-room physician staple it shut so that the show could continue (the event is immortalized by a photo in the band's disc *No Stopping, No Standing*).

DISCOGRAPHY

Boy O Boy (1991)

Shishkabob (1992)

Bobsled (1993)

No Stopping, No Standing (1994)

Forever = 1 Day (1996). This recording documents the ongoing evolution of the group's sound. The first song, "One Day," is an absorbing ska piece. "Lost in the Rain" tones back these elements while engaging the listener with its melody and vocal harmonies. The lilting "Mission Bells" and "Fools and King" are elevated by McGee's warm vocals and the band's honeyed groove. The closer, "Shattered and Torn," represents a return to Fighting Gravity's rock-steady roots.

WEB SITE

www.fightinggravity.com

FIJI MARINERS

- **BRUCE HAMPTON:** *vocals, guitar, chazoid*
- **DR. DAN MATRAZZO:** *keyboards*
- **SONNY NAKAZAWA:** *drums*

In 1994, due to high blood pressure and exhaustion, Colonel Bruce Hampton retired from his role as front man of the band he had founded, Aquarium Rescue Unit. However, after taking some months to relax, Zambi, his creative deity, called to him once again, urging him to assemble a new band. This time he opted for a trio with himself on vocals and a range of stringed instruments, Dr. Dan Matrazzo on keyboards (supplying bass lines with his left hand), and Sonny Nakazawa on drums. The group drew its name from the Pacific island of Fiji, whose natives' communal exchanges and purity of spirit served as an analogue for this project. Of course, the rumor that Fiji sits atop the lost continent of Mu seems equally appropriate, both because it hints at immense structures beneath the surface and because it contains elements of mythology and apocrypha.

Hampton's skewed musings are the heart of the band's presentation. For instance, Hampton describes the Mariners song "Raining in My Car" as a homespun slice of life, asserting that on more than one occasion he has been driving in his automobile on a sunny day while it was pouring inside the vehicle. Also, after mentioning the band's desire to perform in Fiji, he says it could not happen in an even-numbered year. Of course, such observations come naturally to Hampton, whose 1971 *Music to Eat* release with the Hampton Grease Band is reportedly the worst-selling double album in the history of Columbia Records. (This experimental effort is said to have been pitched as a comedy album to some stores.) The question of whether it was in fact Columbia's all-time worst seller is hotly debated: *Music to Eat* may have been vanquished by a yoga album. Still, the underlying spunk and unmitigated weirdness of *Music to Eat* inspired its re-release in 1996. This led Hampton to observe that when he was nineteen he was playing to rooms of mostly forty year olds and that when he was in his forties he began playing to rooms of nineteen year olds.

Fiji Mariners cofounder Matrazzo has an interesting history of his own. He has performed with a number of sterling players, including Clarence Gatemouth Brown and Steve Vai. He has also brought his Hammond B-3 proficiency to the recordings of other artists, including Jimmy Hall. However, the most fascinating tidbit about Matrazzo is that when he was a young man growing up in Japan he belonged to a pop-music group very much akin to the Monkees. Every once in a while someone will attend a Fiji Mariners show and be entranced by the appearance of the Davey Jones of Japan.

The band draws together a number of musical styles, which, along with its penchant for impromptu excursions and digressions, galvanizes listeners in the live setting. Hampton's varied instrumentation allows him to tear up a blues number, provide a bluegrass feel, and sometimes even rock out. Matrazzo's own blizzard of ideas yields some particularly assertive jazz expressions. Sonny Nakazawa's drumming bridges these many realms. Meanwhile, Hampton's slightly off-kilter, stentorian vocals remain a genre unto themselves.

DISCOGRAPHY

Fiji (1996). The band's debut, recorded on vintage analog equipment, reveals its sound to be larger than one might expect, due in part to its members' musicianship and in part to the guest appearances of many admirers (including Count Mbutu, Mike Gordon, and Dave Schools). The opener, "Earth," kicks forward, distinguished by Hampton's vocals and some complementary slide guitar from Derek Trucks. The instrumental "Dolores" is animated by Matrazzo's sprightly keys. "Nowhere Is Now Here" builds on one of Hampton's characteristically skewed aphorisms through some jazzier phrasings. "Raining in My Car" melds a similarly curious account with some southern blues-boogie. Finally, "Pleasure Seeking Fiji Disco

Women'' is an exhilarating, demented disco number employing banjo, chazoid, oboe, tabla, and theremin.

Live (1998)

WEB SITE

www.fijimariners.com

BELA FLECK AND THE FLECKTONES

■ **BELA FLECK:** *banjo*
■ **ROY "FUTURE MAN" WOOTEN:** *synth-axe drumitar*
■ **VICTOR WOOTEN:** *bass*

One afternoon in 1988, Bela Fleck received a phone call from a studio engineer who was recording with a bass player. Fleck listened as Victor Wooten performed through the phone line, and then he invited Wooten to come out and jam with him. A few months later, when the banjo player was invited to perform on a *Lonesome Pine* television special, he assembled a band that included Wooten, Howard Levy on keyboards, and Wooten's brother Roy "Future Man" Wooten on percussion. With the exception of Levy, who has since moved on to other projects, the original lineup remains intact. Each member of the trio is a world-class musician and innovator in his own right, so that their collective efforts are typically exceptional.

Fleck began performing on banjo as a teenager after becoming attracted to the instrument through Earl Scruggs's performance of the theme song to *The Beverly Hillbillies*. While attending New York City High School of Music and Art, he received lessons on the side from a few individuals, including the famed Tony Trischka (the school did not deem banjo to be an acceptable instrument). Following Trischka's recommendation, Fleck moved soon after graduation to Boston, where he appeared with the band Tasty Licks. At age twenty-two, he relocated to Nashville, where he began playing with Spectrum. In 1980, mandolin player Sam Bush invited him to perform with the genre-busting New Grass Revival, and Fleck went on to record five albums with the band, which last performed during an opening slot on the Grateful Dead's 1989 New Year's Eve show. Over the years, Fleck's talents have earned him a series of accolades, including being named "Best Banjoist" five years in a row by *Frets* magazine (after which he was retired to the "Gallery of the Greats"). He has also performed with a range of artists, including Phish, Branford Marsalis, and the Dave Matthews Band.

Victor Wooten is an ingenious player who has encouraged many other bassists to transcend the traditional limits of the instrument. His agile displays support his fellow Flecktones but often soar on their own. As a result, he has won top recognition from *Bass Player* magazine and was the recipient of the 1997 Gibson Award. Wooten has also released a solo recording, *A Show of Hands*.

Future Man supplies percussion on his self-designed synth-axe drumitar. The guitar-shaped instrument is comprised of pressure-sensitive finger pads, which produce digitally sampled tonal and percussion sounds. Future Man slings the drumitar around his neck and stands next to his bandmates, furiously popping. The instrument allows him to simulate a traditional drum kit with just a few fingers; he uses his other digits to produce an array of tones and colors.

The three musicians blend their individual talents to create some novel, liberating sounds. Fleck's instrumentation and background certainly bring an element of bluegrass to the group. However, the band's sound is much more akin to the mid-1970s jazz creations of keyboardist Chick Corea. Any Flecktones show also features some dazzling solo displays. Still, the group's cornerstone may be its awe-inspiring improvisations: Fleck admits that the group frequently launches into its songs without any predetermined resolution in mind. The Flecktones perform an average of two hundred nights a year (at times with guests such as Bush on mandolin or Paul McCandless on saxophone and clarinet), which only serve to augment the group's legendary communication skills.

DISCOGRAPHY

Bela Fleck and the Flecktones (1990)
Flight of the Cosmic Hippo (1991)

UFO TUFO (1992)

Three Flew over the Cuckoo's Nest (1993)

Live Art (1996). Most Flecktones fans find this to be the band's definitive offering. These two discs collect a number of notable performances, many of which feature special guests. Fleck's former New Grass Revival bandmate John Cowan adds vocals to the Beatles song "Oh Darling." Paul McCandless contributes some keening clarinet to an unplugged "Flight of the Cosmic Hippo." Howard Levy appears with his former bandmates for a captivating version of "Sinister Minister." Victor Wooten is showcased during a stirring solo improvisation that ends with "Amazing Grace." Fleck presents a range of banjo styles in "Early Reflection/Bach/ The Ballad of Jed Clampet," ending with a gleeful run though the television show theme song that first inspired him to pick up the instrument. Finally, and perhaps most notably, Fleck welcomes his longtime idol, jazz pianist Chick Corea on both "The Message" and "Cheeseballs in Cowtown."

Left of Cool (1998)

WEB SITE

www.flecktones.com

FOOL'S PROGRESS

- **MATT COCONIS:** *drums*
- **REED FOEHL:** *vocals, guitar*
- **TIM ROPER:** *violin, flute, piano, organ, harmonica, vocals*
- **CURTIS THOMPSON:** *bass, vocals*

Reed Foehl has been contributing songs, vocals, and guitar to Fool's Progress since he formed the band in 1989. Actually, this is not altogether true: from the group's inception through early 1997, it gigged as Acoustic Junction. Indeed, the band developed a national following under that name, touring from coast to coast while performing over two hundred dates a year. The name Acoustic Junction was appropriate at first – when Foehl started things off, the band members performed acoustic-driven folk on stools without a drummer. However, the current quartet's instrumentation and diverse musical offerings exceed the realms suggested by its original moniker, so it has become Fool's Progress, an appellation drawn from the title of a book written by eco-author Edward Abbey (also known for *The Monkey Wrench Gang*).

The band's music is an amalgam of its members' individual interests and experiences. Foehl, the group's principal songwriter, grew up surrounded with sounds – as his parents perform in a bluegrass band (and the singer has had the distinct pleasure of inviting that group to gig with his own band). As a teenager, Foehl did some busking with his acoustic guitar at Boston's Faneuil Hall Marketplace. By contrast, drummer Matt Coconis's extensive performing experience includes some stints playing speed metal. Bass player Curtis Thompson began his musical career on guitar and even eked out a living as a street performer in Boulder, Colorado, an experience he believes strengthened his vocals. Multi-instrumentalist Tim Roper, who graduated from college with a major in violin, has performed with the Fort Collins Symphony Orchestra yet retains a deeper love for powerful, extemporized music.

All of these predilections and proficiencies become manifest in Fool's Progress's live shows. First, due to its folk background, the band maintains a focus on Foehl's songs, which often contain bright, winsome melodies with three-part vocal harmonies. However, Fool's Progress is also a band that welcomes a spirited jam. Utility man Roper often drives these journeys, switching between keyboards, violin, flute, and harmonica within the span of a single song or improvisation. Roper's contributions prove additionally notable, as he will often play his violin instead of lead guitar; many fans find this particularly intriguing when the band works through an infrequent Pink Floyd cover. In all of these endeavors, Roper is joined by his bandmates' own radiant expressions. It is this live energy that distinguishes Fool's Progress, demonstrating the wisdom of its name change – there is quite a bit of electricity at this acoustic junction.

DISCOGRAPHY

Love It for What It Is (1991, as Acoustic Junction)

Surrounded by Change (1993, as Acoustic Junction)

Fool's Progress (1997). This release manifests the band's diverse moods and methods. "Think about It" provides an uplifting message sweetened with Roper's violin. "Broken Mirrors" features some bluesier guitar as well as the soaring vocal harmonies of Jen Hutman. Other notable tracks include the upbeat "East Side Story," which incorporates some swirling keys; the gentle, richly textured "Sugartown," and the spare, lovely "Sometimes I Wonder." The disc closes in pleasing fashion as Foehl's affable vocals and Roper's harmonica enliven the rollicking "Whereabouts Unknown."

WEB SITE

www.foolsprogress.com

FOXTROT ZULU

- **NATE EDMUNDS:** *guitar, vocals*
- **BRAD HAAS:** *bass*
- **NEAL JONES:** *guitar, vocals*
- **TERRYSTON "T.K." KYAN:** *saxophone, vocals, mandolin*
- **JEFF LIGHT:** *trumpet, flügelhorn, vocals*
- **PAUL MILLER:** *percussion*
- **JEFF ROBERGE:** *drums*

Foxtrot Zulu began in 1992 with a group of friends who shared a house in Narragansett, Rhode Island, while attending college. Guitarists Nate Edmunds and Neal Jones had attended high school together and were eager to form a band. They took to rehearsing in their cellar, and, one by one, their various friends dropped by and were added to the mix. (Drummer Jeff Roberge had never really performed on drums until he seated himself behind the kit, eager to join his buddies.) Jones recalls that the group quickly devoted itself to rehearsing and to "playing for anything that people could offer us." By 1995, with the release of *Moe's Diner*, the gig offers had escalated — Foxtrot Zulu bounded out of the state to perform more than 150 dates a year up and down the East Coast.

The band's seven-piece lineup thrives on the strength of twin instrumentation. Edmunds and Jones have developed complementary guitar styles. Percussionist Paul Miller and drummer Roberge pound out interlaced rhythms. Foxtrot Zulu is also enlivened by the brash brass of T.K. Kyan and Jeff Light. Jones affirms that "the band's strengths are the horns and percussion and the way the rest of us work off them."

The group's potent live show features mesmerizing improvisations that expand on ideas suggested by its melodious original compositions. These songs, which are developed collectively, draw from the members' individual partialities for ska, jazz, hardcore, and classic rock. The band cultivates the resulting grooves, which erupt in the concert setting. Jones affirms: "When people come out to see us, they can expect to dance. We supply a lot of energy regardless of the crowd size, whether it be two or two hundred or two thousand. Of course, when people really get into it, we try to play up to their caliber."

DISCOGRAPHY

Moe's Diner (1995)

Burn Slow (1997). On this seventy-four-minute release, the band does a fine job of bringing its scorching live show into the studio. The fiery opener, "Ryders," presents Foxtrot Zulu's full range of flavors — it's rife with harmonies, hooks, and horns. "Moe's Diner" yields some sultry sax, which gives way to a more frenzied display. "Spin Me" works through a number of movements that prove both entrancing and ecstatic. "Watchcat" is a turbulent, funk-flavored workout. "Freight Train" barrels to an appropriate, screeching conclusion.

WEB SITE

www.foxtrotzulu.com

FREDDY JONES BAND

- ■ **WAYNE HEALY:** *vocals, electric guitar, talkbox*
- ■ **SIMON HORROCKS:** *drums and percussion, acoustic guitar, mandolin*
- ■ **MARTY LLOYD:** *vocals, electric and acoustic guitar*
- ■ **MARK MURPHY:** *bass*

Wayne Healy and Marty Lloyd began playing guitar together while still attending high school in the Midwest. The pair eventually made their way to Chicago, where they sought out other musicians who shared their goals and musical predilections, eventually hooking up with Simon Horrocks and the brothers Bonaccorsi (Jim and Rob). This quintet dubbed itself the Freddy Jones Band — an appellation that celebrates neither a band member nor a mutual acquaintance. Despite the recent departure of the Bonaccorsis, the group has endured and has drafted bass player Mark Murphy. Its moniker has come to represent its staying power: the Freddy Jones Band retains a collective identity.

Although the band is bereft of Freddy, it does not lack songwriters, vocalists, or guitarists. On its most recent release, *Lucid*, each band member contributes original material. Observes Horrocks: "With multiple singers and songwriters, the band is a really good forum for bringing lots of different ideas to the table." Vocal duties are shared, predominantly between Healy and Lloyd (when performing the song "Wonder," for example, Healy delivers the verses and Lloyd the choruses). Moreover, the band's sound is built on the dual guitar work of Healy and Lloyd (on *Lucid*, Horrocks joins in on acoustic guitar and on mandolin). All of this is very much in the spirit of the group's name.

Lloyd comments: "The whole point of the band name is that every member is part of the band's identity. There's no single creative source — each of us plays an important role."

The Freddy Jones Band thrives when playing before an audience. In this environment, the guitarists, in particular, really open things up; Healy's melodic phrasings interact with Lloyd's intonations. Of course, Healy and Lloyd also draw in concertgoers with their emotive vocals. The group has gained many devotees over the years while gigging with acts such as Big Head Todd and the Monsters and Widespread Panic. It also retains an avid fan base in its home city; these people will come out for any area show, eager to celebrate the music of the aptly titled Freddy Jones Band.

DISCOGRAPHY

Freddy Jones Band (1992)

Waiting for the Night (1993)

North Avenue Wake Up Call (1995)

Lucid (1997). The band selected former Prince guitarist David Z to produce (he has also worked with Big Head Todd and the Monsters and Kenny Wayne Shepherd). He does a fine job of showcasing the band's fluid guitar attack while emphasizing its inviting compositions. The vibrant opener "Wonder" is a collaboration between Healy and Lloyd built on the pair's vocal exchanges and Healy's guitar accents. Other notable tracks include the urgent, introspective "Waiting on the Stone," the textured "Mystic Buzz," and "Come on Back," featuring Rob Bonaccorsi's gruff vocal turn, which is well supported by bluesy guitar work and some zesty horn fills.

WEB SITE

www.freddyjonesband.com

FREEBEERANDCHICKEN

- **SCATMAN BOYLES:** *drums*
- **KEN JUHAS:** *bass*
- **KIRK JUHAS:** *keyboards*
- **SETH ROSTAN:** *tenor saxophone*
- **CHRIS SULLIVAN:** *electric and acoustic guitar*
- **DAMIAN UBRIANCO:** *vocals, acoustic guitar*

Freebeerandchicken's moniker says much about the band's musical aims. The name reflects a custom the band attributes to bluesman John Lee Hooker of admitting people into shows for free if they brought food and beverages to share with one another. Freebeerandchicken emphasizes this communal spirit at its gigs and in particular the circular flow of energy from audience to musicians. This nexus is heightened when the band launches into one of the many free-form improvisations that constitute the heart of its live performances.

Freebeerandchicken explores a range of musical styles. As the reference to John Lee Hooker suggests, its members have a particular respect for the blues. The group also delves into extended bluegrass romps with some harmonica accents. Saxophone player Seth Rostan also notes: "I listen to a lot of Coltrane and Rollins. As a result, I think a lot of my solos tend to be jazzy." The band links these various genres in its riveting, radiant performances. Freebeerandchicken has honed its collective interplay since it first came together in 1991 (the band's first home was Oswego, New York, but it has since relocated to Albany). All in all, Rostan observes, "We're pretty much a live band, and we value interaction between instruments and freedom within each song. However, while we're free to do what we want, we try to work together to make a cohesive sound. The biggest compliment I think we receive is that our sound is full and that we blend well together."

DISCOGRAPHY

Papa's Waltz (1995)

WEB SITE

members.aol.com/fbandc

FROGWINGS

- **KOFI BURBRIDGE:** *keyboards, flute*
- **OTEIL BURBRIDGE:** *bass*
- **JIMMY HERRING:** *guitar*
- **EDWIN MCCAIN:** *vocals, guitar*
- **BUTCH TRUCKS:** *drums*
- **DEREK TRUCKS:** *guitar*
- **MARC QUINONES:** *percussion*

The term "supergroup" is a product of the late 1960s, typified by the Ginger Baker-Eric Clapton-Steve Winwood collaboration Blind Faith. The creation of Frogwings suggests that the time may be ripe to dust off that term – or, at the least, to come up with a new one capable of evoking the profusion of talent in this lineup. Allman Brothers Band drummer Butch Trucks formed Frogwings in May 1997 to provide himself with another creative outlet when the Brothers were off the road. In so doing, he managed to bring together some of the South's most talented players. For guitar, he tapped Aquarium Rescue Unit cofounder Jimmy Herring and his own nephew, slide whiz Derek Trucks. For bass, he enlisted the estimable talents of another ARU stalwart, Oteil Burbridge (who, as it turned out, would later join the Brothers). Accompanying Trucks on percussion was fellow Allman Brothers Band luminary Marc Quinones (the pair were initially joined by southern rhythm fixture Count Mbutu). Keyboard duties were originally handled by Jana Herbert but have since been assumed by multi-instrumentalist and ARU member Kofi Burbridge. Finally, after the band had worked up a repertoire of instrumentals, Edwin McCain was called in to provide lyrics and vocals.

The group's live performances showcase the collective exponential energy supplied by its individual performers, all of whom thrive in this setting. Frogwings works through original songs – such as the instrumental "Cut Mullet" and "Eyes Give You Away" – as well as several covers – adding a big blues groove to Bob Dylan's "Leopard Skin Pill Box Hat" and tearing up Tower of Power's "Don't Change Horses (In the Middle of a Stream)." Throughout a given evening, the two guitarists exchange lines, supply double leads, and build solos with precision. The percussionists repeatedly lock into steamy, entrancing grooves. Meanwhile, the brothers Burbridge power the engine (with Oteil adding some choice scats as well). McCain also does a fine job, displaying his gifts as a blues vocalist. Together, the members of Frogwings create a maelstrom of music through responsive interplay and communication, which by definition classes the band as a supergroup.

WEB SITE

www.allmanbrothersband.com

FROM GOOD HOMES

- ■ **JAMIE COAN:** *acoustic guitar, mandolin, vocals*
- ■ **PATRICK FITZSIMMONS:** *drums*
- ■ **DAN MYERS:** *saxophone, melodica*
- ■ **BRADY RYMER:** *bass, vocals*
- ■ **TODD SHEAFFER:** *vocals, acoustic guitar, mandolin*

The manner in which it acquired its name says quite a bit about this group. The quintet had been performing at a venue in its hometown of Sparta, New Jersey, when the club owner decided to stop the show a bit early. The disgruntled musicians left their instruments behind and went out for a drink. Later, as they were driving past the club, they decided that they would break into the establishment and tear through a cover of the Replacements's "IOU." When the inevitable happened and the five were brought before a justice of the peace, they were told that they would be let off easy because they were "from good homes." The lesson that one can glean from this story is that, audience or not, authorized or not, this is a group that loves to create music.

From Good Homes delves into folk, jazz, Cajun, and even Celtic music in composing its vivid and engaging material. One critic derisively dismissed its music as "hick pop," a term that the band later appropriated for the title of its 1994 release. However, the group also embraces spontaneity and improvisation — every From Good Homes show features songs that open up into agile, engrossing jams.

From Good Homes also presents some intriguing instrumentation. Both Todd Sheaffer and Jamie Coan perform on acoustic guitars that are deftly miked and adeptly played, creating sounds quite similar to those that can be summoned from the electric guitar. Brady Rymer contributes his own assertive accents on bass. Saxophone player Dan Myers is particularly astute at knowing when not to play, which makes his contributions all the more piquant. Drummer Patrick Fitzsimmons has acquired a reputation for coming up with ingenious ways to accommodate the band's proclivity for acoustic performance. For example, at one early Irving Plaza gig where the band opened for Hot Tuna, Fitzsimmons was not permitted to use a drum kit, so he set himself up with a new percussive implement: a collection of colored cardboard boxes. This creative spirit has permeated all aspects of the band's shows and has brought From Good Homes invitations to share bills with Bob Dylan, Ratdog, and the Dave Matthews Band over the past few years. Meanwhile, the band is also building a solid fan base of its own.

DISCOGRAPHY

Hick Pop Comin' at Ya (1994)

Open Up the Sky (1995)

Live at Waterloo (1997). This four-song EP captures the band expanding on its melodious compositions during a headlining performance at an outdoor venue in New Jersey. The driving "Bang That Drum" opens, a bright song that is invigorated by some robust mandolin. The band extends the groove for nine minutes on "Into the Black," building guitar textures with complementary saxophone. "2nd Red Barn on the Right" is an engaging sing-along with a bluesy flavor. This release closes with the gentle, hypnotic "Rain Dance."

From Good Homes (1998)

WEB SITE

www.fromgoodhomes.com

G. LOVE AND SPECIAL SAUCE

- **JEFF CLEMENS:** *drums, vocals*
- **GARRETT "G. LOVE" DUTTON:** *vocals, guitar, harmonica*
- **JIMMY PRESCOTT:** *acoustic bass*

In the early 1990s, Philadelphia native Garrett "G. Love" Dutton performed his self-designated "hip-hop blues" in a series of Boston bars. Drummer Jeff Clemens took in his show one evening and asked if he might provide accompaniment. Clemens recruited acoustic bassist Jimmy Prescott, and the trio began gigging as G. Love and Special Sauce. The group performed Love's verbose compositions, which feature not only wordplay that evokes Bob Dylan, but also an urban street ethic and vernacular that many associate with rap music. While growing up, Love had immersed himself in both idioms along with the work of bluesmen such as John Lee Hooker. The band slowly became known for its distinctive melange of folk, blues, and rap. The trio appeared on the 1995 HORDE tour and continues to perform with acts such as the Dave Matthews Band and Rusted Root.

G. Love and Special Sauce's absorbing live shows typically captivate audiences for at least two hours. Prescott thumps away at his acoustic bass, aggressively working his way up and down the neck to drive the groove. Clemens adds his own crackling rhythms. Love supplies blues-accented phrasings on his vintage 1939 Dobro. His voice is an additional tantalizing element, with its soulful, sultry drawl. The trio often strips hip-hop down to its essential basis in funk, jazz, and blues. However, the band also, more tangibly, embraces that medium when it occasionally draws in some additional musicians on percussion and Hammond B-3 organ. Throughout all of these efforts, the group supplies entrancing, melodious jams.

DISCOGRAPHY

G. Love and Special Sauce (1994)
Coast to Coast Motel (1995)

Yeah, It's That Easy (1997). On this genre-busting release, the trio both performs alone and welcomes some additional players. The disc opens with the catchy pulsations of "Stepping Stones." The next song, "I-76," is a funky paean to a local highway and the Philadelphia 76ers. "Recipe" presents some full-fledged hip-hop and features the vibrant keyboards of Dr. John. On "Pull the Wool," the band works up nine minutes of hypnotic groove. Meanwhile, Love echoes early-1960s Dylan on the closer, "When We Meet Again," playing harmonica and guitar while Prescott adds bowed bass.

WEB SITE

www.g-love.com

GALACTIC

- ■ **THERYL DECLOUET:** *vocals*
- ■ **ROBERT MERCURIO:** *bass*
- ■ **STANTON MOORE:** *drums*
- ■ **JEFF RAINES:** *guitar*
- ■ **RICH VOGEL:** *keyboards*

It may be unfair to introduce Galactic through a reference to the legendary Meters, but such a comparison is inevitable. First, both groups hail from the distinctive cultural spawning ground that is New Orleans – on Galactic's release *Coolin' Off*, vocalist Theryl deClouet intones "Welcome to New Orleans, Louisiana, home of the hits. And if you're from out of town, welcome to the Third World." Next, Galactic mines some similar music veins to create a predominantly instru-mental funk. Moreover, in 1994, the band's core players – Robert Mercurio, Stanton Moore, and Rich Vogel – learned the Meters's catalog and played a series of shows as the Ivanhoes, naming themselves after the first place the Meters gigged. Nonetheless, Galactic's sound can also be traced to a number of other sources: James Brown and other purveyors of funk; the Stax rhythm-and-blues sound, driven by Booker T. and the M.G.s; a few generations of jazz players, such as Jelly Roll Morton, Jimmy Smith, and Herbie Hancock; and the famed Mardi Gras Indians (whose street revels inspired the Meters as well). So, given such musical and geographical reference points, the band's sound could be labeled "Galactic groove gumbo."

The group first performed in 1993 under the name Galactic Prophylactic, playing mainly to Tulane University students. Then, following the Ivanhoes project, the band grew determined to steep itself further in the sounds of the region. The name attenuation occurred in late 1994 when San Francisco producer Dan Prothero stepped in to produce the song "Black Eyed Pea," which was to appear on Prothero's *Is That Jazz* compilation. The enigmatic deClouet joined Galactic during the *Coolin' Off* recording sessions, when he was invited into the studio to collaborate. He now tours with the band, emerging from the wings and sauntering on stage to lend his vocals at various points during the Galactic set.

Galactic is a band that thrives on the energy of the live show. In this environment, Moore's crackling drums, Mercurio's mercurial bass, Raines's expressive guitar, and Vogel's sprightly keys combine to create a slinky, sensuous, entrancing funk. The horn talents of players such as Ben Ellman and Jason Mingledorff often add vibrancy to the mix. The band works without a set list, moving from groove to groove and song to song depending on the mood of the room and the players. The results are widely admired, and Galactic continues to pull new explorers into its orbit.

DISCOGRAPHY

Coolin' Off (1996). The Galactic core is joined on this release by a three-piece horn section, yielding a collection of simmering instrumental grooves. "Go Go," the representative opening number, gradually introduces the players before giving way to a full funk. Other dynamic tracks include the appropriately titled "Stax Jam," "Church," and the evolving "Everybody Wants Some (Parts 1–3)." DeClouet is here as well, adding his vocals to "Everybody Wants Some (Part 3)" and the resonant social criticism "Something's Wrong with This Picture." *Coolin' Off* also offers CD-ROM enhancements, which include video clips, a presentation on "swamp funk," and Stanton Moore's ruminations about New Orleans dining.

Crazyhorse Mongoose (1998)

WEB SITE

www.fogworld.com/galactic

DAVID GANS AND THE BROKEN ANGELS

- ■ **CLAYTON CALL:** *drums*
- ■ **RIK ELSWIT:** *guitar, synthesizer, vocals*
- ■ **DAVID GANS:** *guitar, vocals*
- ■ **JENNIFER JOLLY:** *piano, vocals*
- ■ **STEVE RAMIREZ:** *bass, vocals*

The name of this group is drawn in part from the Grateful Dead song "Stella Blue." This appellation is certainly appropriate, as David Gans may actually be the world's most famous Dead Head: he has written books on the band and hosts the *Grateful Dead Hour*. Yet long before any of this, Gans was a songwriter and vocalist in his own right. Over the past few years, the California native has decided to refocus his energies on these pursuits. "I really felt it was time to put my own music on the front burner," he explains. "I've been playing around the Bay Area since 1970 in a variety of bands and configurations."

The Broken Angels emerged from a series of jam-infused Berkeley gigs. For these, Gans invited a new collection of players to join him each week and share in the act of musical creation. He remarks, "I had the pleasant experience of introducing people to each other and watching them make magic from scratch." After a year of such performances, he decided to form a permanent band with pianist Jennifer Jolly, guitarist and keyboard player Rik Elswit, bassist Steve Ramirez, and drummer Clayton Call. "The name David Gans and the Broken Angels is like Bob Wills and His Texas Playboys," he adds. "It evokes the image of an American touring band, a great American image. Of course, there is a clue to the Grateful Dead component to those who are aware."

The group is steadily building a following. It has given a number of high-profile performances, most notably a sold-out show at the Fillmore Auditorium with special guests Phil Lesh and Vince Welnick. The quintet predominantly presents original music (some of which appears on Gans's recent release with guitarist Eric Rawlins, *Home by Morning*), but the group also works through covers selected from the Grateful Dead catalog and from those of other artists (Little Feat, Dire Straits). Moreover, as one might expect, the band is quite comfortable with spontaneous exploration, in particular offering some spellbinding segues between songs. The core of the band's sound, however, remains Gans's compositions. "I was a songwriter before I ever picked up an electric guitar and before I ever knew what improvisation was all about," declares Gans. "No matter how good you are at jamming, it eventually comes down to the song."

WEB SITE

www.trufun.com/angels/broken/html

GILA MONSTERS

- **CHARLIE BRAGG:** *guitar, vocals*
- **RICHARD "RH FACTOR" HARDY:** *saxophone, flute, vocals*
- **CHRISTOPHER PELLANI:** *drums and percussion*
- **PAUL PERME:** *vocals, harmonica, percussion*
- **JAVIER WILLIS:** *bass, vocals*

The Gila Monsters is Los Angeles's reigning "Party Gras" band. Says lead singer Paul Perme: "We work hard to make every night an event. People can expect to dance, get a little crazy, and get sucked into the show like a wild tornado." Perme serves as an entertaining front man, a role well suited to someone who initially emigrated to Los Angeles to pursue a career in stand-up comedy and worked for a time as an auctioneer (he employs both of these skills while on stage with the Gila Monsters). The band embraces the sounds of the Neville Brothers and the Meters while giving its own music a slightly harder rock edge.

Perme notes that "There certainly is a New Orleans feel to what we do. We play a mean Mardi Gras mambo, and our friends will often come to our shows wearing Mardi Gras beads." One recent Gila Monsters audience member was Ivan Neville, who supplied an endorsement by sitting in with the band for a set.

The Gila Monsters came into being in 1992 when guitarist Charlie Bragg showed up at Perme's birthday party. Recalls Perme: "I invited him to check out our band. Within two days, he was a member, and he had fired everyone but me." The pair then enlisted a series of players who were committed to vigorous performance — and who met Bragg's stringent standards. Drummer Wendy Colton was the first to pass the test, but she eventually grew weary of touring and passed on drumming duties to the agile Christopher Pellani (who happened to be Colton's percussion teacher). Bass player Javier Willis has emerged as an underlying funk force. Finally, the band's throbbing brass is supplied by RH Factor (a.k.a. Richard Hardy), who previously performed with several of the musicians who later rose to fame in the Dave Matthews Band. All in all, Perme notes, "I'm just real psyched with the direction the band is taking. Aside from the party atmosphere, I think we're really starting to cut it as a live jam band. Every time we play I see more and more people out there taping our shows, which says it all for me."

DISCOGRAPHY

Down in the Pit (1995). The band's debut contains colorful vocal and instrumental expressions. "Walk" is one such splashy offering with harmonica, guitar, and vocals all coming together to produce a funky gumbo. Other strong cuts include the hypnotic "Electric Chair," the bluesy "Still," and the throbbing "Stateside."

New Orleans State of Mind (1998)

WEB SITE

www.gila.com

GOD STREET WINE

- **JON BEVO:** *piano, keyboards, vocals*
- **LO FABER:** *vocals, guitar*
- **AARON MAXWELL:** *vocals, guitar*
- **DAN PIFER:** *bass, vocals*
- **TOMO:** *drums, vocal*

In 1988, God Street Wine played its first gig at Nightingale on Manhattan's Lower East Side (the song "Nightingale," which appears on both *Bag* and *$1.99 Romances*, is a nod to the venue). The group then joined Blues Traveler, Joan Osborne, the Spin Doctors, and many other bands in the burgeoning scene that eventually began to orbit the Wetlands. John Popper even appears on the band's 1989 demo tape, lending harmonica to "Dirty Little Secret." In the intervening years, God Street Wine has traveled far from New York City, crossing the nation and even the Atlantic Ocean to perform up to three hundred shows a year. In so doing, the group has fostered a passionate legion of fans (a number of whom have labeled themselves "Winos"); they exchange news about the band through forums such as an Internet mailing list. The band genuinely appreciates its audience support. As singer/guitarist Lo Faber notes, "By and large there's a lack of any superficial tendencies. It's one of the most uncontrived audiences. We're unhip, and so are they, and all of us are there for the music."

The band's origins reflect a number of entwined friendships. Back in high school, Faber and John Thomas Osander (later Tomo) first began to perform together in a variety of groups. Faber later attended New York University, where he met bass player Dan Pifer. The bassist's own high school career is notable because during it he played in cover bands with Carry Pierce (later of Jackopierce) and Jen Durkin (Deep Banana Blackout's vocalist). Faber and Pifer both finally withdrew from NYU and transferred to the Manhattan School of Music, where they met guitarist Aaron Maxwell. God Street Wine was ultimately completed in the fall of 1988, when the group drew in keyboardist Jon Bevo, a friend of Pifer's from NYU, and Faber's longtime pal Tomo.

God Street Wine flourishes in the live setting. The group's second album, a concert recording called *Who's Driving*, comes with an accompanying essay that extols those moments when band and audience are transported to a different plane. The group's principal navigators tend to be its two guitarists, who exchange leads and engage in a double-barreled attack. Bevo and Pifer prove adept at thickening the sound. Tomo supplies novel rhythmic textures; he is the final contributor to the "chaos," as Faber often characterizes the group's live efforts. "I think our music is a pure product of who we are and what we do," Faber observes. "We're incapable of putting a veneer over ourselves or our music. It's ingenuous. We play so many different kinds of music that sometimes we have trouble honing in on what we do. On any given night we might emphasize country, jazz, blues, gospel, or rock. Or we might just present a mixture of all of those. Some nights, it might be highly improvisational, full of segues from song to song. Or it might just be a collection of tunes. We really try to react to the vibe of the room. We try to react to what's going on — we're sensitive to the moment."

One mystery remains: the source of the band's name. As the story goes, the group had dubbed itself something altogether different back in the fall of 1988 when it first started to send out demo tapes in an effort to secure club gigs. Then, prior to its debut, one young woman misheard the intended moniker and repeated back "God Street Wine?" The name stuck, as has the group.

DISCOGRAPHY

Bag (1992)

Who's Driving (1993)

$1.99 Romances (1994)

Red (1996)

God Street Wine (1997). On this disc, the band, along with producer Bill Wray, endeavored to present the passion and exhilaration of its live shows by limiting overdubs, by recording in analog, and by using vintage equipment. This proved effective, yielding the best of God Street Wine's studio efforts. The memorable melody of "Diana" shuffles along, well supported by slide guitar and organ. "Feather" benefits from the swirling textures supplied by acoustic and electric guitars, keyboards, and John Popper's harmonica. Popper also appears on the alluring "She Comes up Softly." Legendary Little Feat keyboardist Bill Payne lends his considerable gifts to the gentle "Silver." Two other interesting tracks are "Angeline," with its country feel, and "Water," featuring Faber's Dylanesque intonations.

WEB SITE

www.godstreetwine.com

GOV'T MULE

- ■ **MATT ABTS:** *drums*
- ■ **WARREN HAYNES:** *vocals, guitars*
- ■ **ALLEN WOODY:** *bass*

Gov't Mule produces thick, muscular music that certainly earns the group its designation as a "power trio." Its sound perpetuates the rich tradition established by such predecessors as Cream, the Jimi Hendrix Experience, and Mountain. But although Gov't Mule has demonstrated a mastery of moody, midtempo blues, it also delves into jazzier chord progressions. Guitarist Warren Haynes explains that, though he and his bandmates certainly admire all of the aforementioned acts, Gov't Mule is also inspired by the second of the classic Miles Davis Quintets – this group, which featured Ron Carter, Herbie Hancock, Wayne Shorter, and Tony Williams, achieved particular renown for its fluid rhythm section.

The trio came together through its members' associations with the Allman Brothers Band. Drummer Matt Abts and guitarist Haynes were members of the Dickey Betts Band in the 1980s. When Betts returned to the reformed Allman Brothers Band, Haynes also joined the Brotherhood. Allen Woody entered the scene when he became the bass player in this new lineup. Haynes and Woody quickly garnered accolades for their fiery contributions to the Brothers, but the guitarist also hoped to have another opportunity to perform with Abts. Finally, in 1993, during the Brothers's run at the Greek Theater in Los Angeles, Abts, Haynes, and Woody appeared together at a local club for a late-night impromptu take on the Free song "Mr. Big." The three immediately recognized their collective creative potential. Gov't Mule debuted a few months later at the Elizabeth Reed Music Hall in Macon, Georgia.

The players are individual talents who communicate effectively. Haynes, the recipient of multiple *Guitar Player* reader awards for best slide guitarist, executes torrid, serrated leads. His gruff baritone also blends right in. Woody delivers driving, aggressive bass lines, and Abts joins the conversation with his loose, energetic drumming. This synergy eventually led Haynes and Woody to part from the Brothers in 1997 so that they could pursue the Gov't Mule project on a full-time basis.

Gov't Mule is a band that flourishes in the concert setting. Its performances are taped by a fervid following anxious to retain mementos of the group's walloping improvisations. Notes Abts: "Playing live has always been the key for us." Woody adds, "We rely on spontaneity and unpredictability. You can get electrocuted at any time." It is this spirit that brings the band new fans with every show and that keeps those fans riding the Mule train.

DISCOGRAPHY

Gov't Mule (1995)

Live at Roseland Ballroom (1996)

Dose (1998). Producer Michael Barbiero, who has worked with Soundgarden, helps Gov't Mule navigate many terrains on this disc. "Blind Man in the Dark," the crunching opener, incorporates some interesting vocal effects. "Thelonious Beck" is a sinewy instrumental that pays tribute to two of the band's influences. "Raven Black Night" presents the group's reflective, acoustic side. Finally, *Dose* also offers two intriguing covers: a spare, primal take on Son House's "John the Revelator," and a rough reworking of the Beatles's "She Said She Said."

WEB SITE

www.mule.net

GRAN TORINO

- ■ **P.J. ALEXANDER:** *trumpet, flügelhorn*
- ■ **STEPHEN DECKER:** *guitar, vocals*
- ■ **CHRIS FORD:** *vocals, guitar*
- ■ **DEXTER MURPHY:** *trombone, keyboards, vocals*
- ■ **TODD OVERSTREET:** *bass*
- ■ **SCOTT PEDERSON:** *trumpet, flügelhorn, vocals*
- ■ **WHIT PFOHL:** *drums*
- ■ **JASON THOMPSON:** *tenor and baritone saxophone*

A Gran Torino is a grand, stylish, explosive vehicle that runs on all eight cylinders. The band Gran Torino can be described in precisely the same manner. This Knoxville, Tennessee, octet fuses its funk, soul, jazz, and rhythm-and-blues influences to produce sizzling, delectable grooves that rely heavily on the power of its four-piece horn section.

The group came together at the University of Tennessee in 1995. That's where its rhythm musicians assembled and swiftly decided that they needed some brass. Bassist Todd Overstreet recalls, "We went out and approached the horn players. They were jazz majors, and a few played in the school's marching band, the Pride of the Southland. They were happy to get away from some of that structure and join what we were doing." The musicians literally came together as all eight moved into the same house, creating what Overstreet refers to as "a family deal." The band takes a similar approach to songwriting: everyone offers ideas, and the group then sorts through them. Within the band, a variety of influences appears: Al Green, Earth, Wind and Fire, Marvin Gaye, Weather Report, even the Grateful Dead. Gran Torino crafts danceable, soulful rhythms and melodies that are splashed with vivid horn charts.

Most of the band's songs achieve an even greater intensity and vigor in concert. Says Overstreet: "We have a lot of leeway in every song. The songs have structure, but maybe twenty to thirty percent of what we're doing up there is improvised. The solos are never the same from night to night." What does recur, however, is a coherent, focused energy that keeps audience members on their toes with their hips shaking. Overstreet adds, "I think I'm most proud of our musical diversity. There are eight of us up there, and our music reflects all eight of us, each individual's taste and personality."

DISCOGRAPHY

Live at the Chameleon Club (1996)

One (1997). With the first notes of the instrumental "Dopamine," the big, powerful sound of Gran Torino is off and running. This disc is laden with horn melodies, incendiary guitar licks, and smooth vocals. "Telenouvela" follows, a soulful tune, enlivened by the band's brass attack. "When I Grow Up" demonstrates that Gran Torino can also work a fat, funky groove. "Stevland" is another standout soul raveup with catchy horn lines, while "Push" provides a lusher sound.

WEB SITE

www.grantorino.com

GREYBOY ALLSTARS

- **MIKE "ELGIN PARK" ANDREWS:** *guitar*
- **KARL DENSON:** *saxophones, flute*
- **ALAN EVANS:** *drums*
- **CHRIS STILLWELL:** *bass*
- **ROBERT WALTERS:** *keyboards*

The Greyboy Allstars's growing collection of fans owes a debt of gratitude to professional baseball player Gary Templeton. The second baseman was a schoolmate of saxophonist Karl Denson, who, in the late 1980s and early 1990s, was a featured member of Lenny Kravitz's touring ensemble. The San Diego Padres player introduced Denson to a rising DJ named Greyboy (a.k.a. Andreas Stevens). Greyboy had first gained notoriety in 1989 when he was just eighteen: he won a national mixing competition and began spinning a blend of soul, jazz, and hip-hop throughout southern California. Out of this came an invitation to contribute tracks to a CD compilation. Greyboy asked Denson to lend a hand, and the pair collaborated on several cuts. They then resolved to maintain their relationship by forming Greyboy Records.

Denson went on to assemble the Allstars, which was initially intended to serve as the label's house band but soon gained an independent renown. Mike Andrews (a.k.a. Elgin Park) was Denson's first recruit. Andrews had just left his national-touring alternative outfit, the Origin. Bassist Chris Stillwell and keyboardist Robert Walters both joined after leaving a local jazz group, Room 608. The group was accompanied on its debut recording by legendary trombonist Fred Wesley (formerly of James Brown's band and later of the JBs), who occasionally still performs with the Allstars.

The band is building a substantial following with its smooth, inviting grooves that incorporate elements of jazz and funk. As evidenced by the title of its first release, the group defines its sound as "boogaloo," a genre from the 1960s and 1970s that is alternatively described as "soul jazz." There is also a strong improvisatory component to the band's offerings. However, no matter how one chooses to characterize the band, it is the unique blend of all these elements that has prompted dance-happy audiences to envelop themselves in the Greyboy Allstars's enticing music.

DISCOGRAPHY

West Coast Boogaloo (1994)

A Town Called Earth (1997). The band powers its way through many moods and grooves on this disc. Although the ensemble is defined by its sterling musicianship, Denson, in particular, animates songs such as "Happy Friends" and "Toys R Us," and Walters elevates "Quantico, Virginia." Also, while tunes such as "Turnip's Big Move" and "Planet of the Superkids" affirm the group's affinity for funk, the fifteen-minute title track demonstrates the Allstars's improvisational acuity and vigor.

WEB SITE

www.greyboyallstars.com

GRINCH

- **SCOTT ALEXANDER:** *vocals, guitar*
- **STEVE BAILEY:** *guitar, vocals*
- **SCOTT FORSYTH:** *keyboards, vocals*
- **ANDY KUHLMAN:** *bass*
- **CHRIS MAZUR:** *drums*

Grinch first assembled at the University of Delaware in 1992. The group's core membership began performing without a drummer, predominantly at parties. As band members began receiving praise for their intricate music, Grinch started expanding its catalog of original songs. The group also enlisted some percussive assistance and started gigging at local clubs. Over the intervening years, the size of Grinch's venues and its audiences has increased while the band's lineup has generally remained static. One exception has been the addition of former moe. drummer Chris Mazur.

Grinch has become known for its sonic latticework and galvanic spontaneous expressions. Lead guitarist Steve Bailey has proven himself capable of producing dexterous, inventive phrases. Vocalist and rhythm guitarist Scott Alexander lends his own confident accents. Scott Forsyth creates an eddy of grooves on his Hammond. Andy Kuhlman is a skilled enabler on bass as the band moves from folk to funk to blues to jazz. Finally, the band has been energized by the recent addition of Mazur, who is quite familiar with remote musical territories. The results are captivating new listeners as Grinch crosses the nation on tour.

DISCOGRAPHY

Grinch (1995)

Move (1997). This disc focuses on the band's songs while demonstrating Grinch's musicianship. ''Danhtahn'' opens with solid vocal harmonies, percolating keyboards, and soaring guitar lines. "It's Nick/Move" affirms the band's affinity for rapid tempo changes and angular textures. "Getting a Keg" is a bright instrumental. *Move* closes with the swirling "Swoopy."

WEB SITE

www.groundzerorecords.com/grinch.html

GUSTER

- **ADAM GARDNER:** *guitar, vocals*
- **RYAN MILLER:** *guitar, vocals*
- **BRIAN ROSENWORCEL:** *drums, percussion, vocals*

Guster currently contributes its distinctive sound and forceful improvisations to concert venues nationwide. Brian Rosenworcel's thunderous declarations on bongos mesh with the acoustic guitars and vocal harmonies of Adam Gardner and Ryan Miller, yielding infectious results. The band's music often drives performers and audience members alike into apoplectic frenzies (Gardner's sweat-drenched shirts have become an element of band lore).

The group formed at Tufts University in Medford, Massachusetts, in 1992. Dubbing itself Gus, the trio played numerous gigs and even released a four-song demo tape. When it turned out that another band had already claimed the tag, the group added three letters to its name (legend has it that it was one letter per band member, mirroring the group's original name). Indeed, one can occasionally spot those who have long been in the know proudly wearing Gus memorabilia.

Given Guster's somewhat quirky instrumentation and time signatures, one might expect the band's lyrical content to be similarly whimsical. To some degree, this is true, although Miller, who composes most of the lyrics, often pens stories of emotional disentanglement filled with compelling, elliptical imagery. At the same time, the band also revels in its own skewed sense of humor (take a look at the Guster photo in the *AWARE 3* compilation; the musicians' heads are superimposed over those of the Bee Gees). All of Guster's offerings take on additional vibrancy at the trio's generous, exhausting live shows.

DISCOGRAPHY

Parachute (1994)

Goldfly (1998). Producer Steve Lindsey, who has previously worked with such luminaries as Leonard Cohen and Peter Gabriel, was at the helm for this effort. "Great Escape" scampers out first with a lively groove. "Demons" is gentler, percolating fare laced with rich harmonies that belie its dark story of betrayal. String arrangements provide a subtle counterpoint on "Grin" and "Medicine" (Andy Happel of Thanks to Gravity provides the orchestrations and plays violin, and Rudy Dicello performs on cello). The drum machines on "X-Ray Eyes" initially stand out, but they work to convey the narrator's haunting lack of compassion. One final note: *Goldfly* has a bonus track — the goofy "Melanie," which can be located three minutes and sixteen seconds prior to the first song.

WEB SITE

www.guster.com

HEAVY WEATHER

- **BRIAN AYLOR:** *drums*
- **JASON BARNEY:** *percussion*
- **MICHAEL BRESNEN:** *guitar*
- **MONA MICHAEL:** *vocals*
- **CAROLE WALKER:** *vocals*
- **CHRIS WALKER:** *bass, vocals*

Cincinnati's Heavy Weather was formed in 1992 through the efforts of siblings Carole and Chris Walker. The pair brought two different musical perspectives to the venture. Chris was a jazz fanatic whose passion for the Weather Report album *Heavy Weather* inspired the group's moniker. Carole was partial to show tunes. Together they decided to invite a number of players with similarly divergent tastes to join them. One unifying element was to be a commitment to social issues – over the years, the band has performed at a number of consciousness-raising events, including Rock the Vote, Rock for Choice, and the Bring Leonard Peltier Home Tour, a six-week effort mounted by the American Indian Movement in 1997.

Heavy Weather's music is a melange of jazz, reggae, funk, and soul, which in concert is heavily flavored with spontaneous creation. Chris Walker, who supplies some assertive rhythms on bass, has joked that everything the band does is based on improvisation, including getting to its gigs. The siblings are assisted by four gifted players. Brian Aylor and Jason Barney provide a rumbling foundation of percussion. Guitarist Michael Bresnen coaxes a range of tones from his guitar. Mona Michael joins Carole Walker in producing the group's trademark soulful vocal swagger. The results coalesce to yield riveting, danceable, extemporized grooves.

DISCOGRAPHY

The Difference (1993)

As My World (1995). The six songs contained here reveal the band's diverse affinities and performance strengths. Carole Walker's vocals stand out on "Mama Told Me," a powerful horn-infused offering. "What Went Wrong" is carried by fluid, blues-tinged guitar. "As My World" demonstrates the band's jazzier side.

HELLO DAVE

- **BLAKE COX:** *bass, vocals*
- **MIKE HALL:** *guitar, vocals*
- **MIKE HIMEBAUGH:** *vocals, guitar*
- **BRYAN RESENDIZ:** *drums*

Chicago's Hello Dave has built a strong following with its hook-laden compositions, its smooth vocals, its twin guitars, and — above all — its vibrant performances. Mike Himebaugh, the band's principal song-writer and lead singer, is the sole remaining member of the group that recorded its eponymous debut in 1993. The current lineup includes three other like-minded players: drummer Bryan Resendiz, bassist Blake Cox, and lead guitarist Mike Hall. The latter two contribute their own compositions to the band. The resulting collaboration has yielded music that is exuberant and joyous without being cloying.

The group perpetuates an ethos of felicity and transport. Hime-baugh believes that his goal as a performer is "to have the audience members leave with big ol' smiles on their faces. A lot of bands are full of angst, and I think music is entertainment. My mother and stepfather are active in barbershop quartets, and every show of theirs is fun and happiness." When asked about the band's expectations of its audience, Himebaugh remarks, "I don't think they have to do anything except show up. We're supposed to make them have a good time. Of course, when they are, the energy builds back and forth." The group's benevolent nature led it to record *A Hello Dave Christmas with Friends*, which benefited Camp Heartland, a nonprofit organization that assists children with AIDS.

Hello Dave seeks to turn its live shows into mass celebrations. The band creates spirited grooves and then tops them off with bright harmonies. It also supplements its own winsome compositions with covers — a funky take on "Voodoo Chile," for example, or a fevered "Tangled Up in Blue." Chicago audiences are occasionally treated to stripped-down acoustic shows (Himebaugh quips, "There's no real difference except we're sitting down"). Whatever the format, Hello Dave regales its audiences with burnished vocals, gleeful performances, and a kind spirit.

Hello Dave (1993)

West (1996). This release opens in high fashion with the toe-tapping declaration "Golden." Other standout tracks include "Mountains," a celebration of the West; "Brown Well," one of the group's signature songs; and "Believe," which hints at Hello Dave's ability to stretch it out. Poi Dog Pondering's Dave Max Crawford appears on this recording, sweetening the mix with an assortment of instruments (both strings and brass).

16 Tons (1998). This solid offering documents the band's depth. The opening song, "Lust Her," is an endearing shuffle built on Himebaugh's vocals and Hall's sassy guitar. Other notable songs include the radiant "If I Call You Home," the slinky "Barefeet," and the gentler "Family Tree." Hello Dave also welcomes guests on this disc: Tom Murray's fiddle enriches "Freedom," and Brennan Orndorff's lap steel guitar braces "Home." The title track, a cover of Merle Travis's somber staple, is transformed into an upbeat rallying cry.

WEB SITE

www.mountainrecords.com

HIGHER GROUND

- **JOSH BIGGS:** *drums*
- **MICK CHEGWIDDEN:** *vocals, guitar, mandolin*
- **ALAN GLICKENHAUS:** *vocals, guitar, fiddle, banjo, mandolin*
- **CHRIS MISKOW:** *bass*

Although 1997 was a turbulent year for Higher Ground, there are thousands of people rooting for the band. Ever since its formation in 1992, the Portland, Oregon, group has become a community institution. This is a band that actively supports local causes with benefit performances; a December 1995 canned-food drive at its shows netted several hundred pounds of donations. Also important is the fact that Higher Ground produces mellifluent songs enlivened by vital, intricate jams.

The group came together when Alan Glickenhaus and David Kronenberg met at a local bluegrass jam. Glickenhaus had won some regional flat-picking competitions and had appeared with Charles Neville in a Eugene, Oregon, band in the 1980s. A transplanted New Englander, Kronenberg had fronted a band called the Shockers in the 1980s that had gained a following by opening for groups such as the Radiators and the Spin Doctors. Recalls Glickenhaus: "That first day, I just backed him up, and people really took to it." The pair decided to form a band, drawing in Chuck Masi on bass and working through a number of drummers before settling on Oregonian Josh Biggs. The group soon defined the results as "acoustic-fired backroots rock." Glicken-haus remarks, "It was always pretty high-energy music, a pretty fun mix of bluegrass, rock, jazz, and country. We've also been known to take some familiar tunes and give them a bluegrass twist." The band swiftly earned strong audience support; a contingent of tapers was on hand to document each show. Higher ground also found itself opening a run of shows for the Neville Brothers and performing at a number of notable events, including the Oregon Country Fair and the High Sierra Music Festival.

The original partnership came to an end in 1997. Glickenhaus and Kronenberg decided to separate, and the other band members began exploring new avenues and options (Glickenhaus, for instance, started gigging with Blue Honey). However, the group's many fans, longing to hear the band, continued to press its various players to return. Eventually, a revamped quartet emerged: Glickenhaus and Biggs were joined by Chris Miskow on bass and Mick Chegwidden on vocals, guitar, and mandolin. This new lineup embodies the eclec-ticism and enthusiasm of the original band, leading many to hope that the vibe will be perpetuated so that they can continue to seek Higher Ground.

DISCOGRAPHY

Higher Ground (1993)

Portland, Oregon (1994)

Better View (1995)

Sugar Drop (1996)

Live (1997). This release documents the band's triumphant, invigor-ating return to live performance in the fall of 1997. The group tears things up right away with "Goin' Home," as Glickenhaus and Cheg-widden exchange some animated ideas. Other standout moments include the bluesier, searing "Texas Tornado," the gleeful hoedown "Cluck Go the Chicken," and the banjo-inflected "Upum Gulch." Songs such as "Alpaca Sweater" present Miskow's supple bass work set off against Chegwidden's robust guitar and Glickenhaus's sprightly mandolin.

HIPBONE

- **CHRIS BENTLEY:** *alto saxophone, guitar, vocals*
- **AARON BITTIKOFER:** *acoustic and electric bass, vocals*
- **KEVIN BROCK:** *drums and percussion*
- **BRION SNYDER:** *piano, organ, guitar, lead vocals*

Hipbone is quickly carving out a niche for itself with its hybrid groove music. The band's instrumentation initially resembles that of a jazz organ trio, with Brion Snyder on keyboards, Kevin Brock on drums, and Aaron Bittikofer on stand-up bass. However, Chris Bentley steps in on alto saxophone and blows over the top. Many of the resulting songs have a funky feel that is heightened by Snyder's rich vocals, which present the quartet's crisp, literate lyrics. This amalgamation positions the band somewhere within the realms where jazz, hip-hop, funk, and rock intersect.

The group formed in Chapel Hill, North Carolina, in September 1995. Brock and Bentley, fresh out of college, decided to assemble a band. After testing the waters by playing with nearly two dozen musicians, they tapped Snyder and Bittikofer to complete their still-nameless ensemble. A moniker was soon found, however, when a jazz musician the band members heard interviewed on the radio remarked that he thought his music made people move their hipbones.

This certainly describes the North Carolina group's effect as well. Snyder's keyboards percolate while supplying some splashy flourishes. Brock's crackling drums and Bittikofer's rumbling bass anchor the band. Bentley's sax drifts in and out, providing both silky phrases and bebop ferocity. Brock states, "We are interested in music that is both cerebral and accessible." Hipbone succeeds on both counts.

DISCOGRAPHY

Hipbone (1997). The group's debut five-song CD disappoints only in its brevity. Following Snyder's winsome, burbling keyboard introduction, "Everybody" shuffles along, punctuated with some expressive saxophone. "Papa" has a funkier feel that is buoyed by some eruptions from Bentley and a joyous organ break. "Wicked," which features some of Hipbone's incisive lyrics, simmers and then explodes on the strength of the band's collective instrumentation and Snyder's vocal phrasings. Finally, the aptly titled "Ride" scampers along before coming to a more ambient conclusion.

HOMUNCULUS

- **BEN DOEPKE:** *keyboards, vocals, noseflute*
- **CHRISTOPHER ELLISON:** *drums and percussion*
- **CHRISTOPHER "GIL" GILMARTIN:** *bass, harmonica, vocals*
- **KEVIN SHIMA:** *guitar, vocals*
- **MATT WILSON:** *guitar, vocals*

Homunculus is a band that values both bewilderment and humor. When asked to describe what one can expect of his band's live show, keyboardist Ben Doepke says: "If you're coming out to do the noodle dance, you've got the wrong band. We don't do an ethereal thing. We have a lot of fun, but it's not a dreamy, ethereal fun." Indeed, Homunculus will often carom off a deep, funky groove into a vocal-harmony display that echoes late-1960s British psychedelia (there's even a hint of an English accent in there). Adds Doepke, "We love to look out at the audience and see a guy standing there just totally dumbfounded because he doesn't know what's going on. Then he'll realize and get all excited."

Coming out of Bloomington, Indiana, Homunculus has been tweaking audiences since 1995. At that time, two bands – Phatso and Wild Edibles – fused to create the group. Doepke describes the quintet's name as "the mechanism that transforms latent thought into manifest thought. It's the little dude that takes out the sheet music and plays the keyboard for the rest of the body. When you place your hand on the stove, he grabs you by the collar and lets you know its time to cuss and dance around the room. So you have the mental and cerebral stuff crossed with a figure based entirely on nerves and sensitivity." This description captures the essence of the group's music quite well; it draws equally from the Frank Zappa school of ironically detached virtuosity and the Meters's concern with serious grooving. Homunculus's live shows attract droves of repeat listeners eager to hear fresh interpretations of its compositions. Doepke notes, "A lot of the songs have gateways, and we look at each other and decide. We choose our own adventure."

DISCOGRAPHY

Homunculus (1997)

The Pulse of Directed Devotion (1998). This release demonstrates that Homunculus is a band that has plenty of new ideas and is not afraid to use them. The opener, "Get out of the Way," which could well be a metaphor for the band's approach, presents funk guitar, keyboard riffs reminiscent of Traffic, hip-hop phrasings, as well as vocal jams and harmonies. The track "70 West" mates serene singing with pulsing, wah-wah guitar. "Daily Grind" is infused with jazzier tonalities. "A Little Time to Get Down" is another journey from dense grooves through atmospheric abstraction into a guitar soliloquy and then back into thicker rhythms with some burnished vocals as well.

WEB SITE

www.homunculture.com

HONEY CHILD

- ■ **JOE FROST:** *congas and percussion*
- ■ **DINO GISIANO:** *guitar*
- ■ **JULIAN GOLDENTHAL:** *drums*
- ■ **HEATHER HIGGS:** *vocals, percussion*
- ■ **JASON MONTERO:** *guitar, vocals*
- ■ **PAUL RUGALO:** *bass*

Arizona's Honey Child owes its existence to a song. Guitarist Dino Gisiano was at home working on his computer when he heard his wife,

Heather Higgs, in another room strumming a tune she had written. Recalls Higgs, "He came in, and I said 'Listen to this.' When I was done playing it for him, he looked up at me and said 'Okay, we're starting a band.'" With those words, the couple initiated the endeavor that became Honey Child. They had played informally with percussionist Joe Frost and guitarist Jason Montero, and they decided to make this quartet the core of the group. Within a year, the song that Higgs had been working on, "Why Should I," had become the opening track on the band's debut release. She later sang the tune while performing on the Arizona HORDE.

Honey Child appeals to a diverse array of listeners with the varied elements of its sound. Some are drawn to the rippling polyrhythms that undergird most of the group's compositions. Others find the layered guitars of Gisiano and Montero uplifting. Additional supporters are captivated by Higgs; as Gisiano observes, "Heather has a great ability to make an audience believe they're right up there on stage. They really feel involved, and that's all due to her energy." Honey Child's groove-laden live shows have been likened to those of Santana, Black Crowes, and Joan Osborne. The band welcomes these comparisons, although its members emphasize that their music is still evolving. Notes Gisiano: "We feel like a family, and, musicianship aside, we're all growing." Higgs adds, "We're still learning how to express ourselves."

DISCOGRAPHY

Honey Child (1997). The band's live energy is captured in this release, which eschews overdubs. "Why Should I" showcases Higgs's powerful vocals – they glide over the trails crafted by the band's doubled guitar and percussion. Montero contributes vocals to "Breath and Time," and the resulting interplay with Higgs suggests John Doe and Exene Cervenka of X. Other standout tunes include the mellow "Red Moon" and the upbeat, acoustic "What We've Been Through."

WEB SITE

www.honey-child.com

THE HOSEMOBILE

- **JEREMY AVERITT:** *guitar, rhodes piano*
- **CAIN BLANCHARD:** *bass*
- **TIGE CASEY:** *drums, spoken word*
- **ROB RING:** *guitar*

Hosemobile is comprised of four gifted players who revel in collective improvisation. Yet unlike many of today's other thriving jam bands, this group is not attempting to perform songs that will keep its audiences up and dancing. Instead, Hosemobile creates an atmospheric, moody sound built on odd time signatures and grooves that flirt with melody but slam into dissonance before careening away. This is music of fevered, ominous, hallucinogenic reveries.

Hosemobile's sound is intentionally difficult to categorize. The band's efforts will often reference funk, free jazz, and even industrial metal within the span of a single song. Some critics have likened the results to the work of King Crimson and Frank Zappa. Such comparisons are certainly apt, although the group's guitar crunches render its sound current and vital. Jeremy Averitt and Rob Ring lay down both thick chords and light, evanescent riffs. Cain Blanchard's bass negotiates a stream of styles. Tige Casey not only rumbles and cracks on drums but also contributes spoken wordplay. These poems themselves become a metaphor for the band's music; as soon as the images become recognizable, Casey rapidly shifts direction.

DISCOGRAPHY

Six Foot Hater (1996). At the right volume, if you're in the right mood, this one could full-out frighten you. Or, at the very least, bug you. Songs such as "All Round," which seem to situate the listener on recognizable ground, swiftly project themselves elsewhere. The offerings on this disc are confounding and enigmatic; for instance, the vocal sample in "Nellie Is" could represent a range of emotions. In songs such as "Black the Table," Casey's deliberate monotone casts febrile images against the meandering power of the band. This is sinister, compelling music.

HOT TUNA

- **JACK CASADY:** *bass*
- **MICHAEL FALZARANO:** *guitar, mandolin, vocals*
- **JORMA KAUKONEN:** *electric, acoustic, and table steel guitar, vocals*
- **PETE SEARS:** *keyboards, accordion*
- **HARVEY SORGEN:** *drums and percussion*

Hot Tuna has its origins in the nation's capital during the late 1950s. It was there that high school students Jorma Kaukonen and Jack Casady first met and recognized their mutual musical affinity. The pair formed a short-lived band, the Triumphs, which dissolved when Casady headed out West to attend school and Kaukonen entered Ohio's Antioch College. Eventually, Kaukonen transferred to the University of California at Santa Clara (but not before befriending fellow Antioch students Ian Buchanan and John Hammond, two individuals who shared his emerging obsession with the blues). In California, Kaukonen was indoctrinated into the emerging folk scene, which included such future luminaries as Jerry Garcia. Kaukonen also met Paul Kantner and Marty Balin, who joined forces with Casady and him to play and record as Jefferson Airplane; Grace Slick arrived a short while later, replacing original vocalist Signe Anderson. Although Jefferson Airplane focused on the folk-psychedelic realms, Kaukonen and Casady maintained their affection for the blues, which ultimately led them to perform under the name Hot Tuna.

Many of Hot Tuna's initial gigs took place between sets at Jefferson Airplane shows, with Kaukonen and Casady appearing as an acoustic duo. In 1970, the pair released a debut album, a stirring live acoustic performance that earned Hot Tuna additional renown. Three years later, Kaukonen and Casady left Jefferson Airplane to pursue their project full time. By this point, Hot Tuna had become an electric enterprise and had expanded to include drummer Sammy Piazza and violin player Papa John Creach. This lineup toured the nation, performing a number of Kaukonen originals, the blues of Rev. Gary Davis and Mississippi John Hurt, and some timeless Jelly Roll Morton honky-tonk.

Currently, Hot Tuna performs as a galvanic quintet. Michael Falzarano joined the band in the late 1980s and continues to infuse new energy into the group with his guitar and songwriting; he has also performed some notable tandem gigs with Kaukonen. Keyboardist Pete Sears, formerly of Zero and Jefferson Starship, contributes his artistry. Drum duties are now handled by Harvey Sorgen, who has previously worked with such notables as NRBQ and Bill Frisell. This incarnation of Hot Tuna perpetuates the band's original mission by performing a number of searing classics and original tunes unified by the group's collective penchant for improvisation. Hot Tuna has become a featured part of the Further Festival, and in 1996 the group even appeared twice at many festival shows – as an acoustic act and as an electric outfit.

SELECTED DISCOGRAPHY

Hot Tuna (1970)

First Pull Up, Then Pull Down (1971)

Burgers (1972)

The Phosphorescent Rat (1973)

Double Dose (1984)

Live at Sweetwater (1992). Many heralded this release as evidence that Hot Tuna had reemerged in classic form. This acoustic disc also features the contributions of Bob Weir and Maria Muldaur.

Live at Sweetwater Two (1993). Another invigorating set recorded at the fabled California club.

Classic Electric Hot Tuna (1996). This disc documents the closing of the Fillmore West in 1971. The roster of performers includes Casady, Creach, Kaukonen, and Piazza, and together they deliver a riveting electric performance.

Classic Acoustic Hot Tuna (1996). Also circa 1971, this recording showcases the band's acoustic side. The group celebrates the music of numerous American originals while working through its own collective, creative ideas.

Live in Japan (1998)

WEB SITE

www.hottuna.com

HUBINGER ST.

- **BOB CSUGIE:** *bass, vocals*
- **GREG DEBLASIO:** *drums*
- **CASEY GORMAN:** *guitar, vocals*
- **MATT MIKLUS:** *vocals, guitar*

Hubinger St. is named after a New Haven, Connecticut, avenue where the group's members first lived and practiced together. Matt Miklus moved into a house on that thoroughfare and was soon joined by childhood friend and fellow guitarist Casey Gorman. The two began performing as an acoustic duo in local venues, their repertoire largely made up of cover tunes. After they expanded to form a trio by recruiting bassist Bob Csugie, the fledgling group also introduced a broadening slate of original music. Soon afterward, Hubinger St. became a full electric quartet with the addition of Csugie's pal Greg DeBlasio on drums. Hubinger St. soon began to secure an increasing number of gigs in the northeast, including appearances at music festivals such as the Gathering of the Vibes.

The group revels in improvisation. Its live shows feature dynamic jams that at times invoke the Grateful Dead or the Allman Brothers Band while producing inventive tones and textures. Gorman often leads these journeys with some dexterous ruminations on guitar. He is typically joined by Miklus, who responds with his own ringing expressions. Meanwhile, the rhythm section deftly builds on these ideas while anchoring the sound. Between songs, the band's four members often share their skewed senses of humor with the audience. The results have led the group's burgeoning core of fans to rave about the good-natured vibes emanating from Hubinger St.

DISCOGRAPHY

Elasticstarch (1996). The band's debut supplies an abundance of improvised grooves. Each of its seven tracks is at least six minutes in length, and each contains extemporizations. ''Opening Thoughts'' introduces the band to the listener with a spirited, spontaneous jam. ''A Good Life'' is purposefully reminiscent of the Grateful Dead as it muses on the existence of Jerry Garcia. The disc closes with the fifteen-minute ''Life Game,'' which begins as a solid, funky expression and then moves into more exploratory terrain.

Little Solder Boys (1998)

WEB SITE

www.lopa.com/hubinger

HUFFAMOOSE

- **CRAIG ELKINS:** *vocals, guitar*
- **KEVIN HANSON:** *guitar, vocals*
- **ERIK JOHNSON:** *drums, vocals*
- **JIM STAGER:** *bass, percussion*

Although a couple of its concise songs have received radio play, Huffamoose is, at heart, a jam band. The group is comprised of four jazz musicians who decided to play rock tunes. The quartet's jazz training infuses every aspect of its current endeavor, from original compositions to improvisations. In fact, when Huffamoose was preparing to record its 1997 release *We've Been Had Again*, the producer verbally accosted band members and threatened to leave the project if he heard one more jazz chord (he did not stay to complete work on the disc). Still, Huffamoose receives high praise from a number of fellow musicians, including Rich Pruett of Rugby Road, who proclaims, "These guys are our mentors."

Craig Elkins assembled the group in 1992. He was living in Philadelphia and working as a chef in a Mexican restaurant where he had a weekly solo musical slot. However, his boss began encouraging him to put together a band in order to bring in more customers, so Elkins enlisted three local players who were gigging in a jazz combo: drummer Erik Johnson, bassist Jim Stager, and guitarist Kevin Hanson. The quartet began interpreting songs penned by Elkins and Hanson from a jazz perspective. The compelling results have attracted an influx of tapers to Huffamoose's shows. In 1998, the band completed an intensive year of performances by touring with the Mother Hips for a month and then climbing aboard the HORDE for a few dates.

DISCOGRAPHY

Huffamoose (1994)

We've Been Had Again (1997). This disc contains tight versions of songs the band often opens up in concert. "Wait" is the steady, pulsing opener. "James" is a stark, compelling ballad that describes a relationship in suggestive terms. Other notable cuts include the title track, "Speeding Bullet," and "Buy You a Ring."

WEB SITE

www.huffamoose.com

CHARLIE HUNTER AND POUND FOR POUND

- ■ **SCOTT AMENDOLA:** *drums*
- ■ **STEFON HARRIS:** *vibraphone*
- ■ **CHARLIE HUNTER:** *eight-string guitar*
- ■ **JOHN SANTOS:** *percussion*

Charlie Hunter is one of the most creative and confounding guitarists performing today. The former adjective characterizes every aspect of his music, from the format through which he chooses to express himself, to the songs he picks, to the selection of his instrument. Hunter performs on an eight-string guitar of his own devising, and it allows him simultaneously to play both lead and bass guitar while also producing tones similar to those produced by a Hammond organ. As for the second descriptive term, Hunter defies expectation by pursuing a range of sounds that are grounded in jazz but also explore hip-hop, classic rock, and even reggae.

Hunter first garnered national renown with his role in the Disposable Heroes of Hiphopcrisy. He remained with this outfit until it disbanded after recording a hard-hitting debut. From there, the versatile Hunter moved on to form a trio with former Primus drummer Jay Lane and saxophonist Dave Ellis, both of whom have since joined Bob Weir and Rob Wasserman in Ratdog. When Lane and Ellis exited, Hunter expanded his project into a quartet by recruiting drummer Scott Amendola, alto saxophonist Calder Spanier, and tenor sax player Kenny Brooks. This band recorded a few discs – including *Natty Dread*, in which it covered the entire Bob Marley album of the same name (one of this release's many interesting moments is the introduction to "No Woman No Cry," which quotes "Tennessee Waltz"). Meanwhile, Hunter was also performing with T.J. Kirk, a band composed of three guitarists and a drummer that explored the music of Thelonious Monk, James Brown, and Rashaan Roland Kirk.

Pound for Pound is Hunter's newest project. Here Hunter investigates a different rhythmic environment; working alongside Hunter are Amendola, vibraphonist Stefon Harris, and John Santos on percussion. This group creates new textures and timbres while remaining an outlet for Hunter's innovative musicianship and tantalizing improvisations. Once again, Hunter bursts through genres: he offers, for example, a vibraphone-rich cover of Steve Miller's "Fly like an Eagle" yet proudly asserts that the band's release should provide much fodder for hip-hop DJs to sample.

DISCOGRAPHY

Charlie Hunter Trio (1994)

Bing, Bing, Bing! (1995)

Ready . . . Set . . . Shango! (1996)

Natty Dread (1997)

Return of the Candyman (1998). Although Hunter is the nominal leader here, each member of the quartet steps to the fore. Harris's vibes provide an assertive counterpoint to Hunter's eight-string. This recording balances shorter, percussion-fueled exercises with some lengthier explorations. The aptly titled "Shake, Shake It Baby" is a conga-laden example of the former, while the funkier "Turn Me Loose" falls into the second category. "Fly like an Eagle" proves intriguing, due, in particular, to Harris's contributions. "Dope-a-licious" scampers forward to fulfill the many connotations suggested by its name.

WEB SITE

www.shango.org

HYPNOTIC CLAMBAKE

- **DERICK CUMMINGS:** *guitar, banjo, vocals*
- **JIM DOHERTY:** *drums*
- **ZACHARY FLEITZ:** *bass, vocals*
- **MAURY ROSENBERG:** *vocals, accordion*

Hypnotic Clambake may be the only funky, swinging, bluegrass-inflected, jazzy Cajun rock band to feature an accordion. Indeed, one may have difficulty finding a funky, swinging, bluegrass-inflected, jazzy Cajun rock band that eschews the accordion, so Hypnotic Clambake fits that bill, too, during those instances when founder Maury Rosenberg steps over to the piano. Ever since Rosenberg formed the group in 1989 as a rotating orchestra, the band has remained committed to quirky arrangements, superior instrumentation, and lively humor. Hypnotic Clambake's eclectic sound has led the outfit to share the stage with such diverse performers as Bela Fleck and the Flecktones, Public Enemy, Burning Spear, and Ivo Papasov and His Bulgarian Wedding Band.

Perhaps the one unifying aspect to be found within the expansive realm of Hypnotic Clambake is the stellar musicianship of its players. At the center of it all is Rosenberg, who was educated at the Berklee College of Music, became a rehearsal pianist with the Boston Ballet, and went on to perform with the band Border Patrol as well as with cellist Yo Yo Ma. Although Hypnotic Clambake's membership was once more open-ended, the band now tours with a steady roster (however, alumni such as Billy Constable will often join the group when it comes to town). Says Rosenberg: "The band's sound evolves with each musician who comes in and brings their own talent. Right now it's more of a funky, rock and roll band." This is due, in part, to the contributions of guitarist and banjo player Derick Cummings, whose influences range from Johnny Winter to Frank Zappa to Alvin Lee. Jim Doherty, another former Berklee College student who has performed with the Well Babies and Willie (Loco) Alexander, also enriches the mix. Zachary Fleitz, who plays fretted and fretless bass, draws on a background in traditional jazz as well as fusion and Slavic choral music.

Rosenberg sees Hypnotic Clambake as a collective venture between the band and the audience. Accordingly, the group hosts an annual festival it calls O.U.R. (for Outrageous Universe Revival), which draws together a number of similarly unclassifiable, noteworthy bands. Rosenberg remarks, "People get out of the show whatever they bring to it. In terms of expectations, bring something to the show and you'll get something back. There were these people who complained because they'd seen us with a scrub-board player the last time around and we didn't have one this time. I told them that when they see us again they should bring one of their own. I'm not necessarily saying that we should have an audience orchestra, although on some level that would be cool."

DISCOGRAPHY

Square Dance Messiah (1994)

Gondola to Heaven (1995)

Kent the Zen Master (1996)

Frozen Live Vol. 1 (1997). This live release presents a slightly earlier incarnation of the band: a quintet with Mark Chenevert on clarinet and saxophone and Chris Kew (currently with Jiggle the Handle) on bass. The opener, "Smokin' Joe Clark," is a traditional song that Clambake turns into an eleven-minute bluegrass jam with extended solos from each player. Rosenberg's composition "Zyde Coo Coo" follows, featuring some fierce picking and brawny saxophone. "Freedom Jazz Dance" is a glorious nine-minute instrumental with a bad-ass accordion run. "Tie Dye" is a twisted zydeco cautionary tale about living in "burn-out hell." The final track, "421 Breakdown," is as close to a straightforward bluegrass song as Clambake offers.

WEB SITE

www.hypnotic-clambake.com

ILLUMINATI

- **GRISHA ALEXIEV:** *drums*
- **ERIKA ATCHLEY:** *violin*
- **CATHERINE BENT:** *cello*
- **ROBIN BONNELL:** *cello*
- **RUFUS CAPPADOCIA:** *cello*
- **BARBARA CIFELLI:** *soprano saxophone*
- **MARTHA COLBY:** *cello*
- **NICOL DELLI SANTI:** *vocals*
- **JODY ESPINA:** *alto saxophone*
- **EVAN GALLAGHER:** *keyboards*
- **JOE GALLANT:** *bass*
- **ROB HENKE:** *trumpet*
- **DIANA HEROLD:** *vibraphone, percussion*
- **BOB HOVEY:** *trombone*
- **JOHN ISLEY:** *tenor saxophone*
- **JULIA KENT:** *cello*
- **ADAM KLIPPLE:** *piano*
- **ELIZABETH KNOWLES:** *violin*
- **TODD REYNOLDS:** *violin*
- **SQUANCH:** *trombone*
- **ROLF STURM:** *guitar*
- **HIROKO TAGUCHI:** *violin*
- **ROB THOMAS:** *violin*
- **ALEXIS TOMASON:** *vocals*
- **ROB WOLFSON:** *guitar, vocals*

The twentieth of September 1982 was a momentous day in the life of Joe Gallant. It was his first day working as a television sound-effects technician (he would win an Emmy Award in 1996 for his efforts as sound-effects producer on *Guiding Light*). That day also saw the premier performance of Gallant's band, Illuminati. This initial incarnation of the group was a trio, with Gallant's electric bass accompanied by baritone saxophone and drums. Illuminati has, however, long since expanded into a seventeen-piece behemoth, an orchestra that is committed to presenting Gallant's compositions as well as the music of others (most notably the Grateful Dead) while stretching things out through stirring collective improvisation.

The current formulation of Illuminati harkens back to 1970, when Gallant was first introduced to the music of the Grateful Dead. "By now," he explains, "I know the Dead's songs in my bone marrow, on a cellular level." Gallant has taken inspiration from the Dead while writing and performing his music over the years, and so he was elated to appear on Phil Lesh's radio program *Eyes of Chaos*, which was devoted to modern composers (notes Gallant, "Meeting Phil was like holding onto the Empire State Building in a high wind"). In 1993, Gallant arranged a twenty-piece version of "Unbroken Chain" as a Christmas gift to Lesh and the Dead. Two years later, he was asked to arrange the Grateful Dead's *Blues for Allah* album in commemoration of its twentieth anniversary. The successful performances that ensued soon prompted Gallant to work through some additional Dead songs, with *Terrapin Station* as his next major project. Despite some of the logistical difficulties involved in organizing seventeen players, some of whom rotate in and out of the lineup, Illuminati still hits the road to perform numerous Dead arrangements as well as Gallant's own compositions. In summing up his efforts, Gallant comments that "Illuminati's music is my diary and my sketchpad. It is framed triangularly by modern chamber writing, jazz, and improvisation, with an overlay of sound design. My music has been described as a Chinese puzzle box. As it unfolds, every time you open it, you find a chamber. When you open that up, you find a smaller chamber inside."

DISCOGRAPHY

Skin (1991)

Code of the West (1994). On this release, sixty-two musicians perform seven of Gallant's original compositions, weaving together a tapestry of sound that is thematically linked through Gallant's text on the pervasiveness of televised imagery. There is a big-band feel to many of the tracks and an undercurrent of bebop. A number also reveal a dark and moody side as they shift and transform, yielding textures that range from reggae to swing to rock. The disc concludes with a lush twenty-piece arrangement of the Grateful Dead's "Unbroken Chain."

The Blues for Allah Project (1996)

Live Vol. 2 (1997). This is the follow-up to *Blues for Allah*. On it, Illuminati both interprets the music of others and presents some original songs with a swirl of string instruments and brass. Compelling Grateful Dead covers include "The Music Never Stopped" and "Eyes of the World"; both feature vocalists, albeit a female singer in the latter case, a sensible choice that may initially be disconcerting to some Dead Heads. Equally intriguing are Gallant's own compositions, from the pulsing, insistent "Uschi" to the labyrinthine "The Copper Regions."

INASENSE

- ■ **MARC AMBROSINO:** *drums*
- ■ **NOAH CHASE:** *vocals, guitar, percussion*
- ■ **GILAD DOBRECKY:** *percussion*
- ■ **C. LANZBOM:** *guitar, vocals*
- ■ **JAY WEISSMAN:** *bass*

New York's Inasense manages to offer more than explosive, enthralling improvisation. The group provides plenty of this, and listeners who catch the band in midstream — for instance, during the first break of "I Don't Mind" — would certainly laud its players. However, songs such as the lively workout "The Ride" demonstrate that the group does not solely melt its tunes in the tradition of the Allman Brothers Band, but it also embraces some traditional Israeli sounds.

Although both C. Lanzbom and Noah Chase were born in the United States, they traveled to Israel and spent many of their formative years in that country. Lanzbom, schooled in jazz guitar from an early age, went on to earn his living as a popular Israeli session musician. It was in Israel that he met his future partner when he was called in to work on a recording with Chase's father. Lanzbom and the younger Chase struck up a friendship, which expanded into musical realms. When, despite the lucrative nature of his session work, Lanzbom finally decided to commit himself to performing his own compositions, the pair began to assemble a band. They eventually returned to the United States with the hope of finding receptive ears for their music.

Inasense has indeed found enthusiastic listeners. Many of its guitar-based songs build vigorously on rock and blues traditions. Numerous jams are further enlivened by a flurry of percussion. However, the group also evinces its affinity for Israeli music, which originated partially in Spain and is tinged with the flair of that nation's folk musicians. This adds a psychedelic edge to Inasense's sound, particularly when the group delves deeply into an extemporization. In describing his band's live performances, Lanzbom says: "When people come out to see us, they can expect to be dazzled, because I know that I am. Sometimes I'll step back and watch our percussionists go at it. I'll just be hypnotized by what they're doing." Many have said the same about Lanzbom's own guitar techniques. Inasense continues to mesmerize new ears at every show.

DISCOGRAPHY

Inasense (1996)

The Ride (1997). Inasense puts forward a range of ideas on this refreshing release. The title song, a spirited opener, reveals the group's Israeli influences. "I Didn't Know" is bluesier fare marked by Lanzbom's stinging leads. "Space" chugs along with some appropriate psychedelic flourishes. The band also provides a joyous interpretation of the traditional tune "Rider" (known to Grateful Dead fans as "I Know You Rider"). "Oovnay" is a bright instrumental with Middle Eastern rhythms composed by Lanzbom's mentor Rabbi Schlomo Carlebach. The extended "Midnight" allows the band's percussionists to shine.

WEB SITE

www.inasense.com

SHERRI JACKSON BAND

- ■ **GLENN ESPARZA:** *bass*
- ■ **SHERRI JACKSON:** *guitar, vocals*
- ■ **BRIAN MCRAE:** *drums, percussion*

Sherri Jackson's musical career demonstrates that talent and dedication sometimes need to be goosed by serendipity. Jackson entered the University of Colorado at Boulder in 1986 on a violin scholarship. After one semester, she switched to general university studies because she had become disenchanted with some of the personalities that held sway in the music department. Similarly dissatisfied with dorm food, she was interested to hear from an acquaintance on the football team that varsity athletes were treated to sumptuous repasts (and that they shared a measure of collegiality that had been lacking in her first semester). So Jackson resolved to try out for the track team, eventually earning herself an athletic scholarship while becoming a national-caliber sprinter. After breaking her leg during a track meet in Japan, Jackson kept herself busy by joining a female comedy troupe. One day, while dressed up as Diana Ross to perform with the troupe, she attracted the attention of some members of a musical group called Band du Jour. For a laugh, the group's members coaxed Jackson onto the stage and convinced her to join. She toured with Band du Jour for four years, contributing harmony vocals and tambourine. During this period, she also entertained herself by learning to play the guitar – her work on violin served as an initial template – and scribing some songs. By 1994, she had decided to leave the group to focus on her own music.

The Sherri Jackson Band was finally realized when Jackson recruited bassist Glenn Esparza and drummer Brian McRae, both of whom bring their affinity for jazz and funk to the group. The trio's music is built around her vocal phrasings (she has been compared with Sinéad O'Connor and Alanis Morissette) as well as her string attack. In particular, Jackson has earned praise for the tones she summons by plucking and bowing her violin. Jackson shuns repeat extended explorations (a reaction to her stint in Band du Jour, when she often had to beat on a tambourine for twenty minutes at a time), but she does often break free from the dictates of her classical training to improvise, stretching out on both of her instruments. The fervor and passion of the band's live performances won the members a spot on the 1996 and 1997 Further tours, where Jackson often appeared in the show-ending jam sessions with, among others, Bob Weir, Mickey Hart, and Bruce Hornsby.

DISCOGRAPHY

Moments in Denial (1995)

Sherri Jackson (1997). This disc contains a number of engaging melodies and lyrics rendered even more memorable by Jackson's driving vocals and instrumental contributions. She is able to achieve such heights through the strong foundation provided by Esparza and McRae. The group is assisted by John Medeski and Los Lobo member Steve Berlin (who quite capably produced this release). Standout tracks include "Maple Tree," the lilting "Time and Time," and the more forceful "What an Ego."

WEB SITE

www.sherrijackson.com

JAZZ MANDOLIN PROJECT

- **CHRIS DAHLGREN:** *bass*
- **JAMIE MASEFIELD:** *mandolin*
- **SCOTT NEUMANN:** *drums*

The Jazz Mandolin Project, as the name suggests, is an evolving collective originally founded by Jamie Masefield in 1993. The band developed out of Masefield's involvement in Burlington, Vermont's, experimental jazz scene. Masefield, who had attended the University of Vermont (and, for trivia fans, is the great-grandson of England's poet laureate John Masefield), had previously performed in a number of local groups, including the Onion River Jazz Band and the Gordon Stone Trio. The Jazz Mandolin Project came together in the course of some open gigs at a number of area clubs, particularly the Last Elm Cafe, the city's nonprofit community coffeehouse. At these shows, Masefield began to collaborate with a number of players, including Trey Anastasio, Jon Fishman, and Stacey Starkweather (this combo gigged in New England during 1994 as the Jazz Mandolin Project, but later it redubbed itself Bad Hat).

The first incarnation of the Jazz Mandolin Project evolved out of these sessions; Masefield was joined by Starkweather on bass and Gabe Jarrett on drums. This trio balanced Masefield's intricate compositions with an improvisatory ethic. Given the band's instrumentation, its music had a bluegrass feel, but its presiding influence was modern jazz – this became apparent as the group worked through Masefield's songs, some extended extemporizations, and some covers of artists such as Sonny Rollins, Miles Davis, and Duke Ellington.

In 1997, Jarrett and Starkweather opted to move on to other ventures. However, the Jazz Mandolin Project remains a going concern. In the spring of 1998, Masefield fielded a new version of the band, and the Project embarked on a three-week "tour de flux." This trio featured upright bass player Chris Dahlgren, a veteran of the downtown New York jazz scene, and Fishman on drums. These players added their own accents to Masefield's catalog of songs while investigating new territory. The music will continue to develop as Masefield invites new players to join him and infuse their own creative energies into the Jazz Mandolin Project.

DISCOGRAPHY

The Jazz Mandolin Project (1996). This release features the group's long-standing lineup: Jamie Masefield, Stacey Starkweather on electric and acoustic bass, and Gabe Jarrett on percussion. Its ten songs were recorded live in the studio to document the band's creative improvisation. Representative offerings, such as "The Country Open," "The Opera," and "Contois," showcase Masefield's majestic flourishes, Starkweather's inventive rumblings, and Jarrett's crackling expressions.

Tour de Flux (1998)

WEB SITE

www.netspace.org/jmp

JIGGLE THE HANDLE

- **GARY BACKSTROM:** *guitar, vocals*
- **CHRIS KEW:** *bass*
- **GREG VASSO:** *drums, percussion*
- **PAUL WOLSTENCROFT:** *keyboards, vocals*

Jiggle the Handle uses its tight, melodic compositions as a stepping-off point for massive improvisations. Gary Backstrom, guitarist and principal songwriter for the Massachusetts-based group, affirms this goal: "Our shows are a mixture of those elements. I'm happy to write a hook, but we also pride ourselves on our jams. Often we'll know we intend to move from one song to another, but other than that, it's unstructured and unplanned. It's always scary, and sometimes it falls on its face." Often, however, it is inspired and inspiring.

Jiggle's sound is built on a foundation of blues, Latin rhythms, and soul (the palette draws on such luminaries as Carlos Santana, Traffic, and Todd Rundgren). Backstrom's fluid guitar leads are complemented by Paul Wolstencroft's thick, resonant keyboard declarations. Chris Kew constantly pushes the groove with his own chunky bass lines. Drummer Greg Vasso, whose tenure with Max Creek was spent steeped in improvisation, keeps it all moving while adding his own fills. Wolstencroft and Kew are relatively new to the band, and they have brought with them a surge of energy and a profusion of ideas. Backstrom describes Kew, who joined Jiggle after an extended stint with Hypnotic Clambake, as "a powerhouse. He creates a huge, huge pocket. We're happy to walk off and give him a bass showcase so he can blow us away along with the audience." Wolstencroft, who covers both organ and vocals, also contributes his own songs (in his spare time, he organizes a loose, keyboard-based conglomeration called Organically Grown and gigs across New England). Says Backstrom: "Paul has polished our vocal harmonies. And his organ playing rips everyone's head off. I think he's part organ."

The band's creativity is not limited to the musical front. Jiggle the Handle has committed itself to developing innovative ways of interacting with its audience and enhancing the experience of its fans. Backstrom notes, "We receive a great feeling of support from them. We feel like they're part of what we're doing, and we try to express that." One such expression appears on the cover of the band's debut CD, *Mrs. White's Party*, which features a bonus rotating image of Jiggle the Handle's logo. A second is the group's live monthly Webcast. Backstrom comments: "Greg dreamed it up, and now anyone in the world can hear us. We recently heard from people in Germany who tuned in. It's really exciting — it makes me feel like an astronaut."

DISCOGRAPHY

Mrs. White's Party (1997). This collection of studio tracks and live performances offers a whopping seventy-five minutes of essential Jiggle. "Just Can't Get Enough" opens with swirling keyboards and gives way to Backstrom's bracing guitar. Other strong cuts include the slinky "Walk Right out Your Door," the instrumental journey "Vertigo," and "Sowelu," which is enriched by Vasso's contributions. *Mrs. White's Party* comes to a festive end with "Turn Myself Back Home," a reminder to listeners that, though the band can stretch it out, Jiggle the Handle always offers well-crafted songs.

WEB SITE

www.jigglethehandle.com

THE JONGLEURS

- **FORREST GIBERSON:** *bass, vocals*
- **WARREN GLASSMEYER:** *alto and soprano saxophone, vocals*
- **ERIC HASTINGS:** *drums, vocals*
- **JOSH SCLAR:** *tenor saxophone, vocals*
- **MIKE STEGNER:** *keyboards, vocals*

Jongleurs means "jugglers" in French. It's a fitting name for this Miami band, because it juggles a handful of genres. Furthermore, much of the Jongleurs live show is based on improvisation, and the group has proven itself quite adept at keeping its musical balls in the air. In describing the quintet's sound, keyboardist Mike Stegner says, "We had a meeting once and decided to call it 'experimental alternative,' but we're really not sure what that means." In the past, the group has also used jazz, punk, and funk as reference points in characterizing its music as "junk."

The Jongleurs is comprised of piano, bass, drums, and two saxophones. The absence of guitars frees up a lot of room, which is voraciously swallowed up by each of the players. At times, Warren Glassmeyer and Josh Sclar's saxophones take the lead, whether soloing, building a melody through dual entwined expressions, or providing dissonance. Stegner also commands on keys, both by working a steady groove and by interjecting some darker sounds. Forrest Giberson's bass similarly imposes itself, at times in the manner of a lead guitar but more often providing elastic support for the other instruments. Eric Hastings's jazz-flavored drums react to the band's concoctions while working to keep things moving. Although the sound can be somewhat reminiscent of free jazz – or even acid jazz when the band adds its twisted lyric imagery – some songs recall those of hardcore groups such as the Minutemen. Stegner explains that, "In the beginning, everyone was comparing us to Frank Zappa, but, truthfully, when we started we hadn't listened to all that much Zappa. I went out and picked up a bunch of his stuff just to find out what everyone was talking about. And I certainly can see why they had said what they said."

Still, the band continues to defy categorization while creating music that interests its members. Stegner adds, "Sometimes people will be a little freaked out by what we do, but I think we've found a way to entertain people without sacrificing our adventurous side. Our ideal audience would be people like us who don't go out to see a particular style, but go out to see enjoyable music. We've played quite a few punk clubs in our day, along with some jazz rooms and also with a number of jam bands. Through all of it, we just keep in mind what our friends in Day by the River tell us: 'One person at a time, one person at a time.' We really believe that."

DISCOGRAPHY

The Jongleurs (1996)

Five People (1997). This disc documents both the ingenuity and the occasional abstruseness of the Jongleurs. The opener, "Welcome to the Wall Mart," throbs with swaggering horns and twisted lyrics. By contrast, the next song, "One Happy Day in a Midwestern Country Town," is seven minutes of textured soundscape. An offering such as "Calculator" sounds closer to free jazz, while

"Pizza for Brains" would not be out of place on a Frank Zappa album.

WEB SITE

www.rombox.com/~jongleurs

JORDHUGA

- **SCOTT BARWICK:** *bass, vocals*
- **RICHARD E. COCKCROFT:** *keyboards, vocals*
- **MARTY CRIBB:** *drums*
- **STEVE HOFFMAN:** *percussion*
- **TRAVAS HUNTER:** *vocals, percussion*
- **CHRIS LAWTHER:** *guitar, vocals*

The development of Jordhuga is yet another testament to the ineffable creative vibe emanating from Chico, California. The members of the group had originally played together in Columbia, South Carolina, but when some of the band's musicians relocated to the West Coast in 1995 it looked as if the group had delivered its final performance. Explains bassist Scott Barwick: "When I made it out to Chico, all I knew was that I wanted to keep going in music. None of us knew this band was going to happen." However, the arrival of guitarist Chris Lawther proved to be the impetus required for the players to regroup with a renewed vitality and commitment.

Jordhuga dishes up a percussion-laden stew in which melody is an essential ingredient. The four-part harmonies built into many of its songs further distinguish the group. Lawther interjects some supple, subtle guitar ruminations, which are complemented by Barwick's resourceful bass and Richard Cockcroft's keyboard expressions. Jordhuga typically performs two-hour to three-hour shows with the underlying intention of keeping its audiences grooving and shaking. A related band mission is reflected in its name, which it defines as "an evolution of consciousness of earth and spirit." Indeed, Barwick does somewhat understate things when he proclaims: "At heart we're a live dance band. No magic tricks or anything."

DISCOGRAPHY

Jordhuga (1997). Although this debut disc is a studio recording, it does reflect the band's live vigor. The opening track, "Soul Rhythm Dance," typifies Jordhuga's music: it features a spiritual message, an entrancing beat, and sinewy guitar. Other pleasing cuts include the gentle, soulful "You Can Go Swimming," the harmony-rich "Nothing Left to Hide," and the funkier "Grown On."

JERRY JOSEPH AND THE JACKMORMONS

- **JERRY JOSEPH:** *vocals, guitar*
- **BRAD ROSEN:** *drums and percussion*
- **JUNIOR RUPPEL:** *bass*

Jerry Joseph's story is a complicated and compelling one. In 1982, he cofounded Little Women, supplying songs, guitar, and vocals. It began as a reggae-inflected jam band and built a sizable following nationwide. In its early years, the band spent a good deal of time on the road with reggae legends Burning Spear. Gradually, Little Women's music gravitated toward an edgier rock sound; says Joseph, "There was a big tug-of-war within the band, and we may have made some of our best music due to that kind of tension." In 1990, the group was on the cusp of signing a deal with the revitalized Capricorn Records, but the label grew leery when rumors spread of Joseph's heroin use. Little Women split up soon afterward, and Joseph lapsed into addiction. He was invited by Backdoor Records, which had been established by Widespread Panic singer John Bell, to work on a solo album with famed Muscle Shoals producer Johnny Sandlin, but, despite the best efforts of a number of his friends — including his occasional musical partner Woody Harrelson — he could not break free from his drug habit. After many agonizing months, Joseph did finally kick heroin and then resumed his musical career.

The Jackmormons came together in 1996 when Joseph's longtime pal drummer Jim Bone invited him to Salt Lake City to perform. The pair formed a group that began as a quartet and included longtime associate Dave Pellicciaro on keyboards. As for the group's name, Joseph recalls, "I decided that if we're from Utah we might as well pick a name that's indigenous." The band soon accumulated fans, some of whom harkened back to the heyday of Little Women. Unlike that famed earlier band, the Jackmormons do not perform extended improvisations. Joseph describes his new sound as leaner, noting, "At this point in my life, my stuff is about my songwriting." Still, on any given evening, the trio will stretch things out, allowing Joseph to complement his moving, evocative compositions with some expansive guitar.

DISCOGRAPHY

Butte, Mont. 1879 (1996)

Cotton (1997)

Goodlandia (1997). This collection of live tracks highlights the band's strengths, in particular its song craft and tight interplay. "Light Is like Water" demonstrates the Jackmormons's effective use of dynamics. The song simmers, incorporating a lively guitar solo from Joseph and building through his rousing vocals. "Pink Light" and "Watching Me" are two articulate offerings somewhat reminiscent of John Hiatt. "Water Tower," another compelling song, features Joseph digging in on vocals. The closer, "Road to Damascus," presents the band's more open, explosive side during an appearance at the High Sierra Music Festival.

WEB SITE

www.ipeg.com/~kbender/jm.html

JUGGLING SUNS

- **MARK DIOMEDE:** *guitar, vocals*
- **TANK EVELEIGH:** *guitar, vocals*
- **KEVIN KOPACK:** *bass, vocals*
- **CASEY LAPERLE:** *drums, vocals*
- **GUS VIGO:** *keyboards, vocals*

The Juggling Suns began as an entertaining side project for Solar Circus guitarist Mark Diomede. The first version took shape late in the summer of 1995 and was named after Solar Circus's first album. Diomede recalls, "We were not trying to be the next big band trying to break, we were just trying to get back to our roots by playing gigs predominantly comprised of the music we loved." However, in early 1997 two developments occurred. First, Solar Circus broke up after a decade of touring and recording (including five releases on Relix Records). Second, Diomede found himself being pursued by Jon and Marsha Zazula, the founders of Megaforce Records (which had launched the careers of Metallica, Anthrax, and Ministry). The Zazulas were eager to expand into a new genre of music; they had made an initial foray when they brought out Warren Haynes's solo debut, *Tales of Ordinary Madness*, in 1993. A short while later, a revamped Juggling Suns became the flagship band of the Zazulas' new label, Hydrophonics Records.

The Rumson, New Jersey, group has quickly garnered plaudits for its vivid, elaborate improvisations that still offer danceable grooves. Guitarist Diomede often becomes the focus through his energetic exertions, which at times recall Jerry Garcia. Keyboardist Gus Vigo is also capable of taking a jam in an entirely new direction. Bassist Kevin Kopack, who played with Solar Circus during its last two years of existence, interjects his own ideas. Rhythm guitarist Tank Eveleigh may be underappreciated; he adds essential flavors to the band's sound. Drummer Casey LaPerle brings big ears and steady chops to the mix. Says Diomede: "We had that telepathic communication from the first time we got together. Any band that tries to find its way into different realms of musical exploration really depends on those types of interaction. But just as important is the fact that everyone writes and sings. We have a plethora of ideas, and that really keeps things interesting."

DISCOGRAPHY

Living on the Edge of Change (1997). This release was drawn from live performances that took place soon after the band's personnel roster crystallized. It suggests that the members of Juggling Suns were on the same wavelength right out of the box. Also, the eight songs presented here clock in at seventy minutes, demonstrating that the band just doesn't skimp. "Mountain Marlane" has a bright, bluegrass feel. "Obsessions," a reggae-tinged tune, has some engaging Garciaesque tones courtesy of Diomede. "Spin Song" remains lively and upbeat throughout its entire eleven minutes. Finally, the invigorating "Open Road Jam" includes some guest percussion from the inimitable Jonny Z. himself.

WEB SITE

www.webspan.net/~keyz

JUPITER COYOTE

- ■ **GENE H. BASS JR.:** *drums*
- ■ **SANDERS BRIGHTWELL:** *bass*
- ■ **JOHN FELTY:** *vocals, electric and acoustic guitar, mandolin, piano*
- ■ **MATTHEW MAYES:** *vocals, electric and acoustic guitar, guijo, banjo*
- ■ **ROBERT SOTO:** *percussion*

A coyote is a shrewd, scrappy animal that does what it has to do in order to survive. These traits are shared by the Macon, Georgia, quintet Jupiter Coyote. It has toured relentlessly, invented instruments, and even created its own successful record label in order to allow its members to accomplish their collective musical goals.

Jupiter Coyote's "mountain rock" encompasses a panoply of styles and genres. Matthew Mayes, who cofounded the group in Brevard, North Carolina, with John Felty, observes: "We cover a lot of ground – blues, bluegrass, folk, rock. All of that rolled into one burrito." The band also makes use of the distinctive sounds of the guijo, a hybrid guitar-banjo that Mayes himself created. "I put the guijo together," he explains, "because I didn't want to be trapped by the same tones. I think the only other person out there who is playing something like this is Mark Vann of Leftover Salmon."

The group has garnered particular approbation for its live shows. The starting point is the band's melodious original compositions, which present a series of evocative stories. Both Felty and Mayes supply vocals and guitars; Felty will frequently contribute some stinging bottleneck as well. Sanders Brightwell provides sparkling accents on bass. Gene H. Bass Jr. on drums and Robert Soto on percussion give many songs an extra boost. In concert, all of this regularly yields ebullient jams and inspired song-to-song transitions. Affirms Mayes, "We try to link four or five together and then come up for air. It's fun and easy when you've got five horses pulling the wagon."

Another aspect of the Jupiter Coyote story is the manner in which the band has supported itself and several other artists. In 1993, the group created its own label, Autonomous Record. Mayes notes, "It's amazing what you can achieve when you have no options." A number of other bands have recorded on Autonomous as well, including Blue Miracle, Uncle Mingo, and Strangefolk. Mayes's words on the future of Jupiter Coyote may also describe this venture: "It's gonna go where it's gonna go. We're just along for the ride."

DISCOGRAPHY

Cemeteries and Junkyards (1993)

Lucky Day (1994)

Wade (1995)

Ghost Dance (1997). Jupiter Coyote presents a strong collection of songs here. "Tumbleweed" builds on a sharp, driving melody with some animated guitar. "Whoville" is a haunting, spiritual account of Native American peoples (the disc's title and the accompanying essay by Felty describe a Native American ritual of rebirth). "Two Things" is a gentler offering. "Sam Clemens" is a robust composition that concludes with some dexterous rhythmic textures supplied by the band's two drummers.

Here Be Dragons (1998)

WEB SITE

www.jupitercoyote.com

KARMIC

- ■ **JAMIE BLACK:** *keyboards, vocals*
- ■ **GLENN HOUSE:** *vocals, guitar*
- ■ **JOHN LIPPI:** *guitar, vocals*
- ■ **JEFF MARTIN:** *bass, vocals*
- ■ **R.J. NESS:** *drums, percussion*

Karmic's music melds psychedelic imagery, quick-wristed funk guitar, and jazzy piano flourishes reminiscent of Chick Corea. The resulting sonic stew has galvanized audiences in the band's home state of Michigan since 1992. Recently, the group has taken to the road for extended periods, bringing its kaleidoscope to new ears and eyes.

In its original incarnation, the group was known as Karmic Regatta, a primarily acoustic outfit that performed cover material. Then, as new members began to join, not only did the band's name change, but also its focus began to shift. For instance, Glenn House, drummer for Karmic Regatta, stepped to the fore as lead singer and rhythm guitarist for Karmic (in the process, House, who is left-handed, taught himself how to play a right-handed guitar upside down). Another turning point was the addition of lead guitarist John Lippi, a songwriter who provided the group with a fresh jolt by encouraging its members to plug in. Yet more change was triggered by keyboardist Jamie Black, whose development of a profound musical vocabulary also elevates the group.

Karmic has penned a number of memorable melodies and has recently brushed up its vocal harmonies. Above all, though, this is a band that loves instrumental experimentation. Its long jams are seasoned with many elements — from delicate guitar phrasings to spiraling keyboards to perilous bass runs. The group is also quite willing to employ these elements while performing acoustic selections. After all, the quintet's stated intent is to do whatever it can to produce good Karmic.

DISCOGRAPHY

Wha'la in the Field of Flowers (1992)

Sister Chosen One (1994)

Whimsical Stew (1997). Here Karmic offers a Whitman's Sampler of styles and expressions. "Tripping through Time" is a goofy funk tune built on nimble guitar lines and a correspondingly springy keyboard bed. "Cried the Fool" presents some sprightly boogie-woogie. "Foresight" is an extended journey enriched by creative guitar accents and piano riffs that echo Chuck Leavell. "Whimsical Stew" is a burbling instrumental that demonstrates the band's ability to create spacey textures. "Morphing Impressions" turns it over to Black for an unaccompanied piano instrumental with a classical feel.

WEB SITE

www.thejamspot.com/bands/karmic

KEROSENE DREAM

- **DEREK BROWN:** *drums*
- **DAVE COEY:** *vocals, acoustic guitar*
- **JEFF FARNARD:** *bass, vocals*
- **BART FERGUSON:** *vocals, harmonica*
- **BEN STURGILL:** *electric and acoustic guitar, vocals*

Denizens of the Portland, Oregon, groove scene were heartened in late 1996 by the emergence of Kerosene Dream. Prior to this, some of the area's most popular jam bands had folded their tents, including the Strangers, the Renegade Saints, and Nine Days Wonder. Kerosene Dream pulled together the creative forces behind many of these groups, including singer/songwriters Dave Coey and Bart Ferguson and resourceful multi-instrumentalist Ben Sturgill. Drummer Derek Brown, who had previously performed with (the still vital) Rubberneck, and bassist Jeff Farnard, from a local outfit called Haymaker, signed on to complete the Dream. The quintet soon displayed the traits that had marked its antecedents: adroit musicianship and song craft.

Kerosene Dream's melodious original compositions incorporate elements of folk, country, and blues to create engaging roots rock enlivened by pleasing vocal harmonies. Coey maintains that the band devotes much energy to creating music that "supports the lyrical ideas of each song." Nonetheless, in the live setting the band is willing and able to mine some glorious grooves. The results have inspired exuberant dancing at venues throughout the Northwest and at events such as the High Sierra Music Festival.

DISCOGRAPHY

Kerosene Dream (1996). This seven-song release features the earliest configuration of the band: Coey, Ferguson, and Sturgill. Still, through the contributions of the stripped-down trio, this release soars.

From the Sundown Sky (1997). The quintet's debut contains a number of warm, vivid compositions. The opener, "I Can See You," is one such example, with its taste of harmonica and slide guitar. "Arizona Lightening" is held aloft by the band's vocal harmonies. Other standout cuts include the sing-along "'79 Country Squire," the gentler "Last Chance for Glory," and the bright "Outlaw Song."

WEB SITE

www.kerosenedream.com

LAKE TROUT

- **JAMES GRIFFITH:** *bass, vocals*
- **ED HARRIS:** *guitar, vocals*
- **MIKE LOWRY:** *drums*
- **MATT PIERCE:** *saxophone, flute, percussion*
- **WOODY RANERE:** *vocals, guitar*

Lake Trout is committed to creating improvisational music by employing both contemporary sounds and by mining more traditional sources. This group can weave multifarious soul and jazz grooves. Yet Lake Trout may also invite a DJ to the stage: in particular, DJ Who will add some scratches and DJ Shawn will spin beats under the music. The band's collective pantheon of favorite artists reflects this dual focus: Digable Planets and a Tribe Called Quest as well as John Coltrane and jazz guitar dazzler Pat Martino.

The Baltimore-based band began, in 1994, as an instrumental quartet. After a year and a half of gigging in that configuration, it brought in a second guitarist, Woody Ranere, who also sang. As Ed Harris, who supplies most of the group's guitar leads, explains, "We never really intended to add vocals, but Woody just happened to have a voice that contributed an additional texture to the mix." As a result, Lake Trout continues to explore abstract spaces but does so with the aid of verbal poetry. Above all, the group seeks to flavor all of its absorbing journeys with soul, which explains its name – Harris notes that "lake trout is Baltimore soul food."

Lake Trout is an absorbing live band that extemporizes within a mosaic of hip-hop, jazz, and funk. Harris says that he is also pleased with the group's songwriting: "I feel like we have an interesting process – the way our voices chime in as individuals and then as a group. Everybody has written something significant in every piece. That way every song has a lot of interesting colors." The suppleness of the band's grooves is perhaps best evinced by the fact that Lake Trout has been invited to perform behind various artists at area hip-hop showcases. At the same time, the group is celebrated by jazz aficionados and improvisational-rock fans alike.

DISCOGRAPHY

Lake Trout (1997). The band's amalgam of sounds and ideas is well represented on this release. For instance, in the opener, "Cracked," Ranere's honeyed voice calls out, complementing his bandmates' swinging expressions. "Polis" begins with a bebop sax intro and creates an uptempo groove that also features a nimble, metal-flavored guitar solo. Other intriguing tracks include the instrumental "Outswinger" and the laid-back, soulful "What to Do." The delectable epic "Too Sweet" layers smooth vocals over buttery jazz chords.

Volume for the Rest of It (1998)

WEB SITE

www.sbachman.com/laketrout

LARRY

- ■ **JEFF BRADBERRY:** *vocals, washboard*
- ■ **RICK CANNON:** *harmonica*
- ■ **MIKE MCCLUER:** *bass*
- ■ **ANDREW VICKERS:** *drums, vocals*
- ■ **STEVE VICKERS:** *percussion, vocals*
- ■ **TOM VICKERS:** *guitar, vocals*
- ■ **TOM WATTS:** *guitar*

Larry is a band that strives to blend a commitment to technical musicianship with a sense of fun. Accordingly, guitarist Tom Vickers describes the band's stringent work habits while characterizing lead vocalist Jeff Bradberry as "the ringleader for our circus." Although the group aggressively explores its songs, a Larry jam also may gravitate toward the "Dukes of Hazzard Theme" or the "James Bond Theme." It's not surprising that Vickers explains the band's name as "a bad joke that stuck."

The group formed in 1994 when Vickers returned from Colorado to join his younger brother Andrew in Austin. The elder Vickers recalls that, along with bass player Mike McCluer, they would "sit in the garage for hours playing Widespread Panic songs." The band solidified when the trio expanded to include a pair of high school friends, vocalist Bradberry and harmonica player Rick Cannon, as well as a third Vickers brother, Steve, a percussionist. Over the years, the songwriting skills of individual band members have developed, as have their musical-communication skills. Larry currently employs its percussive thrust, dual guitars, and effect-enhanced harmonica to produce a number of rousing grooves. Also, Bradberry's vocals blend in quite effectively while conveying the group's lyrics, which often incorporate an element of humor. The results may be best summed up by the band's motto: "If you love to play in the mud, then you'll love Larry."

DISCOGRAPHY

Live at the White Rabbit (1996)

Here I Am (1997). Although this release presents tight versions of Larry's songs, the band remains on full throttle, yielding a number of robust grooves. The opener, "Razor's Edge," showcases invigorating contributions from each of the band members. Other notable cuts include "90's Hippie," which features a sing-along chorus, the extended "Sleep," and "Manitou Song," which is punctuated by trenchant harmonica.

WEB SITE

www.larryland.com

LEFTOVER SALMON

- **DREW EMMITT:** *mandolin, fiddle, flute, electric guitar, vocals*
- **VINCE HERMAN:** *vocals, acoustic guitar, washboard*
- **TYE NORTH:** *bass, vocals*
- **JEFF SIPE:** *drums*
- **MARK VANN:** *banjo*

Leftover Salmon characterizes its music as "polyethnic Cajun slamgrass." This phrase not only describes the band's sound, but it also succinctly chronicles its origins. Leftover Salmon emerged from the fortuitous amalgamation of two Colorado groups. In 1990, Vince Herman fronted a Cajun/calypso jugband called the Salmon Heads. One evening, some of that group's members couldn't make it to a gig, so Herman put in a call to request the musical assistance of Drew Emmitt's progressive bluegrass outfit, the Left Hand String Band. As a joke, the players decided to fuse the names of their respective groups, thereby creating Leftover Salmon. The moniker stuck, as did the lineup, and the Boulder-based band now performs in excess of two hundred shows a year.

Leftover Salmon creates a tantalizing musical melange. Emmitt is a multi-instrumentalist who will happily pick up an electric guitar, a fiddle, or a flute. He also produces some innovative tones on his electric mandolin, from which he can elicit sounds reminiscent of a steel drum. Vocalist Herman interjects robust phrasings on acoustic guitar while adding washboard accents. Mark Vann is a celebrated banjo player who has taken top picking honors at the Telluride Bluegrass Festival. Bassist Tye North (whose father played on drums in the acid-folk group Holy Modal Rollers) adds an expansive musical lexicon of his own. The band's drummer is the seemingly octo-limbed Jeff Sipe, formerly of Aquarium Rescue Unit (where he was better known as Apt. Q258) and Hellborg, Lane and Sipe.

The hallmark of the band's celebrated live show is spontaneity. Its performances are replete with tantalizing, euphonious jams. On a given evening, one or two of the group's favored genres may predominate. For example, Emmitt may decide to focus on his guitar while the band works through a bluesier rock sound, or he may concentrate on mandolin or fiddle while the band produces a sound that is closer to bluegrass, Cajun, or calypso. Similarly, Vann may put down his banjo to perform on waterphone, an acoustic instrument played with a water-filled bow (this bends notes, creating sounds somewhat reminiscent of a whale song). The band's improvisatory ethic extends to Herman's vocals – he will often supply impromptu lyrics. Spontaneous covers of tunes by the Sex Pistols, Bill Monroe, or Led Zeppelin may further enliven a show. As a result, Leftover Salmon is often followed from gig to gig by a loyal contingent of devotees and tapers (including some on-line denizens who call themselves LoSers), as any show promises a sparkling exhibition of musicianship and humor.

DISCOGRAPHY

Bridges to Bert (1993)

Ask the Fish (1995)

Euphoria (1997). On this release, Leftover Salmon presents an eclectic range of offerings, yet each song bears the band's distinctive musical stamp. "Better" is the kinetic, ska-laced opener. "Mama

Boulet'' displays the band's Cajun side. "Funky Mountain Fog-down" is an animated bluegrass number with some lively fiddle from guest artist Sam Bush. "Highway Song" reveals gentler textures. "Baby Hold On" dishes up the band's vocal harmonies, spiced with a little guitar twang. The sprightly title track, which closes the disc, is taken from the Holy Modal Rollers's catalog.

WEB SITE

www.leftoversalmon.com

LETTUCE

- **JEFF BHASKER:** *keyboards*
- **ERICK COOMES:** *bass*
- **ADAM DEITCH:** *drums*
- **EMILIANO GARCIA:** *tenor saxophone*
- **SAM KINNINGER:** *alto sax*
- **ERIC KRASNO:** *guitar*
- **ADAM SMIRNOFF:** *guitar*
- **RYAN WOODWARD:** *baritone and tenor saxophone*

Lettuce came together in the early 1990s when guitarist Eric Krasno attended Berklee College of Music summer camp. There he started playing with several of the musicians who would ultimately join him in the group. Later, Krasno enrolled at Berklee and reestablished the friendships he had made that summer. When he transferred to Hampshire College, Krasno decided to call on a number of the players he had met to form a group that would make instrumental music. This formal genesis occurred in the fall of 1995, and, since then, Lettuce has attracted a growing audience for its strident mix of funk, jazz, and hip-hop.

Lettuce is comprised of a number of gifted performers, each of whom enriches the mix with his own musical passions. Sam Kinninger, often the group's featured soloist on alto saxophone, is a skilled jazz player who is also drawn to the music of Maceo Parker. Erick Coomes plays six-string bass with a funky flair. Adam Smirnoff primarily supplies rhythm guitar, eliciting some solid rhythm-and-blues tones from his Stratocaster. Ryan Woodward often blows baritone sax, which, Krasno notes, "gives us that 'tower of power' sound." Drummer Adam Deitch, who is also proficient on piano, composes some of the group's songs. A recent addition is keyboardist Jeff Bhasker, who earns special praise from Krasno because, "When we get our ideas together, he's the one who actually writes them down." Meanwhile, Krasno himself composes most of Lettuce's music, plays jazz-inflected funk leads, and facilitates the entire venture. Finally, Lettuce brings in rapper Radio Active to emcee many shows. Audience members continue to be mesmerized, as do fellow musicians. Lettuce is a favorite at Northampton's fabled Iron Horse Music Hall, where it has appeared with Moon Boot Lover's Peter Prince.

DISCOGRAPHY

Lettuce (1998)

LIVING DAYLIGHTS

- **DALE FANNING:** *drums*
- **ARNE LIVINGSTONE:** *electric bass*
- **JESSICA LURIE:** *alto and tenor saxophone*

Seattle's Living Daylights has been performing a hybrid of styles since forming in 1993. Says bassist Arne Livingstone: "We're funky, but we're not a funk band. We're jazzy, but I'm not a jazz player. We're younger musicians who draw on both of these realms, but we really grew up on rock." While high school students in the early 1980s, saxophonist Jessica Lurie and Livingstone formed a rhythm-and-blues group called Musicology. Lurie eventually traveled east to attend college and later spent time in New York performance circles. However, she returned to her hometown in 1992, and the band came together soon afterward. The two longtime friends drew in versatile drummer Dale Fanning to complete their sound.

Living Daylights performs instrumental compositions, most of which are crafted by Lurie and Livingstone; these compositions provide room for each of the group's three players. Lurie's playful, powerful saxophone often blares in a strident manner similar to John Zorn's, but it also emits some more harmonious phrases. Livingstone draws on a range of techniques and effects that incorporate both technical gadgetry and physical ingenuity. Fanning contributes a complementary open style. The results bridge many realms, but as Livingstone maintains, "I think that nowadays people are very receptive to different sound styles. Many of them grew up listening to Indian tabla music on Sesame Street. My ultimate goal is to invent a style of music. I've played reggae, Afro-Cuban, jazz, funk, rock, and rhythm and blues, and I don't want to play any of those styles. I think that with the Living Daylights we may be on the path toward something else."

The group thrives in the live environment and has been hailed for the range and depth of its stunning live improvisations. It has toured the United States and Europe. Remarks Livingstone: "The band's strengths are communication, interaction, and chemistry. On some level, I think that's bigger than the actual songs. 'Kind of Blue' was brilliant because of the elements contributed by its original performers. People can't just play 'Kind of Blue' and suddenly become brilliant."

DISCOGRAPHY

Falling down Laughing (1995). The three members of Living Daylights manifest their individual gifts and cohesiveness on this disc. "Bellice" occupies a jazzy plane between Hank Mobley and Sonny Rollins. The riveting "Trimonk" is a funkier offering. Fanning is set free on "6/8," and Livingstone and Lurie lay down their own deft rhythms. The last cut, "Hip Hop," is an entrancing cauldron of ideas.

WEB SITE

www.speakeasy.org/livingdaylights

MANGO JAM

- **JASON BUSH:** *bass, vocals*
- **BRET ERICKSON:** *drums*
- **JON HERCHERT:** *guitar, vocals*
- **GEOFF PRETTNER:** *percussion, drums*
- **JARED RUSH:** *keyboards*

Mango Jam has long occupied a prominent position in the Midwest improvised music scene. The Minneapolis band formed in 1989 and has shared its ebullient grooves with audiences across the nation ever since. Due to several performances it gave on the Massachusetts island of Nantucket, Mango Jam was selected for the first AWARE compilation. The group has appeared with a number of other bands that share a similar musical spirit, including Blues Traveler and the Why Store.

The quintet's name evokes its music: the mango is a tropical fruit, and the band initially drew on many tropical influences, in particular the sounds of the Caribbean. Principal songwriter Jason Bush hails from Hawaii and enjoys exploring his native island's sounds (which no doubt were much appreciated during the Minnesota winters). Yet, as the band has evolved, it has deemphasized some of these components, relying more heavily on jazz and rock grooves.

One aspect of the band's name that certainly holds true is that its players love to jam. In concert, guitarist Jon Herchert builds on a range of riffs while locking in with bassist Bush. Drummers Geoff Prettner and Bret Erickson have developed their own percussive vocabulary that they interject into every song. Keyboardist Jared Rush is a recent addition to the band and contributes bright accents to the group's improvisations.

DISCOGRAPHY

Mango Jam (1992)

Somewhere in the Middle (1994)

Flux (1996)

Preserves (1998). Mango Jam offers a number of melodious grooves on this recording. The opener, "Pretty Little Town," is a pleasing composition enriched by dulcet vocal harmonies. The drummers and the keyboardist animate "Stay with Me." Other notable cuts include the burbling "Northern Lights," the steady, driving "My Best Friend," and the silken "Cloudy Skies."

WEB SITE

www.mangojam.com

DAVE MATTHEWS BAND

- **CARTER BEAUFORD:** *drums and percussion*
- **STEFAN LESSARD:** *bass*
- **DAVE MATTHEWS:** *vocals, acoustic guitar*
- **LEROI MOORE:** *alto, soprano, and tenor saxophone, flute, vocals*
- **BOYD TINSLEY:** *violin*

The Dave Matthews Band evolved through a series of fortuitous circumstances. Matthews, who was born in South Africa, moved with his family around the world, ending up in Charlottesville, Virginia, in the 1980s. There he secured a job as a bartender at Miller's, a restaurant and jazz club. While working, he witnessed a number of gifted local musicians in action. One of Matthews's earliest public performances was at Miller's: he asked solo guitarist Tim Reynolds, who appeared regularly on Monday nights, if he could join him for a rendition of Bob Marley's "Exodus." At the same time, Matthews had also been composing his own songs (all of which he assigned a number, in order of their creation, which accounts for "#34" on *Under the Table and Dreaming*). By 1991, Matthews had accumulated a slew of tunes that he wanted to record, and so he approached drummer Carter Beauford and saxophone player Leroi Moore, both of whom he had seen perform at Miller's, and asked if they would work with him in the studio. Beauford and Moore listened to the material and consented. Matthews then invited bass prodigy Stefan Lessard to join. Keyboardist Peter Griesar also contributed to the demo (he parted company with the group once it began touring). Violin player Boyd Tinsley played on one song.

The Dave Matthews Band is a union of gifted musicians. Before joining, Beauford had spent a number of years as a jazz drummer, performing with a fusion band called Secrets that gigged from 1984 to 1990. Moore also had been an active member of the area jazz community. Lessard, who was only sixteen years old when Matthews tapped him to join the group, had already distinguished himself as an upright jazz bassist (he actually had to learn electric bass in order to perform with the band). Tinsley was so captivated by the demo tape they'd made that he insinuated himself into the group, becoming a vital member (while still fronting the Boyd Tinsley Band until 1993).

This assemblage of players was so pleased with its synergy that it began playing regular Tuesday-night gigs at a small local restaurant called Eastern Standard. These performances, which melded Matthews smooth vocals, his melodious compositions, and the band's sterling musicianship, soon attracted overflow audiences. The owner of the Charlottesville club Trax invited the group to bring these gigs to his space. This move initiated the band's rise from larger venue to even larger venue while captivating listeners with its original songs and its engrossing improvisations. Many fellow performers (among them Trey Anastasio, Oteil Burbridge, Bob Dylan, Mike Gordon, and John Popper) were similarly impressed and began to join the band on stage. In May of 1995, the Dave Matthews Band was invited to open a series of shows for the Grateful Dead (this led to the band's homage to the late Jerry Garcia – a stirring rendition of "Eyes of the World" – at a Berkeley, California, concert held two days after Garcia's death). The band's popularity continues to swell, yet it remains true to its initial aims: to perform Matthews's songs while exploring a host of rhythms and textures.

DISCOGRAPHY

Remember Two Things (1993)

Recently (1994)

Under the Table and Dreaming (1994)

Crash (1995)

Live at Red Rocks 8.15.95 (1997)

Before These Crowded Streets (1998). The band stretches things out on this release while also welcoming a number of guest performers (including the Kronos Quartet, a classical string ensemble). Another interesting aspect of the disc is that, because the various offerings are divergent in feel and style, some extra long periods of silence are worked in to clean the aural palate. "Rapunzel" is a spirited take on the traditional love story, with some fine contributions from Moore and Tinsley. The band fashions euphonious grooves with "Pig." "Don't Drink the Water" is a foreboding allegory about injustice. In "Wasting Time," the band works through some classic soul sounds. Bela Fleck, who appears on three tracks, works effectively with Tim Reynolds on the Middle East-flavored "The Last Stop." Alanis Morissette contributes some cries to the atmosphere of "Spoon."

WEB SITE

www.dmband.com

MAX CREEK

- **SCOTT ALLSHOUSE:** *drums*
- **ROB FRIED:** *percussion*
- **MARK MERCIER:** *keyboards, vocals*
- **SCOTT MURAWSKI:** *guitar, vocals*
- **JOHN RIDER:** *bass, vocals*

In the spring of 1971, bassist John Rider, drummer Bob Gosselin, and guitarist Dave Reed formed a band, which Rider named Max Creek after a town in the Blue Ridge Mountains of Virginia, where he had grown up. The group began operations in Connecticut, drawing new listeners and new band members alike into the fold. Within two years, keyboard player Mark Mercier had joined the group along with guitarist Scott Murawski (who first sat in with the band in 1972 at the age of fifteen). Percussionist Rob Fried came aboard in 1979, completing a core lineup (along with Rider, Mercier, and Murawski) that has been in place ever since. On 27 April 1996, in honor of the twenty-fifth anniversary of the band, the mayor of Hartford officially proclaimed Max Creek Day in the city (the proclamation reads "Whereas, A Creek concert is a state of mind, a community event which promotes both social and cultural tolerance and individual freedoms in a democratic state . . ."). However, Max Creek is by no means content to rest upon such laurels. Instead, its members continue to write new songs, crisscross the nation on tour, and record.

The group's music draws on a number of influences; its players are trained in classical and jazz. Max Creek's original songs also contain elements of folk, rock, and reggae. Meanwhile, Rob Fried, who is predominantly self-taught, has spanned the globe to indulge his obsession with rhythm instruments. The group's compositions take on lives of their own in the concert setting, where Max Creek experiences what it refers to as "reciprocal energy" from its audiences. Moving from spacey exploratory jams to bluesy shuffles to percussive free-for-alls to blistering raveups, the results vary from night to night, leading numerous fervid listeners to build extensive Max Creek tape libraries.

The band has nurtured a kinship with its audiences that has enabled it not only to endure but also to thrive. For instance, every summer since 1990 it has hosted Camp Creek, a weekend of music and revelry. Notes Rider: "The premise of Max Creek was to create a place to be a family, for like-minded people, and at the same time to give us an outlet for our original music." Mercier adds, "After so many years, we are still absolutely in love with what we do. Max Creek is a living thing, and we have no choice but to go with it."

DISCOGRAPHY

Max Creek (1977)
Rainbow (1980)
Drink the Stars (1982)
Windows (1986)
MCMXC (1990)
Springwater (1998)

WEB SITE

www.maxcreek.com

EDWIN MCCAIN BAND

- ■ **SCOTT BANNEVICH:** *bass*
- ■ **LARRY CHANEY:** *electric and lap steel guitar*
- ■ **DAVE HARRISON:** *drums and percussion*
- ■ **EDWIN MCCAIN:** *vocals, guitar*
- ■ **CRAIG SHIELDS:** *soprano, alto, tenor, and baritone saxophone, keyboards*

While Edwin McCain was growing up in Greenville, South Carolina, learning how to play guitar, he drew inspiration from area folksinger David Wilcox. McCain sought to follow Wilcox's path, performing literate original songs accompanied only by his acoustic guitar. He soon secured some local gigs at which he performed a combination of his compositions and a few covers. In time, however, this would-be acoustic singer/songwriter would find himself opening tour dates for the Allman Brothers Band, singing lead in Butch Trucks's all-star Frogwings lineup, and fronting his own electric band.

In 1992, McCain decided (much like Wilcox before him) to interpret his music with the support of additional players. Although he had performed some gigs with bassist Scott Bannevich, McCain came to believe that his passionate compositions would be well served by fuller instrumentation, so he pieced together the Edwin McCain Band, which gave his emotive vocals an opportunity to soar over the rhythms created by his accompanists. The band also offered McCain, who grew up steeped in the southern rock tradition, the opportunity to delve into some vaster improvisations.

Recently, the band's sound has changed due to the arrival of electric guitarist and lap steel player Larry Chaney. McCain's 1995 disc *Honor among Thieves* and the tour that followed its release featured acoustic guitars. However, these days Chaney tears through electric solos and contributes a few incisive accents. McCain's vocal and instrumental contributions have blossomed with Chaney's support, and the Edwin McCain Band has been invited to tour with both the Allman Brothers Band and Ratdog. The arrival of the new player has also brought things full circle for McCain; in the course of a casual conversation, Chaney revealed that a few years back he was invited into the studio to lend some electric flourishes to the work of David Wilcox.

DISCOGRAPHY

Solitude (1993)

Honor among Thieves (1995)

Misguided Roses (1997). McCain's songwriting skills are evident throughout this release. Guitarist Chaney adds zest to the opener, "See the Sky Again," which has a sharper edge to it than many of McCain's earlier recorded efforts. Yet one of McCain's strengths remains his ability to express emotion articulately, as evinced by the achingly romantic "I'll Be." Fellow soulful vocalist Michael McDonald of the Doobie Brothers helps out on the bluesier "How Strange It Seems" and the powerful "Holy City."

WEB SITE

www.edwin.com

PAT MCGEE BAND

- **CHARDY MCEWAN:** *percussion*
- **PAT MCGEE:** *acoustic and electric guitar, vocals*
- **JOHN SMALL:** *bass*
- **AL WALSH:** *acoustic guitar, vocals*
- **CHRIS WILLIAMS:** *drums*
- **JONATHAN WILLIAMS:** *keyboards*

Early in 1996, singer songwriter Pat McGee decided to assemble a permanent band to help him present his music. He had recently recorded *From the Wood*, a studio release made with a collection of musicians that had demonstrated both McGee's songwriting abilities and his flair for acoustic guitar. Once he had brought together the sextet, however, it rapidly became clear that the Pat McGee Band would be a true collaborative effort.

Although McGee's name is on the marquee, the band derives its strength from its players' collective talents. Pianist Jonathan Williams and guitarist Al Walsh, who appeared together as a duo before they joined McGee, also furnish harmony vocals. At times, Williams's bandmates will even exit the stage, allowing him to put on a solo display. On other occasions, the pianist, bass player John Small, drummer Chris Williams, and percussionist Chardy McEwan will lock for a jam. Small, the lone holdover from McGee's initial release, may be the band's unsung hero, as he contributes his own ideas to a number of songs while holding the music together. Of course, this is not to downplay the role of McGee, whose engaging compositions, skillful guitar work, and smooth vocals shine forth.

The Pat McGee Band is often on the road, typically performing in excess of two hundred shows a year. During one stretch in 1997, it played ninety-nine shows in 106 days. The band keeps the music fresh, fueled by the enthusiasm radiating from its audiences and by its own improvisational skills. Sometimes it will present a medley jam that may include "Pinball Wizard," "You Can Call Me Al," and "The Jeffersons' Theme (Movin' on Up)." Still, it is original songs, performed with verve, that win the Pat McGee Band accolades and new fans.

DISCOGRAPHY

From the Wood (1995)

Revel (1997). The full band appears here, and McGee, who produced the disc, does a nice job of layering the output of all the players to produce a rich sound. McGee's warm voice effectively conveys the sentiments contained in these songs. The first track, "Passion," is a lively, pleasing tune embellished by McGee's guitar, by bright harmony vocals, and by the saxophone of J.C. Kuhl, from Agents of Good Roots. Colorful arrangements elevate several tracks — "Ceamelodic," featuring Julie Murphy's winsome backing vocals; "Straight Curve," with its crisp percussion; and "Can't Miss What You Never Had," with its sprightly keyboards.

WEB SITE

www.patmcgeeband.com

MEDESKI, MARTIN AND WOOD

- **BILLY MARTIN:** *drums and percussion*
- **JOHN MEDESKI:** *keyboards*
- **CHRIS WOOD:** *bass*

Medeski, Martin and Wood prefers to be known as an "improvisational groove band." The trio opts for this description because it is a very open-ended enterprise – it does not align itself with a particular genre of music. Deeply committed to spontaneous musical inspiration, this group aspires to keep its audiences fully engaged.

The band came out of the New York City downtown jazz scene of the late 1980s and early 1990s. Its individual members played with, among many others, John Lurie, John Zorn, and Marc Ribot. Each had also acquired a rich history of musical experiences. For instance, in 1981, when John Medeski was just fifteen years old, famed Weather Report bassist Jaco Pastorius invited him to join a Japanese tour (his mother vetoed the idea). Billy Martin toured and recorded with Chuck Mangione for two and a half years (by the way, Martin is also an accomplished painter who designed the band's logo as well as many of its CD covers). Chris Wood once worked with noted percussionist Bob Moses. Through a series of introductions, the trio came together in 1990.

Medeski, Martin and Wood are inspired by a range of styles and artists in creating their grooves. Along with the aforementioned players, the group lionizes jazz pioneers Albert Ayler, Duke Ellington, and Sun Ra. The trio maintains an affinity for funk (which is evinced, in part, by an occasional Sly and the Family Stone cover). Moreover, the band draws on world music, particularly Afro-Cuban rhythms, and has recently expanded into the realm of hip-hop. The band's adventurous spirit and eclecticism were manifested during the fall of 1996 at a series of weekly parties at New York City's Knitting Factory; these took place without set lists and drew in a series of guest musicians (including Vernon Reid and DJ Logic, who appears on the group's *Combustication* release).

In concert, the band utilizes a full range of instruments to create its signature sound. Medeski, positioned up front, supplies thick, resonant chords as well as some deft boogies as he moves from a Hammond B-3 to a clavinet to an electric piano. Meanwhile, Wood contributes to the ambiance with his own throbbing accents on both electric and acoustic bass. Finally, Martin elicits sounds from an array of percussion instruments. The three place themselves in the tradition of the jazz players of the 1940s and 1950s who improvised on the popular sounds of the day. Still, there is also an abstract component to their music that adds even greater depth to their inviting grooves.

DISCOGRAPHY

Notes from the Underground (1992)

It's a Jungle in There (1993)

Friday Afternoon in the Universe (1994)

Shack-Man (1996)

Farmer's Reserve (1997). This release, which is only available through the band's Web site, presents a more experimental side of the group. The first forty-five minutes offer a heady free-form improvisation followed by a fifteen-minute coda. It is an intriguing effort that fans of the band and those with adventurous ears will want to hear.

A Go Go (1998). Although this is actually a John Scofield disc (the band does not take a hand in the songwriting), the trio's contributions are extensive. Here MMW joins with the famed jazz guitarist to form a quartet. In songs such as "Hottentot" and "A Go Go," the players craft simmering grooves. The collaboration also gives rise to other pleasures, including the more minimalist "Kubrick" and the moody "Deadzy."

Combustication (1998). This release demonstrates the band's extensive range. Songs such as "Sugarcraft" and "Church of Logic" incorporate the scratches of DJ Logic. "Latin Shuffle" supplies a jumping nine minutes during which each player steps to the fore. Other notable tracks include the blues-tinged "Just like I Pictured It," the pulsing "Coconut Boogaloo," and the band's sanctified cover of "Everyday People." A final, intriguing offering is "Whatever Happened to Gus," during which Steve Cannon contributes spoken words in a manner similar to that of Ken Nordine or some of Jack Kerouac's recordings circa the late 1950s and early 1960s.

WEB SITE

www.mmw.net

MERRY DANKSTERS

- **GIBB DROLL:** *guitar, vocals*
- **DAVID GANS:** *guitar, vocals*
- **CHUCK GARVEY:** *guitar, vocals*
- **PETER PRINCE:** *guitar, vocals*
- **DAVE RUCH:** *mandolin, vocals*
- **AL SCHNIER:** *guitar, vocals*
- **ROLF WHITT:** *mandolin, vocals*

It all began with a simple idea. Bay-area singer/songwriter David Gans (who also happens to be the creator and host of *The Grateful Dead Hour*) contacted moe. manager Jon Topper about helping him to secure some East Coast acoustic gigs. "I asked him if he could throw me into a creative situation," Gans recalls. Topper more than met the challenge, and he admits, "Sometimes I can go a bit overboard. First I brought Gans and Chuck (Garvey of moe.) together. Then I thought, 'I bet it would be killer if I could add another instrument to bring it up another notch.'" So Topper invited Buffalo-based mandolin player Dave Ruch (Acoustic Forum) to join in. "Then I started to think, 'Who else would I like to see acoustic? I bet Gibb Droll cranks acoustic.'" And so on. Ultimately, the first incarnation of the Merry Danksters included contributions from members of Moon Boot Lover, Ominous Seapods, Strangefolk, the Gordon Stone Trio, and freebeerandchicken. All this acoustic traveling road show needed was a name. The riff on Key Kesey's Merry Pranksters was suggested to Gans by on-line Well denizen Warren Bograd. Notes Gans: "That original core, Chuck and Dave and me, met for a few days and kicked around some material." The resulting shows themselves proved non pareil, as each night was sequenced differently, with a number of players performing both covers and originals in a variety of formations.

In December of 1997, the group decided to re-create the experience. Gans, Garvey, and Droll returned, along with Peter Prince (Moon Boot Lover) and Al Schnier (moe.), both of whom had played on part of the original tour. Ruch was unable to participate due to tendinitis and ceded his spot to friend Rolf Whitt. Once again, the players met for what Garvey remembers they called "guitar camp." Participants exchanged songs, riffs, and concepts (while showing off a bit as well). The ensuing shows proved just as dynamic as the first ones. The players showcased their individual proficiencies while banding together to lend their picking and vocals to a variety of tunes. Gans sums it up this way: "I always knew it would be tremendously fun, but it was more than I asked for. I played with some brilliant musicians, and I formed a number of beautiful friendships as well."

MIGHTY PURPLE

- **DAVID KEITH:** *drums*
- **JON RODGERS:** *guitar, vocals*
- **STEVE RODGERS:** *vocals, guitar*
- **ADRIAN VAN DE GRAAFF:** *bass*

New Haven, Connecticut's, Mighty Purple started gigging while the band's singer-songwriters – Jon and Steve Rodgers – were still in their teens. The band's history extends back even further than this, however: the brothers have been singing together for as long as they've been able to carry a tune. Bass player Adrian Van de Graaff has been with the band from its inception and, in Jon Rodgers's words, "has been my friend for about as long as I can remember." As a result, the group has developed a chemistry, even a telepathy, along with the ability to create burnished vocal harmonies. The addition of drummer David Keith in 1996 has only widened the possibilities. Indeed, Keith has been a willing participant on those evenings when one band member has spontaneously decided to start performing on another's instrument (leading to an all-out switch).

Whether the band is playing in an acoustic or an electric format, Mighty Purple's focus remains on its songs. In composing their music, band members latch onto winsome melodies and then add complementary bridges and evocative lyrics to craft cohesive musical offerings. However, particularly when performing electric, the group does not confine itself to a single arrangement of a given song. The Rodgers brothers often initiate improvisations, and Van de Graaff and

Keith delve in as well. Says Jon Rodgers: "I'm happy to say we never play the same show twice. Everything would become stale for us if we had to do that. So while the songs come first, we like to open them wide with some intense and emotional jamming."

DISCOGRAPHY

Revolution (1992)

Bohica (1994)

Black River Falls (1995)

Mighty Purple Acoustic (1997). As the title suggests, this release documents the band's acoustic side. This format emphasizes the group's harmonies and the songs themselves. Keith distinguishes himself by contributing some adept percussion, and Van de Graaff adds supple bass. The Rodgers brothers furnish expressive vocals and guitars. Notable tracks include the upbeat opener, "Story," the more atmospheric "Damn the Clouds," the alluring "I Adore You," and "Jimmy Parker," which contains a spirited jam.

WEB SITE

www.horizonmusicgroup.com/mightypurple

MISHAP

- **JIM CHENEY:** *vocals, harmonica, and percussion*
- **MATT RUSSO:** *guitar, mandolin, and vocals*
- **SEAN SCHENKER:** *guitar, vocals*
- **JONATHAN SHERMAN:** *bass, vocals*
- **FRANK TEREMY:** *drums*

Athens, Georgia's, Mishap has proven to be ill named. The group creates music that is the very antithesis of an unfortunate accident.

Belying its name (which also evokes images of a 1980s hair-metal band), Mishap creates buoyant acoustic grooves. The lively, euphonious music this quintet produces is rife with vividly strummed guitars, pleasing vocal harmonies, and percolating harmonica.

The group originated in 1993 at the State University of New York in Genesco when Jim Cheney, Sean Schenker, and Jonathan Sherman (a.k.a. Johnny Diamond) entered a school talent competition equipped with two acoustic guitars and a bass. They won, and this provided the trio with the impetus to continue performing. The three players soon added Matt Russo on guitar and mandolin and started gigging as an acoustic quartet. In 1995, the band decided to relocate to Athens, where it would pursue its musical ambitions on a full-time basis. Soon afterward, the group began to work up a fuller sound with the assistance of drummer Frank Teremy (another SUNY Genesco émigré). Performing whenever possible, Mishap gradually built a fan base from scratch: within two years, the group was filling the Georgia Theater. Its ebullient live shows replete with vigorous jams have earned the band headliner status and plenty of fan support up and down the East Coast.

DISCOGRAPHY

Stuck in the Mud (1996). This is an upbeat, uplifting collection of songs. "Transition" opens, a bright composition punctuated with fluttering harmonica. "Sunshine Song" lives up to its billing with its warm, sparkling guitars. "Independence" stands out due, in part, to the piano work of Day by the River's Walt Austin. The title track initially calls to mind Blues Traveler's "But Anyway," but it soon captivates the listener of its own accord.

Morning Ride (1998)

WEB SITE

www.mishap.com

MOE.

- **VINNIE AMICO:** *drums*
- **ROB DERHAK:** *bass, vocals*
- **CHUCK GARVEY:** *guitar, vocals*
- **AL SCHNIER:** *guitar, vocals*

The members of moe. approach every endeavor with a strong measure of creativity, intensity, and humor. In this spirit, guitarist Chuck Garvey explains that, at any of the band's performances, listeners can expect "the classics, some really cheesy covers, big pauses in between songs when we babble because we like to shoot our mouths off, and an entertaining light show." Although his characterization is accurate, he fails to mention an integral component of the band's appeal: its engaging original songs, which are perpetually reconfigured in the live setting through some adroit collective extemporization. They have earned moe. a faithful, protective fan base that includes a particularly fervid core of Internet devotees (who proudly dub themselves moe.rons).

The band traces its origins to Buffalo in the winter of 1990. It was then that Garvey, Rob Derhak, and three other players formed Five Guys Named Moe (the title of a Louis Jordan song). The group played through the summer but then became a foursome with the loss of its saxophone player; this eventually led the band to change its moniker to moe. In January of 1992, Al Schnier joined, and the band performed with three guitarists for a few months until original member Dave Kessler moved on. Over the years, moe. has worked through a Spinal Tap-esque array of drummers, including original member Ray Schwartz, Jim Laughlin (formerly of Yolk, now involved in other musical endeavors), Mike Strazza, Chris Mazur (now with Grinch), and current member Vince Amico (formerly of Sonic Garden). Amico is sometimes jokingly referred to as "number five" by his bandmates, who have also occasionally lauded his efforts by proclaiming that he has racked up "moe. points."

The band's live vigor is fueled by its synergy. Derhak occupies center stage, slapping and popping as the moment requires. He is flanked by guitarists Schnier and Garvey, who provide biting solos, interlaced leads, and collaborative textures. Amico furnishes a range of complementary accents on drums. Says Garvey: "We have the ability to put together something a bit more powerful or lasting than the individual players might be able to offer. I know there are some nights when I just play things that I shouldn't be able to play. I can recall an evening in Cleveland during our song 'Don't Fuck with Flo' when we just fell into this psychotic seventies Superfly jam. At the drop of a hat, we all just went into it, and we produced some music that we couldn't even have practiced."

The group strives to retain a strong connection with its fans and has to this end devised a number of additional components to the moe. experience. For instance, the quartet accompanied its debut Sony album with a forty-six-minute single of the song "Meat" (a release that further demonstrates the band's improvisational artistry). The group hosts New Year's Eve events, including one epic performance at the Wetlands that lived up to its billing as "breakfast with moe." (Garvey recalls, "We were in that sleep-deprivation zone when we were still playing at seven o'clock in the morning. I basically slept for two or three days after that.") The quartet also performed at the 1997 Further Festival — there its members participated in the show-ending jams and welcomed Bob Weir to the stage for some of their own sets, including a historic run from "Cryptical Envelopment" into "The Other One" and back into "Cryptical." Also, during the spring of 1998, in order to keep its fans entertained while it was off the road recording, moe. even hosted a scavenger hunt on its Web site that offered a range of prizes. As well, the band has retained a loyalty and commitment to some of the clubs that aided its growth by returning to Buffalo to play at Broadway Joe's and appearing at the Wetlands under the billing Monkeys on Ecstasy. (The night after the first such gig, band members asked the audience from the stage, "Did anyone see Monkeys on Ecstasy last night? That was a cheesy moe. cover band.")

DISCOGRAPHY

Fatboy (1992)

Headseed (1994)

Loaf (1995)

Meat (1996). This forty-six-minute single accompanied the release of *No Doy*. It's worth seeking out to hear the band's heady improvisations: ideas zigzag back and forth, are explored, and then are melded with new concepts.

No Doy (1996). This, the band's major-label debut, is a cauldron of playful, volcanic offerings. The first track, "She Sends Me," has a memorable melody, entertaining lyrics, and a musical raveup that becomes an all-out surf frenzy. Opening with Derhak's popping bass, "32 Things" rapidly gains momentum through animated vocal interchanges and instrumental outbursts. "St. Augustine" is enlivened by slide guitar and falsetto vocals. The band's live dynamic is best captured by the twelve-minute run through the odyssey "Rebubula." The closer, "Four," allows moe. to navigate some lusher textures.

Tin Cans and Car Tires (1998)

WEB SITE

www.moe.org

MOON BOOT LOVER

- **JON HAWES:** *bass*
- **ANDY HERRICK:** *drums*
- **JEFF MERROW:** *keyboards, vocals*
- **PETER PRINCE:** *guitar, vocals*

When he was a youngster, Peter Prince wanted to be a superhero. When he grew up, he did the next best thing: he formed a band. The name Moon Boot Lover evokes an image of a science fiction environment. True to this spirit, the band's first two CDs feature art (created by Prince) that approximates the covers of comic books. The releases are even sequentially numbered, just like comics. Prince says that he views each of them as "editions." Moreover, when asked to describe his music, he calls it "Rocket soul. It's a little rock, a little soul, and the 'et' is the extraterrestrial element."

The New York City-based group formed upstate in 1990. The initial core was a feisty force well known for its funky raveups. However, in 1996 that lineup collapsed, leaving Prince alone in his commitment to the band. He rebuilt the group slowly, seeking players who were all on the same page. He brought in bass player Jon Hawes, who had actually performed with the band on its *Live down Deep* release, and who had since been gigging with Percy Hill. Andy Herrick joined following his stint in the band Harpoon. More recently, Jeff Merrow has been added to contribute keyboards and supply some backing vocals.

Moon Boot Lover retains many of its original elements. The group is defined by Prince's muscular guitar and soulful vocals, which will occasionally rise an octave in service of a given piece of music. The funky side of the band's sound lives on, but Moon Boot Lover also, increasingly, emphasizes soul, blues, and some harder edges. Its performance philosophy continues to win it new supporters. Prince notes, "I think it's important to go out there and make each night special and individual. A number of people come out to see whatever that new, unexpected element might be." These elements include both the band's physical presentation and its music. However, Prince also adds: "For a while, I think we became too jam happy. Lately, we've decided to let the melodies that I originally wrote stand on their own." Moon Boot Lover still performs without set lists, though, and it still ascends to the heavens with its epic improvisations. Indeed, although Prince may not actually have been bitten by a radioactive spider, the growing legions of Moon Boot Lover fans would proclaim him a hero anyway. It's good work if you can get it.

DISCOGRAPHY

Outer Space Action (1994)
Live down Deep (1995)

WEB SITE

www.moonbootlover.com

MOTHER HIPS

- **TIM BLUHM:** *vocals, guitar, harmonica*
- **JOHN HOFER:** *drums*
- **GREG LOIACONO:** *vocals, guitar, dobro*
- **ISSAC PARSONS:** *bass*

Mother Hips was the first band in the 1990s to emerge from the Chico, California, music scene and introduce itself to the wider world. In fact, when the group first came together, there wasn't really a cohesive Chico music scene at all. Instead, any number of bands came together at Chico State University (just as Mother Hips did) and began playing cover tunes at school parties and area bars. Bassist Issac Parsons recalls, "When we started, it began as a loose thing because at that time in Chico everyone was playing with everyone. But we quickly recognized that we had something special. Greg and Tim were gifted musicians and lyricists." During this era, many area venues frequently invoked a "no original material" policy, but the exemplary song craft and swelling fan base of Mother Hips led many bars and clubs to abandon that edict.

Ever since its creation in 1991, the group has been winning acclaim for its original music. Mother Hips incorporates elements of folk and blues to produce mellifluent compositions that often display a country aspect as well. Another of the band's signatures is the vocal harmony that Greg Loiacono often blends with Tim Bluhm's leads. Also, Bluhm and Loiacono, who were both English majors at Chico State, bring a poetic spirit to their songs (it was the title of one of Bluhm's compositions that gave the group its name).

However, there is yet another component of the group's popular appeal. In the live setting, Mother Hips ratchets up the intensity, adding ringing twin guitars, resonant bass, and popping drums. At times, the band will crack open its tunes to explore the ideas contained therein, often adding some psychedelic textures. Adds Parsons: "Quite a few of our earlier songs, in particular those from *Back to the Grotto*, had a number of weird time signatures. We continue to play those live all the time." Supportive audiences have kept the band on the road; it has averaged more than 250 shows a year throughout much of its existence. Mother Hips has also traversed the country a number of times — for instance, the group performed a stint on the 1995 HORDE and did a 1998 summer tour with Huffamoose.

DISCOGRAPHY

Back to the Grotto (1992)

Part-Timer Goes Full (1995)

Shootout (1997)

Later Days (1998). On this release, the band focuses on its songs, consigning extended improvisations to the concert setting. Still, this disc is a compelling one. Mother Hips introduces the listener to a number of lives through these story songs. "Gold Plated," which opens, presents a smooth melody, solid harmonies, and absorbing lyrics. Other appealing efforts include "Esmerelda," "Spotless as You," and "Payroll Peter."

WEB SITE

www.motherhips.com

MOUNTAIN EXPRESS BAND

- ■ **DAVE AMOS:** *vocals, guitar*
- ■ **GARRETT BISHOP:** *bass*
- ■ **SCOTT COGGINS:** *mandolin, vocals*
- ■ **ADAM MCARTHUR:** *percussion, vocals*
- ■ **DENNIS WARE:** *drums, vocals*

The Mountain Express Band describes its music as "rhythmically cultivated organic groovegrass." The phrase proves quite evocative of the group's sound. Rhythms are abundantly supplied by drummer Dennis Ware and percussionist Adam McArthur. The pair lock with bassist Garrett Bishop to provide a deep bottom in any given song, but they also detour into their own complementary passages whenever the moment strikes them. The band's music is informed by the bluegrass tradition, as manifested by Scott Coggins's mandolin prowess. Principal songwriter Dave Amos often leads the group full tilt into tantalizing explorations with his supple electric-guitar work.

The Columbia, South Carolina, band began as an acoustic bluegrass duo comprised of Amos and Coggins. In time, however, the pair decided to expand their sound, influenced in part by their regard for the music of the Grateful Dead. Most Mountain Express Band members did their share of touring with the Dead and freely acknowledge their debt to that group. The quintet also venerates such icons as Bill Monroe and Sam Bush and has built its following in the South through its ability to bridge these two realms. The group has performed on the main stage at the Black Mountain Music Festival with such diverse luminaries as Merl Saunders, Peter Rowan, and Del McCoury. The quintet has held its own in these presentations, drawing from its well of more than fifty originals to perform music that reflects its traditions yet tweaks them as well. The Mountain Express Band exuberantly crafts this zestful amalgam, its own rhythmic groovegrass.

DISCOGRAPHY

Been a Long Haul (1997). Following the sounds of the band's tour bus attempting to start, "Uptown Blues" introduces the quintet in a spirited manner. The next cut, "9 Lb. Hammer," demonstrates the group's ability to transform folk traditionals into upbeat, bluegrass-flavored raveups ("Little Maggie" and "John Hardy" also receive this treatment). "Foothills" is a lively, winsome instrumental that features the band's full range of flavors, particularly Coggins's high-stepping mandolin. The epic "Shines" showcases the quintet's improvisatory side, with Amos's guitar often taking the lead in a manner reminiscent of Jerry Garcia. The release closes with "Sitar Jam," which, in lieu of a sitar player, features the band's propulsive percussive duo.

WEB SITE

www.carolinaglobal.com/mxb

NATIVE

- ■ **MATHEW HUTT:** *vocals, guitar*
- ■ **MIKE JAIMES:** *guitar, vocals*
- ■ **MATT LYONS:** *bass*
- ■ **DAVE THOMAS:** *drums*
- ■ **JOHN WOOD:** *percussion, vocals*
- ■ **CHRIS WYCKOFF:** *keyboards, vocals*

Native has enlivened the New York City music scene since 1993. It grew out of the friendship between British expatriate and would-be actor Mathew Hutt and drummer Dave Thomas, who met while they were working at an area hotel. The pair recruited guitarist Mike Jaimes and bassist Matt Lyons to their fledgling outfit, and the foursome immediately began rehearsing and writing material. Lyons recalls, "We were rough, but it was pretty clear we had something right from the start. Matt brought in a number of strong songs, and Mike is this incredible soloist — we just feed off him." Percussionist John Wood heard the results and came aboard soon afterward. Native's personnel roster was completed by keyboardist Chris Wyckoff, of whom Lyons remarks: "He's just nuts. It was hard to find a keyboardist who could hold his own with a guitarist of Mike's caliber, but Chris is the guy."

Native layers elements of jazz, soul, and funk over a percussive tapestry, and although it composes euphonious melodies its members are also advocates of the all-out jam. During a two-year stint of weekly gigs at the Soho venue McGovern's, the band built a reputation for itself. Within this supportive environment, Native felt free to engage in animated musical interactions and experiments. Says Lyons: "We used it as our laboratory. We'd play until four in the morning, working through a lot of ideas and material. Then, since we tape all of our shows, we were able to go back and listen to decide what worked and what didn't." The results continue to win the band supporters — Native now regularly draws crowds to its shows at the Wetlands and at venues throughout the northeast.

DISCOGRAPHY

Native (1994)

Live from Marmfington Farm, Vol. 1 (1997). This disc documents the band's radiant live show. Native's percussion section drives the opening track, "Simon," which also features smooth vocals and Santanaesque guitar. "Barefoot Girls" is another interesting offering that hints at 1960s psychedelia. "Down to the River" has a bright, catchy melody. The band really stretches things out with a seventeen-minute run that includes a percussion jam, its own "Something Worth Remembering," and a nimble take on "Fiyo on the Bayou."

WEB SITE

www.nativenyc.com

DAVID NELSON BAND

- **BILL LAYMON:** *bass, vocals*
- **DAVID NELSON:** *vocals, electric guitar*
- **MOOKIE SIEGEL:** *keyboards, accordion, vocals*
- **BARRY SLESS:** *pedal steel guitar*
- **ARTHUR STEINHORN:** *drums*

David Nelson has had quite a storied career. In the early 1960s, he joined Jerry Garcia and Robert Hunter in the Wildwood Boys, and thereafter he remained a key member of the Bay Area music scene. He added guitar to three of the Grateful Dead's classic albums: *Aoxomoxoa*, *American Beauty*, and *Workingman's Dead*. Nelson was also a founding member of New Riders of the Purple Sage, singing lead on the band's song "Panama Red." In the mid-1980s, he performed with the Jerry Garcia Acoustic Band and was on hand for the group's heralded 1987 Broadway run (and the resulting *Almost Acoustic* album). Yet instead of coasting on the strength of such accomplishments, Nelson has continued to write songs and create new sounds on stage with his own band.

The David Nelson Band is committed to perpetuating the improvisational spirit that first thrived on the West Coast in the late 1960s and early 1970s. The band is comprised of a number of players who emerged from that supportive musical scene. Pedal steel wizard Barry Sless was a member of the San Francisco outfit Kingfish (which Bob Weir joined in the mid-1970s). Keyboard player Mookie Siegel performed with Kingfish and appeared for a while in Ratdog. Bass player Bill Laymon was a member of New Riders of the Purple Sage, along with drummer Arthur Steinhorn. As a result, this band is adept at working collectively to fashion expansive, majestic, psychedelic music.

These efforts remain vibrant as the DNB interprets new songs, many of which Nelson has written with his former bandmate Hunter.

DISCOGRAPHY

Limited Edition (1995)

Keeper of the Key (1997). The group's penchant for improvisation is well documented on this release, which is drawn from a 1995 live performance. The quintet takes things out pretty far during the segued "See So Far/Sage and Egg." A few of the songs on this disc are collaborations with Hunter, including the country-tinged "John Hardy's Wedding" and the burning "Kick in the Head #9." The band also offers enthusiastic readings of Bob Dylan's "Wicked Messenger" and the Grateful Dead's "The Wheel."

WEB SITE

www.nelsonband.com

NEW BROWN HAT

- **FELL HERDEG:** *bass*
- **FRANK KOVAC:** *guitar*
- **JULIE PRUNIER:** *vocals*
- **CRAIG WOERZ:** *keyboards*
- **KYLE YOUNG:** *drums*

The staying power of New York's New Brown Hat is striking: four-fifths of the band has been in place since 1987. Although that span of years may not, in itself, seem inordinately impressive at first glance, it becomes rather astonishing once one recognizes that the members of New Brown Hat have been playing together since they were in junior high school. In fact, drummer Kyle Young and keyboardist Craig Woerz started the group while they were performing together in their grade school jazz band. They recruited bassist Jared Hart and callow guitarist Frank Kovac to join the fledgling band. Vocalist Julie Prunier completed the lineup soon afterward when Kovac spotted her in a junior-high performance of *The Sound of Music*. The band began gigging, first under the name XYZ and then as Steel Wood. In 1992, Hart decided to move on, and the next year the group brought in Woerz's college friend Fell Herdeg to replace him. The quintet marked the occasion by renaming itself New Brown Hat.

The band members perform with the confidence and instincts of musical friends who have been playing together throughout their adult lives. Herdeg maintains that "the fact that we all know each other really helps when we're stretching things out, because we have a handle on the general direction and aims." The bassist also believes that the group's camaraderie shows through on stage: "I think one thing that distinguishes us is that everybody out there is just having so much fun." For instance, while her fellow bandmates are working a jam, Prunier will often move to the side of the stage to dance, reveling in the music.

The most distinctive feature of the band's sound may be Prunier's clear vocal tones. The classically trained singer hits notes and holds them with a purity and richness. Woerz's keyboards also remain a steady presence in the group's music. Kovac will often step forward to deliver splashy guitar phrases, complemented by the interlocked Herdeg and Young. "Our emphasis is on the songs," says Herdeg, "but we do a good amount of jamming within those songs." This has earned the band a number of avid supporters as well as appearances on the 1997 HORDE tour.

DISCOGRAPHY

Live to DAT (1995)

Dandelion Wine (1996). The clear production of this studio release effectively highlights the band's individual strengths, in particular Prunier's voice, but New Brown Hat's collaborative flair also shines through on these lush songs. Notable cuts include "Stillwater," with its message of personal hurt; "Tracks," which is enlivened by Woerz's keyboards; and "He Doesn't Know," with its pleasing melody and groove. "Rise and Fall" ends the disc on a liberating note with some exuberant phrasings from each of the band members.

WEB SITE

www.newbrownhat.com

NEXT STOP WILLOUGHBY

- **BRIAN AVIGNE:** *guitar, vocals*
- **PETE AVIGNE:** *drums*
- **STEPHEN GARCIA:** *vocals, guitar*
- **FRANCIS JARAMILLO:** *bass*

Next Stop Willoughby began performing under the moniker Rubber Soul while its members were still in high school. At that time, the group mainly presented covers of other artists' material, but it also introduced some original songs written by guitarists Brian Avigne and Stephen Garcia. In 1996, the group initiated a transformation by gradually phasing out covers while placing additional emphasis on improvisation. Comments Avigne: "Although we played Dead songs, I wouldn't say we were a jam band until we started playing our own material. So, in some ways, I guess I pushed everyone into it." In early 1998, to mark this development, the band jettisoned the name Rubber Soul and became Next Stop Willoughby, an appellation inspired by an episode of *The Twilight Zone.*

The Detroit group garnered loyal supporters due to the creativity it brings to its performances and its gig selections. Next Stop Willoughby presents musical tableaux, as Avigne composes songs in a range of styles, including bluegrass, funk, blues, and jazz, in order to compel himself and his bandmates to learn how to play them. Preferring to present these tunes in slightly atypical environments, the group has refused many club dates. Instead, it hosts its own gigs with other bands in more fan-friendly atmospheres (remaining sensitive to the fact that many of its supporters are below the legal drinking age).

DISCOGRAPHY

Hang a Sign (1997). This disc, which the band recorded under its original name of Rubber Soul, collects a number of pleasing melodies and performances. It begins with an instrumental, "King Richard," which yields to the lively, funky "Alexis." Other notable cuts include "Weight of the Day," the gentler "Imitation of Self," and the banjo-abetted title track. Vocalist Krista Basque, who is no longer with the group, brightens a few tunes, including "Tea for Time."

OLD DEAD BUG

- **ROD BRETON:** *percussion*
- **DAVE DORMAN:** *drums*
- **DARREN HOME:** *bass*
- **VICTOR MANNING:** *guitar, vocals*
- **GEOFF NIXON:** *guitar, vocals*
- **STEVE SMITH:** *harmonica, vocals*

Old Dead Bug is, quite literally, named after a large, deceased insect. One evening, a few of the group's members were walking along the beach in their hometown of San Jose, California, when they happened upon an intricately carved stick. When they picked it up, they discovered that the marks had actually been etched by an arthropod. They saw fit to name themselves after the old dead bug that had created those "grooves."

The band first started creating its own grooves in the late 1980s. Most of Old Dead Bug's members had attended high school together, but the group didn't crystallize until after they had completed their education at San Jose State. At that point, vocalist Geoff Nixon brought the various players together to create a music that reflected their interest in blues, rock, and Latin rhythms. Guitarist Victor Manning supplies all of these elements with his deep musical vocabulary. Harmonica player Steve Smith, whom bassist Darren Home describes as a "good, crazy freak," adds some interesting tones with his effect-enhanced harmonica. Drummer Dave "Stormin'" Dorman plays with such incendiary force that when he first rehearsed with the band he fell backward off his stool and put a hole in the wall behind him yet still leapt back to continue the song. Percussionist Rod Breton infuses the mix with his affinity for salsa music. Home describes the group's live shows as "good dancing fun jam times" – which is just another way of saying that this band gives good groove.

DISCOGRAPHY

Monkeys by Nature (1997). This disc contains a number of bright, lively tunes. The opener, "Julian Street Song," is a vivid collaborative jam. Other strong tracks include the funky, harmonica-accented "Messenger," the spacier "Don't Bother," and the gentle folk song "Sanctified Soul."

WEB SITE

www.odb.com

OMINOUS SEAPODS

- ■ **BRIAN MANGINI:** *keyboards*
- ■ **TED MAROTTA:** *drums and percussion, vocals*
- ■ **DANA MONTEITH:** *electric and acoustic guitar, vocals*
- ■ **TOM PIROZZI:** *bass, vocals*
- ■ **MAX VERNA:** *electric and acoustic guitar, vocals*

An Ominous Seapods show is far more than just a musical experience. Audiences can also expect visual stimulation: the five band members will often take the stage wearing masks, costumes, or other accoutrements of their own devising. Additionally, the humor of the players often celebrates the absurd, resulting in some memorable, spontaneous interactions between each other and between band and audience. Finally, the group has been known to transform its gigs through its own twisted themes, such as the time it hosted an eight-track release party. But make no mistake – the Seapods is not simply a prop band. These guys can rip.

The group first came together in 1989 when two State University of New York at Plattsburgh students, guitarists Dana Monteith and Max Verna, performed at an open-mike night hosted by a local club called the Monopole (the band references the venue in its song "Leaving the Monopole.") The pair eventually decided to work with a full band, bringing in bass player Tom Pirozzi, who confides: "I was the area bass slut, I would play with anyone. But eventually I decided to stick with these guys and keep it going." Soon afterward, the band members traveled south and settled in Albany, where they solidified their lineup with keyboardist Brian Mangini and drummer Ted Marotta. Over the past few years, the Seapods has become a national touring band, assisted, in part, by some avid on-line supporters. Says Pirozzi: "The Internet knows no geography. And we have some really loyal fans on the Podnet who have taken it upon themselves to get the word out and to spread tapes. So we've walked into a bar in Iowa City where the place is just packed full of people who have heard about us, know our music, and are excited to have us there."

The band's music is a collaborative venture. Although most of its songs are contributed by Monteith and Verna (Pirozzi writes a few as well), they are often transformed and enhanced in the live environment, in which the band thrives on spontaneity, adding new wrinkles and mutations (a favorite word of the band). Verna's guitar is often up front, producing soaring, spiraling leads. Rhythm guitarist Monteith adds hyperactive, funky fills and steps forward on occasion. Pirozzi navigates the band through fresh territory. Keyboardist Mangini contributes what Pirozzi describes as "macabre, sci-fi textures." Marotta supplies a steady backbeat, although he will sometimes stretch out as well. This music is further animated by the band's manic collective wit, rendering any Ominous Seapods show a uniquely entertaining experience.

DISCOGRAPHY

Econobrain (1994)

Guide to Roadside Ecology (1995)

Jet Smooth Ride (1997). Lo Faber of God Street Wine produced this release, which demonstrates that, aside from the band's splashy stage show, the Seapods can write strong songs. The opener, "Waiting 4 the Bomb to Drop," is a catchy, funky offering. "Some Days" is an entrancing tune, somewhat reminiscent of early Talking Heads. The exuberant title track is further energized by strong vocal harmonies and keyboards. Pirozzi sings lead on his own "Branch's House," which effectively incorporates acoustic instrumentation and electric exultation.

Matinee Idols (1998)

WEB SITE

www.netspace.org/seapods/

ONE STEP BEYOND

- **BRYDEN BAIRD:** *trumpet*
- **DAVID GONCALVES GOUVEIA:** *percussion*
- **SANDY MAMANE:** *bass*
- **ANDY SCOTT:** *guitar*
- **LOUIS SIMAO:** *keyboards*
- **DEAN STONE:** *drums*
- **BRADIE WEST:** *saxophone*

Toronto's One Step Beyond routinely accomplishes a goal matched by few contemporary bands that perform all-instrumental music: its shows become all-out, frenzied dancefests. The group performs heavily rhythmic, horn-infused, jazz-based, funk-abetted original compositions that exhilarate both its devoted supporters and first-time listeners. Guitarist Andy Scott reflects: "We have a pretty strong live show. It's certainly not a relaxed atmosphere. There's a lot of energy. Sometimes I'll look out and see a few hundred people out there dancing to our jazz. It's a pretty remarkable thing that occasionally I take for granted."

The septet's list of accomplishments also includes its ability to circumvent some of the logistical obstacles of being a national band committed to live performance. Explains Scott: "It's really hard to tour Canada because it's so huge and the big cities are widely dispersed. It takes eighteen hours to get from Toronto to Thunder Bay, and that's not exactly a metropolis." Still, ever since it evolved out of a weekly club gig in 1995, One Step Beyond has crossed the country more than a half-dozen times, performing at jazz festivals from Vancouver to New Brunswick. The band has made successful forays into the United States, performing at venues such as the Wetlands and Boulder's Fox Theater. One Step Beyond has also opened for moe., Galactic, and Merl Saunders.

The group's music blends the predilections and propensities of its seven players. Scott views himself as a jazz guitarist, citing Pat Martino as a personal favorite. By contrast, bassist Sandy Mamane enjoys the sounds of James Brown and seeks to perpetuate a rhythm-and-blues/funk ethic. Percussionist David Goncalves Gouveia has an affinity for Santana. Scott views these varied influences as crucial to One Step Beyond: "We're bringing together sounds. We fuse Latin rhythms with jazz, rhythm and blues, gospel, and soul. The term 'fusion' has taken on a stigma of being math music, everything's in 7/4, but that's really what we're doing in the purest sense."

One Step Beyond (1996)

Life out There (1997). The band's mellifluous compositions and ebullient performances are well represented on this release. The first cut, "12 Miles to San Diego," is enlivened with buoyant horns and vivid keys. "Life on Asteroid B-612" features deft guitar work and sparkling brass. "Swungin'" lives up to its title, projecting the full flavor of the band, as do offerings such as "Noblesse Oblige" and "Lookout!"

OROBOROS

- **WILL DOUGLAS:** *drums*
- **JIM MILLER:** *guitar, vocals*
- **MICHAEL ROTMAN:** *percussion, keyboards, acoustic guitar, vocals*
- **SCOTT SWANSON:** *bass, vocals*

Oroboros is a mythological snake that bites its own tail, a symbol of continuity and change. The Cleveland band of the same name also embodies these qualities. Jim Miller, founder and sole original member, has been gigging with Oroboros since 1980. In the intervening years, the band has gone through a number of personnel changes but continues to thrive, performing with soul and vigor.

The group has mounted many standout shows in the course of its existence. Miller has particularly fond memories of the night when former Quicksilver Messenger Service guitarist John Cippolina joined Oroboros for two complete sets: "It was amazing. Here was a guy I had idolized growing up, and we're playing double leads together like we'd been doing it for years. What a gifted player he was." Another highlight occurred the night before the 1994 HORDE tour. Miller had invited his fellow HORDE participants to join Oroboros at a Cleveland nightclub. John Popper and Sheryl Crow showed up, and Miller played guitar for seven songs with members of the Allman Brothers Band. Yet another standout event was the nine-show tour of Thailand that took place after Oroboros had been invited to perform at the 1996 Southern Thailand Jazz Festival. Back at home, the band has become well known for two of its traditions: an annual benefit festival for a Cleveland medical clinic and the group's yearly free St. Patrick's Day performance.

Oroboros's musical palette blends percussion-driven polyrhythms, a strong feeling for the blues, a hint of country, and a sprinkling of psychedelia. Notes Miller: "We love to jam, but we consider ourselves songwriters as well. I mean, as far as my songwriting goes, my idols were the Beatles. It's always been my first goal to write a great song. So when we play live, you'll hear two things: you'll hear concise songs, but you'll also hear us take it out there where we don't know where we're going." Miller often leads the journey, but, at times, the audience is swept away by the propulsive power of the group's drummers. This music energizes band members and concertgoers alike, and Miller's enthusiasm for the band, what it has accomplished, and what it has yet to achieve is palpable. "We started in the skinny-tie era and we're still at it. We just want to keep doing what we love."

DISCOGRAPHY

Different Feeling (1985)

Psychadeli (1988)

First Circle (1991)

Serpent's Dance (1994)

Shine (1996). This live recording captures the band in a slightly earlier incarnation with a second guitarist and underscores the reasons for its staying power. Miller's guitar work rings forth throughout the release. The band's percussion erupts on numerous cuts as well. Oroboros's ability to craft catchy, pleasing songs is showcased on songs such as "Calliope," "Sunshine Sally," and "You Shine."

WEB SITE

www.oroboros.net

PELE JUJU

- **TRACE ASHLEIGH:** *percussion, keyboards, vocals*
- **MOLLY HIGBIE:** *guitar, keyboards, vocals*
- **DANA HUTSON:** *vocals*
- **DEB LANE:** *drums*
- **ANNIE STEINHARDT:** *bass*
- **BRINDLE SWEIGART:** *percussion*

The "Wild Women of World Beat" came together in 1985 during a jam session in Molly Higbie's living room. Since then, Santa Cruz's Pele Juju has worked to become a dazzling, radiant live band. The two components of the group's name evoke its essence. *Pele* is the Hawaiian volcano goddess, which suggests both the group's female constituency and the rumbling percussion that undergirds all of its music. *Juju* is the West African word for magic, reflecting the group's synergy (as well as the fact that several band members have worked and studied in that part of the world).

Pele Juju strives to provide its audiences with an uplifting experience. When it performs without a supporting act, the group will often deliver three sets of energized and energizing music. Dancing is vigorously encouraged through example: vocalist Dana Hutson often uses her feet to express her appreciation for Pele Juju's invigorating sounds — in fact, she throws her whole body into it, exulting in the act of musical creation. The group blends a number of styles to produce its Afrobeat, from reggae to funk to soul. Of course, it's propelled by the percussive triad of Trace Ashleigh, Deb Lane, and Brindle Sweigart, who are occasionally joined by Hutson. Their sounds are complemented by Annie Steinhardt's dexterous bass and Higbie's guitar and keyboards. The band often brings in additional players; most recently, Shelley Doty has provided incendiary guitar, and Jayn Pettengill has injected sizzling saxophone (taking over for Elaine Beggelman, who no longer joins the band on tour). Pele Juju latches onto some ecstatic, extended grooves, often leaving its audiences both rejuvenated and exhausted.

DISCOGRAPHY

Pele Juju (1992)

Rhythm Rite (1996)

Live! (1997). Here Pele Juju explores its true métier, creating spirited, invigorating jams for a reciprocally enthusiastic audience. The band swiftly accelerates on the opening track, the ebullient "Anikewa." The song that follows, the Cajun-flavored "Happy to Be Alive," is ignited when guest guitarist Shelley Doty begins layering bottleneck guitar behind Beggelman's saxophone. The ballad "Magic" proves similarly notable, as the band changes the tempo and Hutson's soulful vocals elevate the offering. "Kryptic Postcards" works a groove for nearly eleven minutes fueled by driving percussion and catalyzed by keyboards, guitar, and vocals.

WEB SITE

reality.sgi.com/pelejuju

PERCY HILL

- ■ **JOE FARRELL:** *vocals, guitar*
- ■ **AARON KATZ:** *drums, vocals*
- ■ **JOHN LECCESE:** *bass, vocals*
- ■ **NATE WILSON:** *keyboards, vocals*

The vivid, vibrant grooves of Percy Hill have been bringing fans to their feet ever since the band came together in 1993. In particular, Joe Farrell's ringing guitar leads and Nate Wilson's lively keyboards routinely prompt much spirited physical expression.

Percy Hill started out as a six-piece band whose members were students at the University of New Hampshire. The Wilson brothers, Nate and his elder sibling Zack, got things rolling by approaching four friends they knew and respected from the area music scene. The band's name was respectfully lifted from a friend's father, Percy Hill, who had offered other suggestions to the group when it was struggling to find a suitable moniker. The lineup quickly gelled; the guitarist's and keyboardist's songwriting and performance talents were compounded by the rhythm guitar and vocals of Tom Powley and the vigorous percussion of Zack Wilson. Nate Wilson describes the band's music as a mix of "Latin, funk, soul, and bluegrass. We've always listened to different kinds of music and kept an open mind." The group swiftly distinguished itself with its volcanic, enveloping improvisations as well.

Early in 1998, however, as its various players decided to move in different directions, the band reconvened as a quartet. The remaining players, the younger Wilson and Farrell, welcomed drummer Aaron Katz and bass player John Leccese. They had been students together in the University of New Hampshire music program, and Katz was known for his work with the popular jam band Vitamin C.

Percy Hill has perpetuated its four-part vocal harmonies and maintained its venturesome spirit. Notes Wilson: "Our songwriting is much deeper now. Along with Joe and I, Aaron also composes on guitar and keyboards. And, whereas before many of our songs were used as a catalyst for a big jam, now we're focusing on each tune a bit more." As the band forges ahead with a strong sense of its musical direction, the lone area of uncertainty may be the future of Zack Wilson, who will continue to join the group for some area gigs. His brother confides, "It's a tough decision for him. He'll always be part of Percy Hill. We'd love to have him."

DISCOGRAPHY

Setting the Boat Adrift (1993)

Straight on 'til Morning (1995)

Double Feature (1997). This epic two-CD release, which features the long-standing six-piece lineup, manifests Percy Hill's intensity and spontaneity within the live setting. These qualities swiftly become evident as the opener, "Been So Long," simmers and explodes; guitarist Farrell leads the seventeen-minute journey. "Setting the Boat Adrift" is one of the many vital offerings animated by Nate Wilson's keyboards. "Othello" is fueled by the dynamic created by drummer Dylan Halacy and percussionist Zack Wilson. "Sooner or Later," a winsome composition in its own right, proves even more notable for Nate Wilson's engrossing instrumental expressions, which at one point riff on a familiar Stevie Wonder song.

WEB SITE

www.percyhill.com

PHISH

- **TREY ANASTASIO:** *guitar, vocals*
- **JON FISHMAN:** *drums, vocals*
- **MIKE GORDON:** *bass, vocals*
- **PAGE MCCONNELL:** *keyboards, vocals*

"Vermont's phinest" has been dazzling appreciative audiences since the fall of 1983. The band formed when University of Vermont students Trey Anastasio and Jeff Holdsworth started jamming on their guitars in dormitory common rooms. Resolving to create a band, they asked dormmate Jon Fishman, a drummer, to join them and put up notices for a bass player. Mike Gordon responded, and Phish's journey was under way. During May of 1985, the band performed at Goddard College in Plainfield, Vermont. Keyboard player Page McConnell came to listen and was quite taken with the group; he eventually managed to convince its members to let him join. When Holdsworth graduated the following spring, he moved on, leaving the Phish lineup that remains today. The group then began to gig more actively, soon winning a regular slot at a Burlington bar called Nectar's. There Phish slowly gained a sizable following, moving on to fill larger venues.

The loyalty and the dimensions of its phan base continue to increase due to the individual artistry, collective prowess, and wonderfully bent senses of humor of Phish's players. Just as important, the band has never stopped striving to reinvent itself and add new components to its shows. For instance, early on, band members took barbershop-quartet lessons to improve their vocal harmonies. Similarly, the quartet performed a number of gigs with horn players as a jazz group, determined to learn from the experience. During the summer of 1995, band members climbed onto stools to perform an instrumental with four acoustic guitars. That fall, they repeated the exercise on keyboards. Such efforts have led to some occasions when, in midjam, they will rotate onstage to perform on each other's instrument. Many of these ventures have been motivated by Phish's goal to become "egoless," to lose individual identity while crafting communal music. The most successful endeavors have been described as achieving "the hose," a phrase originally attributed to Carlos Santana, who once stated that while Phish played he envisioned the crowd as a sea of flowers, the music as water, and the band as the hose.

Over the years, Phish has often labored to break down the barriers between itself and its audience. In the early days, band members would often walk directly off the stage and into the crowd after a performance to engage listeners in conversation. As the venues have become larger, Phish has had to seek alternative methods of fostering this communication. In the fall of 1992, the Big Ball Jam was initiated. For this, the group tossed four large inflated balls into the audience, each of which corresponded to a particular band member; by striking a particular ball, an audience member could elicit sounds from a particular musician – the audience could literally play the band. Then there was the Band-Phan Chess Game, which took place in the fall of 1995: a large board was suspended behind McConnell, dropped down before the show so the group could move a piece, and then lowered before the start of the second set so that an audience representative could do the same. In the spring of 1992, Phish also shared its Secret Language with the audience, a series of musical clues that elicited certain responses from band and phan alike. Also, in the spring of 1994, when Anastasio's ankle was in a cast, the group invited audience members on stage to join Gordon in the pair's trampoline routine.

Phish has also become known for its festive holiday concerts. On October 31, 1994, it inaugurated a new tradition by donning a unique Halloween costume – a set of music comprised solely of another group's recordings. That year, the band invited its supporters to vote for the album, with the balloting remaining a secret until Phish emerged to perform the Beatles's *White Album*. The next year, Phish presented the Who's *Quadrophenia*, and in 1996 the band selected its own offering – the Talking Heads's *Remain in Light*. Since 1989, the band has also hosted a series of New Year's Eve performances that feature three sets of music along with some bonus visual revelry: in 1993, the quartet was lowered into giant clams prior to midnight; in 1994, band members climbed into an oversized flying hotdog, which then sailed across the Boston Garden; in 1995, they incorporated a time-machine scenario into their act; and, in 1996, they dropped thousands of balloons on the crowd.

Finally, Phish has solidified its relationship with its supporters through its annual music festivals. This practice was started in August 1996, when the band hosted seventy thousand fans at the Clifford Ball in Plattsburgh, New York. A year later, the event was labeled the Great Went and held in Presque Isle, Maine, at the northeastern tip of the state. In 1998, the festivities returned to Presque Isle under the title Lemonwheel. At these events, along with three sets of Phish each day, the band affirms its audience appreciation through any number of extra flourishes, including fireworks, air shows, rides, interactive art exhibits, a radio station, guest orchestras that perform during the dinner hour, and late-night surprise Phish sets.

DISCOGRAPHY

Junta (1989). Originally a cassette, this recording was rereleased as a two-CD set in 1992 with some additional tracks (the live music is from 7/25/88, not 5/3/88).

Lawn Boy (1990)

A Picture of Nectar (1991)

Rift (1993)

Hoist (1994)

A Live One (1995). This double live package collects a number of notable performances from the fall of 1994.

Billy Breathes (1996)

Slip Stitch and Pass (1998). This disc presents the band in concert at Hamburg, Germany, on March 1, 1997. It also documents an evolution in the band's sound: Anastasio's solos are deemphasized, and he frequently acts as rhythm guitarist. This direction may best be detected in the band's churning, funky take on "Wolfman's Brother," which segues fluidly into the ZZ Top slow-burner "Jesus Just Left Chicago" (one of three covers on the disc – the others being the a cappella "Hello My Baby" and the Talking Heads's "Cities," which had been a Phish live staple in the late 1980s). Longtime favorite "Mike's Song" makes its recorded debut with some bonus quotes from the Doors's "The End" and Pink Floyd's "Careful with That Axe Eugene." Another first-time offering is the ebullient "Weekapaug Groove," which briefly incorporates the Rolling Stones's "Can't You Hear Me Knocking."

The Story of the Ghost (1998)

WEB SITE

www.phish.com

POI DOG PONDERING

- **EDDIE CARLSON:** *bass*
- **ROBERT CORNELIUS:** *vocals*
- **DAVE MAX CRAWFORD:** *keyboards, trumpet*
- **LEDDIE GARCIA:** *percussion*
- **STEVE GOULDING:** *drums*
- **KORNELL HARGROVE:** *vocals*
- **DAG JUHLIN:** *guitar*
- **PAUL MERTENS:** *saxophones, flute, piccolo, clarinet*
- **ARLENE NEWSON:** *vocals*
- **FRANK ORRALL:** *vocals, guitar*
- **SUSAN VOELZ:** *violin, vocals*

Poi Dog Pondering has evolved through a series of journeys. This certainly holds true from a geographical perspective. Poi Dog began as a street band in Hawaii, then relocated to Austin, Texas, and eventually made its way to Chicago, its current home base. From a musical standpoint, the group has transformed itself from a busking acoustic outfit into a techno-infused, multimedia juggernaut. However, at its heart remains Frank Orrall, whose winsome compositions and generous, life-affirming spirit have animated Poi Dog from the moment of its inception.

These days, the band incorporates elements of salsa, soul, folk, funk, techno, and the music of Orrall's native Hawaii; the eleven-piece dynamo crowds onto the stage to serve up this fricassee. Orrall is a frenetic front man who supplies most lead vocals. Susan Voelz, one of the remaining original members of Poi Dog, will frequently step forward on violin (Voelz has also initiated a solo career with her releases *13 Ribs* and *Summer Crashing*). Fellow longtime contributor Dave Max Crawford moves from keyboards to trumpet with an occasional display on accordion or trombone. Paul Mertens is a versatile horn player who blows a full range of saxophones. Lead guitarist Dag Juhlin is a nimble player who also performs with his own band, the Slugs. Percussionists Leddie Garcia and Steve Goulding add flavorful rhythms. The vocals of Robert Cornelius, Kornell Hargrove, and Arlene Newson infuse the group's sound with additional primacy and power.

The sheer size of the band coupled with the exuberance of its members creates a festive atmosphere, which is regularly enhanced by additional features. When in Chicago, Poi Dog incorporates a student dance troupe, House O Matic. Luke Savisky will sometimes project film loops behind the group (Orrall has some familiarity with this medium, as he provides an entertaining turn in the movie *Slacker*). At times, the band also employs the stylings of several DJs. In July of 1996, Poi Dog Pondering teamed up with Chicago's Grant Park Symphony Orchestra to provide a free show for fifty thousand fans.

DISCOGRAPHY

Poi Dog Pondering (1988)
Wishing like a Mountain, Thinking like the Sea (1989)
Volo Volo (1991)
Pomegranate (1995)
Liquid White Light (1997). This double live release captures the full, tantalizing sound of the band. There are a number of resplendent instrumental exertions and excursions here amid a collection of songs that spans the group's career. Longtime favorites include the bright, twisted "Living with the Dreaming Body," "Ta Bouche est Tabu," "Everybody's Trying," and the throbbing "Jack Ass Ginger." The band's funkier edge is manifested in songs such as "Diamonds and Buttermilk" and "Platetectonic." Other strong offerings include "Sandra at the Beach," "God's Gallipolli," and "Complicated."

WEB SITE

www.poihg.com/poi

POST JUNCTION

- **JON FADEM:** *guitar, vocals*
- **ROB FORD:** *drums*
- **OZZIE JONES:** *bass*
- **DON NEWKIRK:** *keyboards, vocals*
- **JOHN PEZIK:** *trumpet*
- **JOE VAGLIO:** *saxophone*
- **MARK WEISS:** *guitar*

In 1994, Jon Fadem completed his first year of medical school. However, before entering the next phase of his training, he elected to take a year's leave of absence to perform his music. He assembled

Post Junction, a collective committed to producing sounds in the spirit of some of Fadem's heroes: the Meters, Parliament Funkadelic, and Band of Gypsies. Recalls Fadem: "When we first got started, all we did was get together and play 'Who Knows' [Band of Gypsies] for an hour at a time. Hendrix really expressed what we were trying to do, which was to fuse soul, rock, and funk." The group swiftly earned a following in New York City as people began grooving to Post Junction's original, funk-based, jazz-tinged compositions. Fadem's leave of absence has long since become permanent.

The band's sound has filled out. Post Junction began as a trio, with Fadem providing guitar and vocals. Rhythm guitarist Mark Weiss soon came aboard to add some denser textures to the mix. By 1996, the quartet was being buttressed by Ozzie Jones's rumbling, inventive bass and Rob Ford's popping drums. A year later, the band added the Post Junction Horns, Joe Vaglio (saxophone) and John Pezik (trumpet). Noted musician and producer Don Newkirk (who appears on De La Soul's *3 Feet High and Rising*) then joined as well, furnishing keyboards and many of the vocal leads.

Post Junction remains committed to exploring and expanding on the funk of the 1970s. This is not surprising, given the fact that another of Fadem's idols and influences is the veritable musical Magellan Miles Davis. The group performs songs such as Sly and the Family Stone's "You Can Make It if You Try" and P-Funk's "Standing on the Verge of Getting It On," which Fadem believes are funk standards in the same sense as jazz standards. Meanwhile, Fadem also strives to compose songs that are harmonically complex but still capable of keeping the dance floor grinding. He describes the sounds of Post Junction as "music for your mind and body." Although he may not have officially joined the medical fraternity, Fadem is nonetheless a holistic healer.

DISCOGRAPHY

Post Junction (1996). Although this debut disc does not feature the Post Junction Horns, it is still a solid offering that documents a good portion of the group's current live show. Jones's bass is solid throughout, and Weiss's rhythm guitar ably supports the sound. The instrumental "Vibe," which opens, is a thick funk with a hint of blues courtesy of Fadem. "Time for Some Answers" is reminiscent of vintage Sly and the Family Stone. "Waiting for You" is jazzier fare, and "Stare into the Hole" demonstrates the band's effective dynamics.

WEB SITE

www.postjunction.com

PUDDLE JUNCTION

- **BRIAN ASHER:** *guitar, vocals*
- **TROY DYE:** *bass*
- **MICHAEL GAMMON:** *drums*
- **ROB LAMONICA:** *keyboards*
- **DOUG STEIN:** *vocals*

Puddle Junction came out of one of the jam sessions that seem to proliferate in Chico, California. The quintet initially played for its own edification and entertainment before making its public debut on Halloween night 1995. The frenzied twirls of those in attendance on that evening have trailed after the band ever since. In characterizing the group's music, singer Doug Stein says: "I like to call it serious fun. We're trying to educate ourselves about ourselves and bounce that off other people who are doing the same thing. I mean, our ultimate goal is to get everyone in the room to shake their asses, but we'd like them to dance while their knowledge is growing."

Puddle Junction has gained particular renown for its rousing improvisations. Lead guitarist Brian Asher brings a range of effects pedals and distortions to his fluid performances. Keyboardist Rob Lamonica employs his classical training while keeping his hands awhirl. The two are well supported by the rhythms crafted by bassist Troy Dye and drummer Michael Gammon. Stein is up front supplying his own galvanic expressions. "In a lot of ways," reflects Stein, "the Puddle Junction experience is all about energy. The most satisfying nights have been those when everyone comes out exhausted and digs real deep to find the energy they never thought they had."

DISCOGRAPHY

Reinvent the Wheel (1996). Puddle Junction went all out to turn this release into a full multimedia package. The enhanced disc includes live footage, animated sequences, and a band biography.

Of course, the music itself proves entertaining as well; witness vivid offerings such as "Find a Reason" and "Feel Your Soul." The band's affinity for blues shines through on "Fruits of Your Labor" and the irreverent "Trucker for the Lord." Other interesting tracks include the boogie-woogie "High Flyin' Mama" and the Doors-esque "Pagan Lament."

WEB SITE

www.netgate.net/~puddlejunction/

PUDDLEDUCK

■ **DAVE HEDEMAN:** *acoustic guitar, percussion, vocals*
■ **DARREN MOXIN:** *guitar*
■ **JASON SELL:** *drums, percussion*
■ **BOBBY SUTTON:** *guitars, vocals*
■ **DAVE WATKINSON:** *bass*

As founding member Dave "Gomer" Hedeman describes it, Puddle-Duck began "as a bunch of friends at James Madison University messing around in a cellar and playing some songs we knew." In March 1994, they decided that their first public performance would be at an open-mike night hosted by a local venue. When they attempted to sign up, however, they encountered a problem. A club employee asked them what they called themselves, and a brief moment of panic ensued. "We'll get right back to you," the not-quite-a-band-yet responded. After thumbing through a dictionary, they were left with two contenders: "Salt Wedge" and "Puddleduck." The latter won out, and so it was PuddleDuck and not Salt Wedge that took the honors in the *Richmond Musical Journal*'s Favorite Band Poll in January of 1998.

PuddleDuck is particularly vital in the live setting. There, the band builds its sound around Bobby Sutton and Darren Moxin's twin guitar attack, which is pushed by Jason Sell's precise drumming and Dave Watkinson's steady bass. Hedeman livens the mix on acoustic guitar and percussion. PuddleDuck juxtaposes furious jams with shorter, harmony-rich tunes to give audience members a moment to catch their breath before it charges off again. Hedeman describes the band's music as "southern funk, which takes the Allman Brothers Band as a starting point and moves out from there." Other influences that can be detected in PuddleDuck's recorded efforts and live shows include Curtis Mayfield, Parliament Funkadelic, and John McLaughlin.

DISCOGRAPHY

Best Things in Life (1995)

Fly (1997). This release proves that PuddleDuck not only possesses technical skill but can also construct appealing melodies. The disc is laden with hummable compositions, such as "Carolina" and "Round and Round." Other tracks – in particular, "Everyday," "Slow Down," and "Farewell" – layer vocal harmonies and multiple guitars over a funky backdrop.

WEB SITE

www.pipeline.com/~puddleduck

QUIVER

- **JASON BRUNER:** *drums, vocals*
- **DAVID FULFORD:** *keyboards*
- **ROB LORD:** *bass, vocals*
- **VASILI SIMMONS:** *guitar, vocals*

Virginia Beach bass player Rob Lord and keyboardist David Fulford assembled the first version of Quiver in 1994. The pair's intent was to create a band that would craft original music inspired by their favorite performers, including Medeski, Martin and Wood, jazz organist Jimmy Smith, and the Sun Ra Arkestra. From the start, the group was committed to writing its own songs, asking, "Without original music, what would cover bands do?" Lord and Fulford drew in drummer Jason Bruner along with guitarists Garrison Kloss and Tommie Thomas and began securing gigs throughout the region. Citing family considerations, Kloss and Thomas withdrew from the enterprise after a few years, and Quiver was reduced to a trio. Early in 1997, the three were introduced to Vasili Simmons, who had studied jazz guitar with John D'earth at the University of Virginia. They welcomed him into the fold, and he has gone on to sharpen and invigorate the band's sound.

The group describes its sound as "fuse music" because it bridges a number of genres. Fulford is a resourceful keyboardist, capable of executing adroit, rousing runs while layering textures. Simmons is not only a well of jazz-inflected phrasings but also a source of explosive rock declarations. Lord, a very active bass player, regularly carries the band into funkier territory. Bruner is the utility musician who spryly navigates through all of these environments. The sounds they manufacture are often quite tantalizing, as Quiver is particularly adept at robust, collective improvisation.

DISCOGRAPHY

Smile (1996)

Cup of Gold (1998). This disc introduces listeners to the band's various styles, which are unified by its in-the-pocket grooves. Following a spoken word over a throbbing musical interlude, Quiver bursts into the funky "Chi-Town." Other solid cuts include the bright "Carpe Diem" and the keyboard-driven instrumental "Positive Release." The spirited "Suntide II" features guest appearances by guitarist Keller Williams and drummer Mike Williams (of the Gibb Droll Band). The release closes with the entertaining "I Saw Jimi Hendrix on the Wall," which begins as cocktail jazz but soon expands into sharp, pulsing vocal and instrumental intonations.

WEB SITE

www.quivernet.com

THE RADIATORS

- **CAMILE BAUDOIN:** *guitar, vocals*
- **FRANK BUA:** *drums*
- **DAVE MALONE:** *guitar, vocals, percussion*
- **REGGIE SCANLAN:** *bass*
- **ED VOLKER:** *vocals, piano, keyboards*

In January 1978, New Orleans-based bandmates Ed Volker, Camile Baudoin, and Frank Bua invited their two favorite players from another local group, Dave Malone and Reggie Scanlan, to join them for a jam session. The summit that followed lasted for more than five hours. The next day, Malone and Scanlan left their band and the Radiators saga began. More than twenty years later, the group continues to go after it with the same verve and intensity, still barnstorming across America and tearing it up live.

The band's sound is very much a product of its home city. Its list of influences is a roster of the Big Easy's greatest musical citizens: Jelly Roll Morton, Professor Longhair (the subject of the band's lively eulogy, "Long Hard Journey Home"), Allen Touissant, Earl King, the Meters, and Dr. John. It is a testament to the Radiators's own musical prowess that the group has been given an opportunity to play with most of these individuals. In the process, the band assimilated some aspects of these performers' sounds, using them to craft its own Cajun swamp boogie.

Another important facet of the Radiators's experience is distinctly piscine. Early in the band's career, Volker took to drawing fish and using these sketches on the flyers he made to promote the band's shows. The imagery of the group's original songs soon came to feature marine life (for instance, "Law of the Fish" and "Suck the Head" – advice for eating crawfish). The bandmates also began calling each other "fishheads," an epithet that became a backhanded term of endearment. The group's devotees soon appropriated the word and further identified the Radiators with such imagery; for instance, the fan-crafted collection of set lists modeled after the Grateful Dead's Dead Base is entitled the Bouilla-Base.

Radiators fans are fascinated with the group's set lists because the quintet has an exhaustive musical repertoire. At a moment's notice, the band can whip out and work through hundreds of songs, many of which are originals. Its members' individual tastes yield covers that range from "Hi-Heeled Sneakers" to "Tears of a Clown" to "New Speedway Boogie," as well as one notable segue from "Sympathy for the Devil" to "Route 66." Indeed, fishheads have been known to throw down a buck apiece and a list of songs before a show, with the jackpot going to the person who comes closest in his or her predictions (sumptuous dinners have been won on the strength of two or three matches).

Of course, musical diversity alone does not explain such loyalty. The Radiators love to perform live, energetically stretching out their songs. The band's scorching jams are often fueled by dueling guitars, as Baudoin's sassy slide provides a counterpoint to Malone's fiery leads. Volker will also take charge, moving from nimble boogies to soulful declarations. Scanlan's bass and Bua's percussion are yet another source of acclaim. Indeed, the Radiators's live shows very much capture and re-create the revelry associated with the band's home city, prompting longtime supporters and new converts alike to travel long distances in order to go fishing.

SELECTED DISCOGRAPHY

Law of the Fish (1987)

Zigzagging through Ghostland (1989)

Total Evaporation (1991)

SNAFU (1992)

Bucket of Fish (1994)

New Rock Ages (1995)

Songs from the Ancient Furnace (1997). This is a greatest-hits collection culled from the group's Sony releases (the first five discs listed here). It supplies a tasty helping of Rad stew, including, among other things, a chunky live offering of the band's concert mainstay "Love Is a Tangle."

Live at Great American Music Hall (1998). High Sierra Records released this disc on January 28, 1998, the twenty-year anniversary of the band's first live gig. It demonstrates that the group has lost none of its initial enthusiasm over the years and certainly has learned a trick or two. Most of these songs are presented on disc for the first time. "Devil's Dream" is a sampling of New Orleans funk that references the city. "You Can't Miss What You Can't Measure" is a bluesy track embellished with some fine turns on guitar and keyboards. Also notable are "Last Getaway"; the guitarists' sweeping contributions on "Lucinda" (which offers a taste of *The Magnificent Seven*); and the closer, "Rainbow," which is well grounded in soul.

WEB SITE

www.radiators.org

RADIO I-CHING

- **TED KRAUT:** *guitar, vocals*
- **ELIZABETH LANDAU:** *vocals*
- **JASON LEVIN:** *bass*
- **EVAN OSBORNE:** *keyboards*
- **DAVE WEBSTER:** *drums*

Radio I-Ching is named after a game once practiced by Neal Cassady and the Merry Pranksters. While Cassady was driving the Pranksters in their day-glo 1939 International Harvester school bus, Furthur, he would randomly select a radio station and his passengers would attempt to guide their conversation into whatever they heard coming over the airwaves. The Venice, California, band selected this moniker because it represents a heightened awareness of the moment and an ability to anticipate; Radio I-Ching attempts to accomplish both of these goals through its live music.

The group's melodious original compositions incorporate elements of funk, folk, and rock. They are typically presented through the band's energetic, deeply grooved live performances. In concert, the primary focal point is often Elizabeth Landau, who transports listeners with her rich, clear voice. Her contributions are accented by guitarist and principal songwriter Ted Kraut, who has been working with Landau for some time as they are brother and sister. Notes Kraut: "Sometimes when I tell people that she's my sister, they say, 'Right on. I get that feeling too. I know what you mean.' I have to explain, 'No, she really is my sister.'" Speaking about keyboardist Evan Osborne, Kraut points out that he "does some really interesting left-handed stuff. He adds some lively boogies." Bass player Jason Levin and drummer Dave Webster also make vital contributions to the band's high-energy improvisations. The results have marked Radio I-Ching as one of Los Angeles's preeminent live bands (its song "Look Away" has also been featured on the television show *Party of Five*). "When people come to see us," says Kraut, "they can expect to hear some really good music, but there won't be the same grooves the whole time — there will be different types of tunes that span the emotional spectrum."

DISCOGRAPHY

Emo's Choice (1994)

Sigh (1998). This release concentrates on the band's songs. In fact, the only time the group stretches out here is during a robust cover of Los Lobos's "Dream in Blue." Landau's vocals prove captivating throughout, but they particularly carry the sultry "Catbird" and "My Heart Is Broken." Other fine tracks include "Look Away," "Belinda," and "Sigh."

WEB SITE

www.lama.com/radioiching.html

RATDOG

- **JEFF CHIMENTI:** *keyboards*
- **DAVE ELLIS:** *saxophone*
- **MATT KELLY:** *harmonica, guitar*
- **JAY LANE:** *drums*
- **ROB WASSERMAN:** *bass*
- **BOB WEIR:** *vocals, guitar*

Ratdog traces its origins back to a Willie Dixon performance at the Mill Valley, California, club Sweetwater. Two of the people in attendance that night were guitarist Bob Weir and bass player Rob Wasserman. Both shared a reverence for Dixon and were introduced to one another by the club owner. Weir, of course, had met Jerry

Garcia in the early 1960s, and together they had formed the acoustic Mother McCree's Uptown Jug Champions, which later plugged in and became the Warlocks, which in turn evolved into the Grateful Dead. Wasserman had spent a number of years early in his career playing with David Grisman and went on to perform with Rickie Lee Jones and Lou Reed. Shortly after the initial meeting between the two musicians in the fall of 1988, Wasserman released his acclaimed album *Duets*, and Weir showed up at a Wasserman jam session where the pair worked through half a dozen songs together. Afterward, Weir suggested that they form an acoustic pairing to open for the upcoming Jerry Garcia Band shows (some of the results are documented on *Weir/Wasserman Live*). It was the beginning of a beautiful friendship.

Weir and Wasserman toured together sporadically over the ensuing years, their gigs dependent on the Grateful Dead's tour schedule. In 1995, the duo expanded into a quartet. One addition was harmonica player and guitarist Matt Kelly, who had spent a number of years playing with T-Bone Walker and with Weir in Kingfish. The other was Jeff Lane, the original Primus drummer and a former bandmate of Charlie Hunter (Lane had been recommended by Primus's Les Claypool, who appears on Wasserman's *Trios*). The next step in the group's development was the addition of saxophone force Dave Ellis, who was also a founding member of the Charlie Hunter Trio. For a while, the lineup was completed by legendary pianist and septuagenarian Johnnie Johnson (best known for his long partnership with Chuck Berry). When the band moved away from a bluesier sound into more exploratory realms, however, keyboard duties were assumed by Jeff Chimenti.

Ratdog draws on the ingenuity and facility of its players to deliver dynamic shows that often approach two and a half hours in length. The set list ranges from Weir's songs with the Grateful Dead to those he created outside that circle to some traditional blues covers to some evolving Ratdog compositions. Weir typically spends much of the evening on his electric guitar, but he may also pick up an acoustic instrument to perform a few stripped-down offerings. Sometimes Ellis's saxophone becomes the focus as he supplies leads to Weir's rhythm guitar (when the band performs a Grateful Dead song, Ellis often transposes and transforms some of Garcia's renowned solos). Wasserman will frequently take center stage for a singular journey conducted through a variety of techniques; in the course of this, he may hint at a work in progress, a rock anthem, or even a Grateful Dead classic. Kelly, the only Ratdog member predominantly versed in the blues tradition, manifests this predilection through both his harmonica and his occasional turn on vocals. Yet the one unifying element of any Ratdog show is the group's commitment to extemporization.

Regardless of the song, its members are constantly, collectively, creatively working on the fly.

DISCOGRAPHY

Weir and Wasserman Live (1997). Although not a Ratdog release, this live offering presents a collection of songs currently performed by the full group. It is also an intriguing document of the first collaboration between the pair, in the fall of 1988. "Walkin' Blues" is given a particularly invigorating reading. The moving "Heaven Help the Fool" is also presented with verve. Other standout tracks include the winsome instrumental "Blue Sky Bop," the Ratdog standard "Easy To Slip," and the pair's take on "KC Moan." Also notable is the Weir-Wasserman-Willie Dixon composition "Eternity," which was recorded at the 1992 memorial tribute to the great bluesman.

WEB SITE

www.dead.net

MICHAEL RAY AND THE COSMIC KREWE

NEW ORLEANS COSMIC KREWE
VICTOR ATKINS: *piano*
CHUCK BARBER: *percussion*
EDDIE DEJEAN: *drums, vocals*
JONATHAN FREILICH: *guitar*
TIM GREEN: *saxophone*
CLARENCE JOHNSON: *saxophone*
JOSHUA PAXTON: *keyboards*
MICHAEL RAY: *trumpet, synthesizer, vocals*
LARRY SIEBARTH: *keyboards*
MICHAEL SKINKUS: *percussion*
JIMBO WALSH: *bass*
MARVIN WILLIAMS: *bass*
ANDREW WOLF: *bass*

NORTHEAST COSMIC KREWE
GRISHA ALEXIEV: *drums*
STEVE FERRARIS: *percussion*
DAVE GRIPPO: *saxophone*
DON GLASGO: *trombone*
BOB GULLOTTI: *drums*
ADAM KLIPPLE: *keyboards*
MICHAEL RAY: *trumpet, synthesizer, vocals*
STACEY STARKWEATHER: *bass*

Michael Ray is the unifying force behind the two musical collectives that perform as the Cosmic Krewe. Both the New Orleans and the Northeast Cosmic Krewes create "jazz you gotta dance to in the Sun Ra tradition." Like their music, the rosters of both groups remain open-ended; the list of performers who have appeared as Krewe members includes Marshall Allen, Mark Ribot, Jon Fishman, and Trey Anastasio (Ray has also joined Phish's Giant Country Horns along with Dave Grippo and Don Glasgo). Despite the particulars of his group's formation, Ray smoothly orchestrates a menu of free-form musical exploration and butt-shaking "jazz funk for the future."

Ray's sound reflects his personal and musical journeys. In 1978, the trumpeter joined the Sun Ra Arkestra's free-jazz odyssey as "Intergalactic Tone Scientist." Soon afterward, he also became a member of Kool and the Gang. He remained with that outfit for ten years, helping to create popular hits such as "Celebration" and "Get Down on It." All the while, he was leading a peripatetic existence – he traveled from coast to coast, attending Sun Ra's grueling thirteen-hour rehearsal sessions and then resuming a life of relative leisure on the road with Kool. Ray now draws on both influences with the Cosmic Krewe, although he is particularly interested in perpetuating the legacy of Sun Ra. Thus, although the Krewe's music contains elements of soul and funk, it also upholds the Arkestra credo that "space is the place."

Ray offers additional flavors through his full neon-sound performances. During these, he embraces a full pageantry: stage sets, Jill Kelly's elaborate costumes, and choreographed dancers. Meanwhile, Jerry Theiro's neon sculptures are dispersed around the venue, altering hues and pulsing rhythmically at Ray's direction – specific vibrations are associated with particular colors. The resulting spectacle, elevated by the performance of the Krewe, seems to stimulate previously inaccessible regions of the brain, carrying audience members away to cosmic realms.

DISCOGRAPHY

Michael Ray and the Cosmic Krewe (1994). This release suggests the full dimensions of the band's musical mission and reflects its (inter)stellar musical chops. "Discipline 27" and "Islands in

Space" offer noteworthy arrangements of Sun Ra's expansive free-form jazz (Ray incorporates Gregory Boyd's steel pans to interesting effect). "Champions," written with Kool and the Gang, is an explosive funk number livened by Ray's trumpet and Adam Klipple's keyboards. The band's capacious sound is also showcased in Ray's swinging "Charlie B's," the New Orleans celebration "Beans and Rice," and the rousing "Echoes of Boat People."

WEB SITE

www.satchmo.com/CosmicRay/

THE RECIPE

- ■ **TOM BATCHELOR:** *guitar, vocals*
- ■ **GREG LOWLEY:** *drums*
- ■ **TIM PAGE:** *bass*
- ■ **JOE PRITCHARD:** *vocals, guitar*
- ■ **MARK RAPSON:** *violin, fiddle*
- ■ **TOM WHELAN:** *percussion*
- ■ **KRISTEN WOLVERTON:** *vocals*

The Recipe is among the leading lights of the emerging Morgantown, West Virginia, music scene. The band defines its sound as "primal-acoustic roots rock," and its live shows demonstrate the force of this approach. Vocalist Kristen Wolverton comments, "Sometimes when I'm up there and the band's playing I'll just stop dancing and listen. They'll blow me away. These guys are huge." Vocalist/guitarist Joe Pritchard adds, "At our shows, people are usually up and dancing right away, and our goal is to keep them going till we're done." The Recipe accomplishes this through the collective talents of its seven members. The group's vocal harmonies stand out: Pritchard and Wolverton often swap lines while contributing to each other's lead. Classically trained violinist Mark Rapson's fiddle provides some pleasing embellishments. Pritchard adds that the drummers may be the Recipe's secret ingredient: "If you're not drawn in by Kristen or the vocal harmonies or the songs, then Tom and Greg, they're gonna get you."

The band balances its various skills and affinities in the concert setting. Pritchard describes the experience as "an amusement park ride, with plenty of peaks and valleys." Although the band emphasizes its individual songs, part of the group's appeal arises from its jams.

Says Pritchard: "We can break it down and let the bass roll. Then we'll just toss it around like a bluegrass band. Some of the best stuff occurs when Kristen starts scatting, just her and the drums." The Recipe's live shows are also popular for those moments when Wolverton cuts loose with a Jefferson Airplane cover or a Janis Joplin song such as "Piece of My Heart." In fact, fans have lately taken to chanting "Janis" during the band's set with the hope of goosing it down that path. Wolverton remarks: "Of course, I appreciate it, that's an honor. But, on the other hand, I don't just want to snitch somebody else's voice. I really love it when they start calling for Recipe tunes. That's the music that moves me." As the band extends its touring orbit, more and more fans will be moved to ask for the Recipe.

DISCOGRAPHY

Love Marble Hoe Down (1996). This disc is a solid representation of what the band can do. The opener, "In Season," displays both the group's vocal powers and Rapson's warm fiddle. "Aurora Borealis" is an appealing composition that chugs along, with a catchy chorus built on Wolverton's riffs. "Spill" provides a gentle, folky change of pace. "Out of the Rain/The Almanac" proves a showcase for the band's percussionists and hints at the power of the band's live show.

Night of the Porch People (1998)

WEB SITE

www.therecipe.net

REFRIED CONFUSION

- **JAY CAMPHIRE:** *piano and organ, lap steel guitar, vocals*
- **JOE DEBOTTIS:** *drums*
- **CARTER EVERETT:** *guitar, vocals*
- **RUSSELL GASPARD:** *guitar, mandolin, violin, saxophone, vocals*
- **STEVE KOWALCHUK:** *percussion*
- **RYAN WALSH:** *bass*

Central Florida's Refried Confusion produces music that lives up to its name. Percussionist Steve Kowalchuk declares: "It's a good description of what we're doing. At times there's a certain amount of confusion, with six people who actively want to contribute their own ideas. And we're cooking new stuff all the time as well." The band does not confine itself to a set list, preferring to let inspiration and the feel of a given improvisation guide it from song to song. Over the years, band members have developed a series of hand signals to help them keep the jams alive by varying keys and times. Says Kowalchuk: "We work really hard at it. We spend quite a bit of time on this aspect of our shows because it can be a fine line between chaos and something very, very cool."

Every member of Refried Confusion contributes musical ideas, and most offer songs as well; the sounds that ensue are a product of the players' proclivities and performance strengths. Guitarist Russell Gaspard has a college degree in classical guitar performance. Carter Everett holds a B.A. in jazz guitar from the University of North Carolina. Keyboardist Jay Camphire is a multi-instrumentalist who often performs on pedal steel. Drummers Kowalchuk and Joe DeBottis, who have been playing together since the group formed in 1992, work to present dynamic, entwined rhythms. Bassist Ryan Walsh, also a founding member of the band, alternately adds structure and adornment. Kowalchuk observes: "Some of our tunes certainly are based on classical themes. But, oftentimes, even within such a song, you'll hear a jazzy run. And if you listen to all of our stuff, you'll also find elements of folk, blues, rock, and ragtime."

While maintaining an extensive touring schedule, the band has hosted many memorable gatherings at its home in the woods of Apoka, Florida, which it has dubbed the Refried Ranch. Sometimes the group will invite several other performers to come over and jam, and the music will blast until two in the morning, at which point the undertaking will turn acoustic until ten the next day. The group's 1997 Halloween show at the ranch effectively demonstrated the band's appreciation of its fans, as well as its own adventurous spirit. Kowalchuk notes, "Sometimes to work through our chops we'll pick out an album and play it. Well, we came out for this show, and it was just pouring outside, and it had been dumping for a while. We talked about it, and we decided to give those people a treat. So we went out and played all of Frank Zappa's *Hot Rats* followed by all of Pink Floyd's *Animals*. Then we took a break and came back with a second set of our own stuff."

DISCOGRAPHY

Bean (1996). Here the band presents a varied set of offerings that reflects its musicianship. "Roll" is driven by Refried Confusion's twin guitarists and by Gaspard's growling vocals. "Abalone" is a more subdued expression with a bluesier feel. "Iguana" has some funky flavors. The instrumental "No Gritty Residue" bookends an extended jazzy interlude with some languid expressions. The disc closes with the textured "Diamonds and Jade."

WEB SITE

www.refriedconfusion.com

RUBBERNECK

- **MIKE BARBER:** *trumpet, vocals*
- **BRIAN FOXWORTH:** *drums, vocals*
- **JOHN MORROW:** *saxophone, flute*
- **PABLO OJEDA:** *bass, vocals*
- **RICARDO OJEDA:** *vocals, guitar*
- **JOEY PORTER:** *keyboards, vocals*

Rubberneck describes its music as "lunk." Portland, Oregon, resident Ricardo Ojeda, who formed the group with his brother Pablo in 1992, notes, "Our sound is a fusion of Latin and funk. When we play the Latin stuff, we try to kick it as hard as we can, and when we get funky, we do it with Latin rhythms." The Ojedas were immersed in both types of music while they were growing up. Born in Chile, they moved to the United States as kids and began to explore a full range of sounds. Ricardo Ojeda started his musical training very young, spending many years studying jazz guitar until he realized that he just didn't love it. He finally turned to the music that did move him when he and his brother created Rubberneck. Ricardo explains that the band's name "comes from the old Stax and Motown stuff where the bass players in the background are grooving their necks and biting their bottom lips because they're just kicking so hard."

The band has expanded and contracted over the years, embracing anywhere from four to eight players. It is currently a sextet. Says Ricardo: "These people are the right mix, the right vibe. They really love to jam, too, which is important. We're into the rhythms of everything. That's what makes funk funky and adds the Latin to Latin. It's those pulses that move people and keep the music alive." One of Rubberneck's supporters and a rhythmic force in his own right is Santana percussionist Raul Rekow. He took in the band's show one evening, enjoyed what he heard, and later joined Rubberneck in the studio to add congas to its disc *El Nino*. Rekow has since appeared with the group in concert, adding propulsive artistry to the "lunk."

214

DISCOGRAPHY

Nosotros (1995)

El Nino (1997). This release effectively presents the band's distinctive sound. The disc opens and closes with two thick funk offerings built on nimble guitar, elastic bass, strident horn arrangements, and a piano talkbox. "Diga Me" reflects the band's Latin influences, as does "Toda Pa Ti," both of which feature Rekow. Other notable tracks include the darker "Break You" and the powerful "Completely."

WEB SITE

www.rubberneck.com

RUGBY ROAD

- **KENNY KEARNS:** *vocals, keyboards, harmonica, percussion*
- **RICH PRUETT:** *drums, vocals*
- **DEREK SMITH:** *guitars, vocals*
- **BRUCE VUURENS:** *bass, vocals*

Pennsylvania's Villanova University was the point of origin for Rugby Road. At that institution, singer/keyboard player Kenny Kearns first met guitarist Derek Smith. The pair formed a band with starting points provided by an eclectic group of favored artists that included Brian Eno, Charles Mingus, Stevie Ray Vaughan, and members of the Allman Brothers Band. After rehearsing and arranging a number of Kearns's compositions and a handful of covers, the group snared its first gig. An oversight was revealed when the band finished a song and someone inquired as to the group's name. "What street are we playing on?" Kearns questioned. "Rugby Road," he was told. "Done," he responded, and the band has kept the moniker ever since.

The group's appealing original music often invites comparisons with that of Steely Dan. However, unlike that tour-shy outfit, Rugby Road is not chained to the studio — it thrives in the live setting, where it can transform its original compositions. Drummer Rich Pruett notes, "When we play live, any song can open up at any given moment — and most of them do." He adds that at present the quartet particularly venerates the artistry and improvisational skills of jazz musicians. "Recently," Bruce Vuurens elaborates, "our music has incorporated a rising number of jazz chords, but it's definitely not something that only jazz heads would like." This certainly rings true: some of the group's songs introduce funk riffs, and many of its improvisations have a blues flavor. In fact, it is this amalgamation of sounds that has led an increasing number of individuals to attend the group's shows armed with taping equipment.

DISCOGRAPHY

Times Already Happened (1996)

Different Degrees (1998). Tight, appealing takes on the songs that Rugby Road opens up in the live setting are primarily presented here. "Thatsfine" is the lone exception, beginning with some nimble funk, then progressing into a guitar-fueled jam animated by percussion. Other winning cuts include the lurching "Goodsign," which also offers some stalwart guest saxophone; the bluesy, slide-fed boogie "Austin"; and the melodious ballad "Outofmyway."

WEB SITE

www.rugbyroad.com

RUSTED ROOT

- **LIZ BERLIN:** *violin, percussion, vocals*
- **JOHN BUYNAK:** *guitar, percussion, flute, mandolin*
- **JIM DISPIRITO:** *percussion*
- **JIM DONOVAN:** *drums, vocals*
- **MICHAEL GLABICKI:** *vocals, guitar, mandolin*
- **PATRICK NORMAN:** *bass, percussion, vocals*

Perhaps the word that is most commonly used in association with Rusted Root is "tribal." This term describes the polyrhythms the band produces, which draw upon the drum-based traditions of other cultures. It also characterizes the vibe the band creates, which evokes those ritual performances from other parts of the world during which collective dancing blurs the boundary between performer and audience. Finally, the word is appropriate because many of the band's followers join it on tour, becoming part of a small nomadic society.

"Tribal," however, does not describe all aspects of the band's music. Its sound has many dimensions. Rusted Root often shifts both keys and time signatures within a given song. It also employs a passel of acoustic instruments to create its vibrant grooves, including flutes, finger cymbals, rattles, recorders, and violins. Michael Glabicki's vocals become a rhythm instrument as well – Glabicki emits an array of sounds, from yelps to coos. Liz Berlin works up her own vocal percussion, contributing scats to the mix. Furthermore, over the course of the group's two-and-a-half-hour shows, players will often exchange musical roles; John Buynak and Patrick Norman, in particular, move back and forth with facility.

The band originated in Pittsburgh in 1990. Two years earlier, guitarist Glabicki had decided to concentrate his efforts on songwriting. When he was finally satisfied with what he had written, he concluded that his compositions needed additional accompaniment. So, after hearing about a local battle of the bands, he pulled together a quartet with the help of high school acquaintance Berlin and her friend Jim Donovan. They rehearsed for two weeks and won the preliminary round. Before the finals, however, the original bassist dropped out, and Norman stepped in. The group placed fourth in the competition, but a collective commitment had been initiated. During the year that followed, the band fulfilled its pledge to practice together every day of the week – no exceptions made for holidays. Eventually, the group decided to expand its sound a bit further, adding Buynak and second vocalist Jenn Wertz (who remained with the group until the summer of 1995, when she left to form her own band, Lovechild). The Rusted Root lineup crystallized in 1993 when skilled hand-drummer Jim DiSpirito joined.

Exuberant percussive melodies have earned the group plaudits from both its fans and its musical peers. A number of notable bands have invited Rusted Root to perform with them, including the Allman Brothers Band, Page and Plant, and the Grateful Dead. A 1997 tour with Santana (on the heels of Rusted Root's recorded cover of "Evil Ways") saw the entire band emerge from the wings during the headliner's set; twelve musicians blended their talents during songs such as "Exodus" and "Get Up Stand Up." Over the past few years, as a result of the band's invigorating live shows and appealing compositions, the Rusted Root tribe has expanded to become more of a global village.

Cruel Sun (1992)

When I Woke (1994)

Remember (1996). On this disc of varied offerings, many cuts are propelled by the band's ubiquitous percussion. In both the kinetic "Sister Contine" and the twangy "Virtual Reality," Rusted Root builds on absorbing melodies. Glabicki's mandolin meshes well with his vocal expressions in the spiritual "Faith I Do Believe." Other notable songs include the meditative "River in a Cage" and the darker-toned "Voodoo."

WEB SITE

www.rustedroot.com

THE SAMPLES

- **KENNY JAMES:** *drums, vocals*
- **SEAN KELLY:** *vocals, guitar*
- **ALEX MATSON:** *keyboards*
- **ANDY SHELDON:** *bass, vocals*
- **ROB SOMERS:** *guitar, vocals*

The Samples debuted at a Boulder, Colorado, club named Tulagi's on Easter Sunday 1987. Childhood friends Sean Kelly and Andy Sheldon formed the band after moving west from their home state of Vermont. Placing a notice at the University of Colorado, they recruited drummer Jeep MacNichol and guitarist Charles Hobelton (Hobelton would remain with the group until 1991). Soon afterward, keyboardist Al Laughlin saw the band perform and persuaded its members to let him join. The group's name was derived from the fact that its members once subsisted on the free tidbits offered by the local King Soopers grocery store.

Quickly distinguishing itself on the strength of Kelly's soaring vocals, its mellifluous original compositions, and its urgent live shows, the band began to draw crowds eager to hear its radiant, often reggae-tinged music. By September of 1992, the Samples had developed a large enough following to headline a show at Red Rocks. The next summer, the group was a featured act on the first full-scale HORDE tour. It has continued to record and perform, appearing on *The Tonight Show* and at a special concert for President Clinton.

In the summer of 1997, the Samples introduced a new lineup after Laughlin and MacNichol parted from the group. Guitarist Rob Somers was already well known to many Samples devotees. A childhood friend of Kelly and Sheldon, Somers had appeared with them in their first group, the Last Straw, and had gigged with Kelly. Keyboardist Alex Matson was another Kelly tour veteran. Finally, the band welcomed Kenny James, a ubiquitous Boulder drumming force. The new outfit was immediately put to the test, playing a series of live dates. Most longtime fans agree that the current quintet has perpetuated the group's engrossing sound and vibe.

DISCOGRAPHY

The Samples (1989)

Underwater People (1991)

No Room (1992)

The Last Drag (1993)

Autopilot (1994)

Outpost (1996)

Transmissions from the Sea of Tranquillity (1997). This release provides an introduction to the new Samples. Recorded over two months in 1997, its two discs contain twenty-seven songs, most of which are concert performances. *Transmissions* includes a number of old favorites, including "Giants without Hearts," "The Last Drag," "Did You Ever Look So Nice," and "Feel Us Shakin'." Other stand-outs are a spare, poignant reading of "Indiana," a cover of John Lennon's "Watching the Whales," and the lush new offering "Sacred Stones." This collection is a fine starting point for new listeners, but its alternate arrangements, new tunes, and concert cuts should also appeal to established Samples fans.

Here and Somewhere Else (1998)

WEB SITE

www.war.com

SANTANA

- **RODNEY HOLMES:** *drums*
- **TONY LINDSAY:** *vocals*
- **KARL PERAZZO:** *percussion*
- **RAUL REKOW:** *percussion*
- **BENNY RIETVELD:** *bass*
- **CARLOS SANTANA:** *guitar*
- **CHESTER THOMPSON:** *keyboards*

Carlos Santana is one of today's most expressive performers. His percussion-rich band produces elevating spiritual music that pulls together the sounds of many cultures. This ensemble energizes audiences through Santana's guitar artistry and its players' collective capacity for ebullient, engrossing improvisation.

The guitarist spent his preteen years in Mexico. Music permeated his home life: his father, Jose, was a mariachi violinist; his grandfather had been a mariachi player as well. In 1955, when the Santana family moved from the small town of Autlán to the city of Tijuana, Carlos was exposed to some of the music that would remain with him forever: the blues of T-Bone Walker, John Lee Hooker, and B.B. King. He swiftly moved away from the violin, which he had been learning, and started playing guitar. In 1960, at his mother's urging, the family relocated to the United States, finally settling in San Francisco. By 1966, the guitarist had started gigging in the Bay Area with a septet, the Santana Blues Band, interpreting traditional blues songs but infusing many of them with Latin rhythms and his own distinctive phrasings. One early champion of this music was promoter Bill Graham, who, in 1969, agreed to help the organizers of the Woodstock Music and Art Fair on the condition that the band be invited to perform. It was at this festival that Santana serenaded the nation for the first time.

The band has remained a vital force for years due to the contributions of many gifted players. Raul Rekow first joined Santana on congas in 1976, and he continues to contribute percussion; he has also performed recently with Rubberneck. Karl Perazzo has played timbales with a range of other players, including Tito Puente and Dizzy Gillespie; in the fall of 1996, he added flair to a number of Phish shows. Bass player Benny Rietveld, who grew up in the Netherlands and later studied music in Hawaii, has also toured with Miles Davis. Keyboardist Chester Thompson enjoyed a long stint with Tower of Power before joining Santana in 1983. Tony Lindsay has been enriching the Santana mix with his tenor vocals since 1991. Finally, although he does not take vocal turns, Carlos Santana unquestionably sings with his guitar. He has often said that he does not actually play the instrument — rather, he transmits its sounds, he channels a musical spirit that resides elsewhere. Many listeners would agree. Santana and his band are clearly tapping into some animating force that transforms their shows into vibrant, cleansing experiences.

SELECTED DISCOGRAPHY

Santana (1969)

Abraxas (1970)

Santana III (1971)

Caravanserai (1972)

Lotus (1974)

Amigos (1976)

Zebop! (1981)

Freedom (1987)

Spirits Dancing in the Flesh (1990)

Sacred Fire (1993)

Milagro (1992)

Dance of the Rainbow Serpent (1995). This three-disc set serves up the essential Santana. Its package is enhanced with a vivid sixty-page booklet that provides insight into many of the songs through the artist's own words.

Live at the Fillmore (1997). This two-CD recording documents the band performing a 1968 concert at the Fillmore West prior to Santana's coming-out party at Woodstock. The performance is raw yet animated and suffused with energy. There are tantalizing, revealing takes on the group's early staples here, including "Soul Sacrifice" and "Jingo." Other intriguing offerings that have not heretofore made it onto disc are "Chunk a Funk" and "Fried Neckbones."

The Best of Santana (1998)

WEB SITE

www.santana.com

MERL SAUNDERS AND THE RAINFOREST BAND

- ■ **MICHAEL HINTON:** *guitar*
- ■ **VINCE LITTLETON:** *drums, percussion*
- ■ **MARIANA ROSMIS:** *Vocals*
- ■ **MERL SAUNDERS:** *piano, synthesizers, vocals*
- ■ **MICHAEL WARREN:** *bass*

Merl Saunders is an enduring musical force. He began his professional music career in the 1950s, performing both jazz and pop piano with such figures as Miles Davis and Johnny Mathis (one of Mathis's first gigs was as a vocalist in Saunders's band). Then the keyboardist began playing the blues with such notables as B.B. King and Michael Bloomfield. This, in turn, led him to some associations in rock circles: he started to work with a whole new set of musicians, including members of the Grateful Dead. In the 1980s, Saunders divided his time between gigs with the Dinosaurs (a band that included Peter Albin, John Cippolina, Spencer Dryden, and Barry Melton) and scoring duties for television programs such as *The Twilight Zone* and *Tales from the Crypt*. These days, Saunders records and tours with his current outfit, the Rainforest Band, while guesting with other acts, among them Phish and Blues Traveler.

Saunders may be best known for his collaborations with Jerry Garcia. The Grateful Dead guitarist appears on Saunders's *Heavy Turbulence* and *Fire Up*, and the two musicians were given joint billing for their *Live at the Keystone* performance. This fruitful union was revitalized with *Blues from the Rainforest*: in 1989, Saunders called on Garcia to help him re-create the natural sounds of the rainforest and to interpret the expressions of trees mourning the destruction of this environment. The resulting mélange of guitar and synthesizer (embellished by the likes of such diverse and established artists as Buddy Rich and Mickey Hart) was widely hailed for its creativity and passion.

Saunders's live shows draw on his various associations. While on tour with the Rainforest Band, he will often move from the rhythm-and-blues "Hi Heel Sneakers" to a Grateful Dead cover such as "Sugaree" and then work through a few of his own compositions. Jessica, his trusty 1962 Hammond B-3 organ, resounds throughout the evening. Saunders has long stated that one of his aims is to elevate people through music. With the animated performances of the Rainforest Band, he goes a long way toward realizing this goal.

SELECTED DISCOGRAPHY

Heavy Turbulence (1972)

Live at the Keystone (1973)

Fire Up (1974)

Blues from the Rainforest (1990)

Save the Planet So We'll Have Some Place to Boogie (1991)

It's in the Air (1993)

Still Having Fun (1996)

Fiesta Amazonica (1997). This is Saunders's follow-up to *Blues from the Rainforest*. As with that release, he assembles an all-star cast to produce a lush environment of sound and mood with a New Age feel. This time, his efforts have more of a world-beat flavor, as evinced by the Latin-tinged opener, "Forest Dance," which is sung by Mariana Rosmis. The title track fulfills its appellation with fervent percussion and joyous fills by Saunders and guest guitarist Steve Kimock. Saunders takes over lead vocals for "Child's Play," an entrancing song that bears a message of hope. He also pays tribute to his departed friend Garcia with the plaintive instrumental "Nostalgia for Jerome." The release concludes with "The Ayahuasca Zone," one final collaboration with the Grateful Dead guitarist in which Saunders and Vince Welnick layer keyboard effects over some spacey tracks that Garcia, Bob Weir, and Bill Kreutzman had contributed to a Saunders *Twilight Zone* score.

WEB SITE

www.merlsaunders.com

SCHLEIGHO

- **SUKE CERULO:** *guitar, flute, vocals*
- **ERIK EGOL:** *drums*
- **JESSE GIBBON:** *organ and Rhodes, vocals*
- **DREW MCCABE:** *bass, vocals*

Schleigho describes its sounds as "music for the minded." Drummer Erik Egol explains: "Our music appeals to the adventurous. It doesn't really fit into any genre, and it's pretty in your face, pretty up front. You don't see people tapping their feet, but there's a number of them throwing themselves around quite a bit." The band performs songs with atypical time signatures that draw on a number of styles, including samba, funk, and fusion. Schleigho is often hailed for its explosive extemporizations, many of which build from ethereal passages. Notes Egol, "One of us will jump off a musical cliff, and everyone will follow instantaneously until things run their course. Sometimes that takes five minutes; sometimes that takes a half-hour."

The band originated in Westchester County, New York, in the late 1980s. Egol and bassist Drew McCabe met when they were playing together in a youth symphony. The pair formed a band with keyboard player Jesse Gibbon, but the project fell apart when all three went off to college. However, in 1993, Egol, who was studying at the Berklee School of Music, urged his former bandmates to join him in Boston. They heeded the call, and, after they had drafted guitarist Suke Cerulo, Schleigho was born. However, due to the intensity and perfectionism of these players, the group practiced for a year, writing an entire set worth of material before seeking its first gig. That commitment has since been translated into more than two hundred shows a year.

Schleigho's live shows build on the imagination of its players to yield atmospheric composed passages, furious impromptu jams, and vice versa. Within the span of a few measures, the band may move from phrasings that recall John McLaughlin to others that echo Carlos Santana to still more that hint at Frank Zappa. The results are challenging, but they often prove inspiring to the initiated. Says Egol: "We're on the road so often that we only have a chance to write a new tune or two per month. As a result, we're always trying to do things with the songs we have. Some people call it demented, but it's a good kind of demented."

DISCOGRAPHY

Schleigho (1995)

Farewell to the Sun (1997). Collected here are seven songs that span nearly seventy minutes – three studio tracks and four live cuts. Both categories are marked by elaborate arrangements and torrid improvisations that often veer off into new planes without warning. Notable cuts include the throbbing title track, the combustive "D-Funk," the rippling instrumental "Trash Compactor Phobia," and "50% of the Battle," which closes with some hip-hop touches – in particular, an extended *Star Wars* rap.

In the Interest of Time (1998)

WEB SITE

www.schleigho.com

SCREAMIN' CHEETAH WHEELIES

- **STEVE BURGESS:** *bass*
- **MICHAEL FARRIS:** *vocals, harmonica, guitar*
- **TERRY THOMAS:** *drums and percussion*
- **BOB WATKINS:** *guitar*
- **RICK WHITE:** *guitar*

The Screamin' Cheetah Wheelies formed in Nashville in early 1991. Several of its founding members belonged to other bands but were inspired to put together this project as a creative outlet. The band's first session yielded not only some invigorating jams but also a few original songs, including "Shaking the Blues," which would later become a signature tune. The five players swiftly committed themselves to the project, bucking musical trends in the country capital.

Although the musical side of things came together fairly quickly for the quintet, the players found themselves unable to select a suitable moniker. Sizzle Donkeys and Big Pickle in a Jar were on the table for a while, yet neither stuck. Finally, the band found its appellation in a *Far Side* cartoon. The image, dubbed "Cheetah Wheelies," presented a number of the speedy cats racing in the flats and popping onto their hind legs. "Screamin'" was then added – an evocation of Michael Farris's vocals as well as the band's guitars.

Screamin' Cheetah Wheelies references a few genres and styles in crafting its energized sound. Farris explains that the band's influences include James Brown, Mahalia Jackson, Al Green, acid jazz, and Mississippi Delta blues. All of these are translated through the band members' individual proficiencies. Farris's raspy voice is up front, complementing the strident dual guitars of Rick White and Bob Watkins. Bass player Steve Burgess and drummer Terry Thomas undergird the band's variegated offerings. The group earned itself a plum spot on the 1994 HORDE tour, and the Screamin' Cheetah Wheelies continues to barnstorm the nation, drawing from its cauldron of southern swamp soul.

DISCOGRAPHY

Screamin' Cheetah Wheelies (1993)

Magnolia (1996). This release presents a number of solid offerings. "Backwoods Travelin'" is absorbing roots rock rife with tremoloed guitars and harmonica. "Gypsy Lullaby" features Farris's kinetic vocals and some stinging slide. "I Found Love" tantalizes with a taste of funk and bluesy guitar runs. "You Are" is an intriguing change of pace, an amalgam of soul and jazz influences.

WEB SITE

www.wheelies.com

SISTER HAZEL

- **JEFF BERES:** *bass, vocals*
- **KEN BLOCK:** *vocals, acoustic guitar*
- **ANDREW COPELAND:** *vocals, acoustic guitar*
- **RYAN NEWELL:** *electric and acoustic guitar, vocals*
- **MARK TROJANOWSKI:** *drums*

Sister Hazel is named after a woman who ran a rescue mission in Gainesville, Florida, in the 1970s and 1980s. When the band came together, founding member Ken Block recalled the television commercials for Sister Hazel's safe haven he'd seen while growing up. He decided that this woman's name would reflect the kind of human compassion he hoped the fledgling band could express. Block has long been committed to humanitarian causes, and he holds a master's degree in counseling psychology. The name choice was apt: throughout its career, the band has raised funds and made its own donations to a number of charitable organizations, including Big Brothers and Big Sisters of America and the American Cancer Society.

Of course, Sister Hazel also makes music, and has been since 1991, when Block and Andrew Copeland met before a college football game and began strumming their guitars. Their first official performance was at the wedding of Copeland's sister Diane, and soon afterward the pair began gigging around northern Florida. In 1993, they drafted bass player Jeff Beres to enrich their sound. A year later, the lineup was completed with the arrival of electric guitarist Ryan Newell and drummer Mark Trojanowski. Sister Hazel soon committed itself to the road, touring the length of the East Coast. The plaudits it received earned the band a tour spot with the Allman Brothers Band.

The group's music displays a range of textures. Some songs are enlivened by acoustic exchanges between Block and Copeland. Many more are marked by Newell's stinging slide counterpoints. Still others are embellished by four-part vocal harmonies. This blend of elements, particularly within the context of the band's charged live show, is attracting new listeners to the ranks of the Hazel nuts.

DISCOGRAPHY

Sister Hazel (1995)

Somewhere More Familiar (1997). Sister Hazel's melodious repertoire is well represented on this release. "Just Remember" opens things with some sassy bottleneck guitar that is well complemented by acoustic strumming. "All about You" features rich vocal harmonies that support an appealing melody. "Wanted It to Be" engages the listener with clear, vibrant guitar tones. The disc closes with the quirky, catchy sing-along "Starfish."

WEB SITE

www.sisterhazel.com

SISTER 7

- **DARRELL PHILLIPS:** *bass, vocals*
- **SEAN PHILLIPS:** *drums*
- **PATRICE PIKE:** *vocals, guitar, percussion*
- **WAYNE SUTTON:** *guitar, vocals*

Sister 7 has been forced to jam from the outset of its career. Its four players originally came together during a fortuitous 1991 open session at Dallas's Club Dada. After solidifying their commitment during some area shows, they moved south to Austin. There Sister 7 played the Black Cat Lounge, a club that required its headlining acts to perform for a minimum of three hours. The group ultimately thrived in this atmosphere, all the while honing its improvisational skills. Sister 7 later took these lessons to the road, where it now performs over 250 gigs a year.

Energetic live shows remain the band's hallmark. These days, the quartet presents both open-ended songs and more concise numbers. Guitarist Wayne Sutton contributes varied expressions, at times supplying a steady funk beat like a rhythm guitarist and at other times digging in and tearing it up. The band's extensive live experience allows the Phillips tandem – bass player Darrell and drummer Sean – to lock behind a groove or to create one of their own. Patrice Pike supplies captivating sounds with vocals and percussion.

The group's aggressive touring schedule and vigorous live performances won it a national following – under its original name, Little Sister. After five years of playing and recording under that moniker – within that span, it released two discs and made some high-profile HORDE appearances at the invitation of Dave Matthews and John Popper – the band decided to rename itself because on the road it would occasionally run into another group with the appellation Little Sister. The quartet elected to keep Sister and add Pike's lucky number, seven. As it turned out, the impulse to change demonstrated a certain synchronicity: a search subsequently revealed that six other bands had used the name Little Sister – what is now Sister 7 had been the seventh.

DISCOGRAPHY

Free Love and Nickel Beer (1994)

Little Sister/Sister 7 (1995)

This the Trip (1997). Producer Danny Kortchmar worked with the band to distill its live power into a more compressed format. Tunes such as "Say Good-Bye," "Bottle Rocket," and "Shelter" effectively accomplish this goal. The title track slinks along, then gives way to some crunching guitar and complementary intonations from Pike. Psychedelic flavorings spice "Shelter," while "Under the Sun" is an inviting, funky shuffle.

WEB SITE

www.sister7.com

SKIN

- **MAYA DORN:** *vocals, guitar*
- **EDWIN HURWITZ:** *bass*
- **STACEY LUDLOW:** *percussion, vocals*
- **DAVE WATTS:** *drums and percussion*

Skin's music may not altogether defy description, but it certainly precludes succinct characterization. Vocalist and principal songwriter Maya Dorn began her performing career as a folksinger. As a result, along with her gift for melody she possesses a knack for storytelling. Percussionist Stacey Ludlow is proficient on a range of percussion instruments, from congas to driftwood to rebar. Bassist Edwin Hurwitz and drummer Dave Watts first played together in 1989 as members of the funk-laced group Shockra. The band's music also incorporates odd time signatures, jazzy vocal stylings and scats, along with a strong element of improvisation.

The Boulder, Colorado, quartet came together in late 1994 after Dorn had encountered Watts through the city's supportive musical cooperative. The pair recognized the possibilities inherent in a collaboration, and soon invited Ludlow to join them. In the summer of 1995, Hurwitz relocated from Massachusetts and completed the Skin lineup. The band was soon earning plaudits from area performers as well as a rising swell of listeners. Hurwitz heaps particular praise upon Dorn: "Maya is more or less self-taught. She hasn't worried about fulfilling any traditional expectations as a performer or songwriter." The latter part of this description certainly applies to the band as well, which draws from folk, funk, jazz, and global groove without inhabiting any of those realms. Adds Hurwitz: "The other night, we played before a group of people, and some of them seemed kind of bothered by what we do. They couldn't deal with any music that didn't lend itself to instantaneous recognition. We appeal to people with open minds.

People who come out and see us have the opportunity to experience dancing in their bodies in many different ways."

DISCOGRAPHY

Don't Buy the Man Another Drink (1997). This is less a series of songs than an atmosphere of sound and story. Dorn's vocals are subdued as she delivers a number of verbose accounts while the band pulses behind her. Each of the players contributes to the sonic environment – Hurwitz furnishes funk-inflected digressions, Watts makes fluid statements, and Ludlow contributes on percussion. The opener, "History," fuses all of these efforts as Dorn relates the story of a father who is bruised and distanced from his family. Her poetic expressions in "Corner of Iris" are supported by a keening saxophone that trails in and out. The message of poverty contained in "Trucks and Ducks" is juxtaposed with Watts's marimba. "The Deep That Covers the Earth" is an effects-laden instrumental bass collaboration between Hurwitz and guest Stacey Starkweather.

WEB SITE

www.indra.com/~edwin/skin.html

THE SLIP

- ■ **ANDREW BARR:** *drums, percussion*
- ■ **BRAD BARR:** *guitar, keyboards, vocals*
- ■ **MARC FRIEDMAN:** *bass*

Over the past few years, the music of the Slip has galvanized listeners throughout New England. The trio references a variety of musical traditions to create its signature sound. Brad Barr's guitar moves from nimble jazz expressions to heavier blues declarations. Younger brother Andrew's drumming manifests his affection for African poly-rhythms; the group is often joined on stage by members of Abdoul Doumbia's percussion ensemble. Marc Friedman's bass contributions testify to his grounding in 1970s funk and his passion for the music of jazz masters Bill Evans, Rahsaan Roland Kirk, and Thelonious Monk. Additionally, although many of the Slip's compositions are instrumentals, some are elevated by Brad Barr's soulful vocals. All of these individual predilections and proficiencies are utilized in the course of the Slip's resourceful extemporizations. Friedman notes, "One of the thrills in playing in this band, and I would imagine one of the thrills in seeing us play live, is watching us create. We're up there constructing new segments and defining new spaces."

The Slip's music can be deceptive. At times, it burbles forward as the three musicians lay down a simple groove. Then an individual player may interject his own commentary, carrying the improvisation outward while continuing to reference the original phrase. Although such initiatives require heightened listening skills and acute concentration if the jams are to maintain focus, the results are often compelling. Friedman affirms, "We're getting bigger ears every time we play together." He also heaps particular praise upon drummer Andrew Barr: "He's doing things that people don't recognize. He's working with time signatures that are unfamiliar to those who normally listen to 4/4 music, but he does it so effortlessly that it becomes totally enjoyable to anyone."

Some have described the Slip's music as baited with "subliminal hooks." These hooks seem to be working: the band is blessed with a passionate fan base. Buses filled with supporters have accompanied the band from Boston to the Wetlands in New York and even out to Colorado. The group has responded generously: at its 1997 New Year's Eve extravaganza, the Slip performed for seven and a half hours.

DISCOGRAPHY

From the Gecko (1997). Although this is a studio effort, the band's exploratory nature is not hampered. There are a number of improvisations here, and the Slip plays out its ideas to their conclusions. Several guest saxophonists also enrich the musical texture. Like the lizard of the disc's title, many of the instrumentals scamper along, propelled by Andrew Barr's elegant drumming. Friedman's understated bass moors these songs, creating room for Brad Barr's guitar phrasings. Meanwhile, Brad Barr's robust vocals invigorate tunes such as "The Weight of Solomon" and the sublime "Eube."

WEB SITE

www.theslip.com

SLIPKNOT

- **JOHN BRIGHAM:** *bass, vocals*
- **GREG DEGUGLIELMO:** *drums and percussion*
- **JEREMY ESPOSITO:** *drums and percussion*
- **LARRY MANCINI:** *guitar, vocals*
- **BRUCE MANDARO:** *guitar, vocals*
- **MARK MUNZER:** *keyboards, vocals*

Slipknot's debut release, *Slip into Somewhere*, was nearly twenty years in the making. In the late 1970s, guitarist Bruce Mandaro was inspired by the Grateful Dead to assemble a group named after the Jerry Garcia-penned instrumental that bridges "Help on the Way" and "Franklin's Tower." This Boston-based band was initially devoted to interpreting the sounds of the Grateful Dead. Over the years, however, Slipknot has expanded its repertoire, introducing a series of original compositions that contain some stylistic similarities to the music of the Bay Area icons while forging an individual identity.

Slipknot's particular prowess lies in crafting inventive, involved improvisations; it doesn't mimic any other group but works to create dense, diverse jams that are unique to any given performance. Together, guitarists Mandaro and Larry Mancini carry the band into novel musical territories. Bassist John Brigham, who has been with the group since 1983, is a versatile player who is often the beacon that guides the rest of the band home from its elaborate journeys. Mark Munzer, a member since 1990, adds resonant, plangent keyboards. The band's two drummers, Greg DeGuglielmo and Jeremy Esposito, were both trained at the Berklee School of Music and possess a gift for group improvisation; they have previously performed with, among others, Max Creek and Jiggle the Handle. Slipknot tours throughout the northeast and offers Boston-area fans biannual musical events appropriately titled Slip into Summer and Slip out of Summer.

DISCOGRAPHY

Slip into Somewhere (1997). The group's debut features several pleasing compositions. "Clear the Sky" is the bright opener. "Better Back Off" is animated by Munzer's keyboards. "The Clouds Are Spinning" displays pedal steel flourishes of guest Buddy Cage. "Let's Go" closes the release with some lively Garcia-flavored guitar accents.

WEB SITE

www.knotbuzz.com

SMOKIN' GRASS

- **ADAM FREHM:** *dobro, vocals*
- **JASON KOORNICK:** *mandolin, vocals*
- **DOUG PERKINS:** *guitar, vocals*
- **MICHAEL SANTOSUSSO:** *bass, vocals*
- **KINGSLEY TURNER:** *drums*

Smokin' Grass has described itself as a "freak-out bluegrass dance band." This phrase certainly hints at the band's essence, but it doesn't fully characterize the group. The quintet's music situates it within the tradition of bands – such as New Grass Revival – that have stretched the limits of the genre (NGR's alumni include Sam Bush and Bela Fleck). The band's repertoire includes original songs, traditional bluegrass tunes, and a list of covers such as "Octopus' Garden," "It Takes a Lot to Laugh, It Takes a Train to Cry," and "Caravan." All the while, Smokin' Grass prides itself on its ability to keep its listeners' limbs in motion.

The group formed in Burlington, Vermont, in 1994, performing biweekly gigs at local venues. Over time, as its artistry and interplay evolved (along with its personnel), Smokin' Grass began gigging throughout the northeast, and it has recently begun making southern forays. The band appeals to many listeners through the three- and four-part vocal harmonies that enliven many of its songs. Jason Koornick's vibrant mandolin is often up front along with Perkins's guitar expressions. Adam Frehm furnishes bluesy dobro intonations, and Michael Santosusso drives the engine on electric bass. The resulting spirited picking and lively tempos elicit enthusiastic audience responses (and plenty of dancing).

DISCOGRAPHY

Take Yer Pick (1998). The band balances instrumentals and vocalized songs on this release. "Opus #1" has a bright bluegrass feel. The title track is a lively instrumental with Jason Crosby guesting on fiddle. "Some Funky Grass" fulfills its promise with Perkins's electric guitar and guest David Cast's alto saxophone. "Jillian" is a gentle, lilting composition. The group also presents its interpretations of Duke Ellington's "Caravan" and Bob Dylan's "It Takes a Lot to Laugh, It Takes a Train to Cry."

WEB SITE

www.together.net/~koornick

SOUP

■ **LEE ADKINS:** *bass, vocals*
■ **BRAM BESSOFF:** *drums and percussion*
■ **KEVIN CROW:** *guitar, vocals*
■ **ANDREW MARGOLIUS:** *accordion, harmonica, vocals*
■ **ERIK ROWEN:** *vocals, guitar*

Atlanta's Soup crafts its compositions with a thoughtful, playful attitude and presents its music guided by the same spirit. Its debut album, *Laughing at Fables*, contains a number of sound effects that are thematically linked, as well as cover art that incorporates elements from each of the songs (some of which are more abstract and obscure than others). Soup's second release, *Breakdown*, includes a sixteen-page booklet that links many of the songs. The band is also known for its theme shows that typically revolve around one of its tunes. For instance, one concert focused on the group's composition "Professor Plumb's Last Dance," which riffs on the board game Clue. During this show, band members dressed up as Clue characters; every concertgoer was handed an envelope with three Clue cards, and those who held the winning combination won prizes. Clearly, Soup goes to great lengths to enhance its fans' engagement with its music.

However, these efforts would be far less significant if the band members were not such adroit songwriters and performers. Soup's music is animated by smooth vocals, solid musicianship, catchy melodies, and lyrics that often evoke quirky themes. The group, which came together when vocalist/guitarist Erik Rowen and drummer Bram Bessoff moved to the South from New York in 1995, mainly performs with acoustic instrumentation. Kevin Crow equips his acoustic guitar with a number of effects. Additionally, in lieu of keyboards, the band has chosen to use an accordion, played by Andrew Margolius. Soup thrives on the jam and endeavors to introduce some novel extemporized textures into every performance. This philosophy carries over into other phases of its live show. Says Rowen: "We never play the same set twice. All of our set lists are ad-libbed, and we feed off the audience in deciding which way to go."

DISCOGRAPHY

Laughing at Fables (1996)

Breakdown (1998). This disc, which is loosely unified on a thematic level around the breakdown of the band's van, collects a number of vivid, appealing compositions, many of which are flat-out funny as well. For instance, the hooky "Jefferson" is an entertaining sing-along account of the nation's third president. "Leisure Suit" is a funky offering that pays homage to the sounds of the 1970s. Other fine moments include "Sovereign State," with its accordion accents and falsettos, the spirited break in "Marvin Wright," and the lively "Sally's Sister," which contains engaging vocal riffs and harmonies.

WEB SITE

www.soupkitchen.com

SOURWOOD HONEY

- **CHRIS CONNER:** *vocals, acoustic guitar*
- **RYAN GOFORTH:** *vocals, acoustic guitar*
- **CALE HERNANDEZ:** *drums and percussion*
- **BOB HYLTON:** *bass*
- **JESSIE JEFFCOAT:** *electric guitar*

Sourwood Honey is not altogether comfortable with the notoriety it has gained for its expansive jams. The band freely admits that, particularly in its formative years, it would often embark on twenty-minute journeys in the tradition of the Allman Brothers Band. Ultimately, however, band members began to think that such excursions detracted from the songs that they had so carefully crafted. So recently Sourwood Honey has scaled back these efforts, and now every tune does not automatically become the basis for a free-form improvisation. Nonetheless, the band retains the ability and the inclination to tear it up once in a while in the southern-fried tradition.

The Lexington, South Carolina, quintet began as an acoustic duo featuring Chris Conner and Ryan Goforth. The pair honed their skills as a songwriting team, strumming their guitars and creating vocal harmonies. In 1993, they drew together some electric players to form Sourwood Honey. Jessie Jeffcoat's vigorous turns on guitar proved particularly tantalizing. Bob Hylton's supple bass and Cale Hernandez's crackling drums completed the group. Due primarily to Conner and Goforth's melodious, contemplative compositions, Sourwood Honey has been compared with a range of country-influenced performers from Gram Parsons to Son Volt. Still, the band's live shows manifest a southern flair for improvisation.

DISCOGRAPHY

Big Neon Hounddog (1996)

Oxydendrum Arboretum (1998). The band's song craft comes through clearly on this disc, which is fortified by some strong musical arrangements. The opener, "Follow Me Down," is an engaging, introspective composition enriched by Jeffcoat's piquant guitar. "Part II" is a breezy slice of Americana with a Nashville feel. Two additional, intriguing, seemingly mistitled songs are the countrified "Blues for You" and the electric romp "Folk Song." *Oxydendrum Arboretum* also offers an invigorating cover of Country Joe McDonald's "Save the Whales."

WEB SITE

www.sourwoodhoney.com

STIR FRIED

- ■ **BUDDY CAGE:** *pedal steel guitar*
- ■ **JAMES ALVIN HARRISON:** *bass*
- ■ **CHRIS LACINAK:** *drums*
- ■ **JOANNE LEDIGER:** *vocals*
- ■ **JAN LONDON:** *guitar, percussion*
- ■ **VIN LORENZO:** *percussion*
- ■ **JOHN MARKOWSKI:** *vocals, guitar, percussion*

New Jersey's Stir Fried embraces the sound and spirit of the 1960s and early 1970s, seeking to translate it for audiences of the 1990s. The band pursues this legacy in part because founding member John Markowski's father, Thomas Jefferson Kaye, was a songwriter and producer who performed with a number of that era's leading lights, including Jerry Garcia. Another reason is that Stir Fried's roster includes New Riders of the Purple Sage veteran and pedal steel magician Buddy Cage. Finally, the band has maintained a working relationship with fiddle player Vassar Clements, who is best known in some circles for his work with Garcia, David Grisman, and Peter Rowan in Old and in the Way. Given all of this, it's not surprising to hear Markowski sing, in his spirited composition "Love and Peace," that he would like to return to 1969.

Stir Fried, however, is by no means solely a retro outfit. This ever-expanding septet creates a collage of grooves that builds on Markowski's original compositions (along with some favorites from his father's catalog). The group blends gospel, funk, blues, soul, and bluegrass and elevates it all through improvisation. Cage remarks, "I've known Vassar since the Old and in the Way days. So the first time he comes out with the band, he sidles up to me and asks, 'What keys? What are the chord changes?' I laughed and told him, 'It's better you don't know." It's that spirit that keeps things interesting. And let me tell you, Stir Fried is real interesting."

The group, which formed in 1993, embraces a number of talented complementary players. Joanne Lediger's well-controlled vocals animate many songs and provide a warm counterpoint to Markowski's rough-hewn baritone. Guitarist Jan London supplies subdued phrasings and picks up a bottleneck for some biting leads. Stir Fried's feisty rhythm section pushes the music forward. Cage deftly paints between the lines (and out of the lines as well, when the spirit moves him). On occasion, the group will add horns to intensify the bluster. All in all, Cage notes, "I serve the music, and so do they. That's the ultimate test for me. And when I'm playing with this band, we're all serving the music. That's what makes my endorphins go off."

DISCOGRAPHY

Stir Fried (1997). This, the band's debut, demonstrates its facility with a series of styles. "I Know There's Someone Else" features burbling guitar and mighty horns. "Hoe-Bus" has a swampier feel and some gospel flavors. Lediger cuts loose on "Beaten Path 2," which also presents guest Derek Trucks on slide. Finally, following the well-named "Bug Jam," the release closes with the hypnotic aural odyssey "Collection Box."

WEB SITE

www.stirfried.com

GORDON STONE TRIO

- ■ **ANDY COTTON:** *bass*
- ■ **JOSH STACY:** *guitar*
- ■ **GORDON STONE:** *banjo, pedal steel*

Gordon Stone has long been a fixture in northeastern picking circles. For a number of years in the late 1980s and early 1990s, the banjo player performed as part of the Burlington, Vermont, bluegrass band

Breakaway. In 1994, he decided to branch out, to find new sounds that moved him. So he enlisted area mandolin player Jamie Masefield and bassist Stacey Starkweather, who at that time were also performing together in the Jazz Mandolin Project, to join him in a trio. Their aim was to present instrumental acoustic music that bridged boundaries, incorporating aspects of bluegrass, jazz, Latin, and funk. Furthermore, given the propensities of these musicians, improvisation also became an integral component of the trio's live performances.

The Gordon Stone Trio soon made a name for itself with the novel, nifty textures it created. It received a flurry of gig offers. However, due to Masefield's and Starkweather's other touring commitments, Stone was forced to refashion the lineup. These days, guitarist Josh Stacy adds his own accents to the group, particularly an affinity for the blues. Bass player Andy Cotton supplies phrasings that often reflect the jazz and funk he has performed with Michael Ray and the Cosmic Krewe. Although Stone's outfit continues to perform as an acoustic trio, it also invites drummers to participate in some of its performances, among them Gabe Jarrett and Jon Fishman (who is simply returning the favor, as Stone has appeared on stage with Phish and performed on *Picture of Nectar* and *Rift*). Audiences continue to be enthralled with the group's expansive musical vocabulary, songwriting proficiency, and inventive jamming.

DISCOGRAPHY

Scratchin' the Surface (1981)

Touch and Go (1995). Stone appears with a variety of players on this release, which features drums and horns on a number of tracks. The bright opener, "South Wind," demonstrates Stone's gift for melody and is infused with complementary brass. "Monkey Wrench" resembles a New Orleans-flavored bluegrass number. The title track is a lusher offering that extends over thirteen minutes. Two of Stone's friends contribute compositions and appear on this release: Mike Gordon joins him for a duet on the abstract "Fraction," and Masefield plays on his "Ballad for Gordon."

Even with the Odds (1998)

WEB SITE

www.gordonstone.com

STRANGEFOLK

- ■ **REID GENAUER:** *vocals, guitar*
- ■ **ERIK GLOCKLER:** *bass, vocals*
- ■ **LUKE SMITH:** *drums and percussion*
- ■ **JON TRAFTON:** *guitar, vocals, mandolin*

Strangefolk is a grassroots musical success story. These denizens of the Green Mountain State (Burlington, to be precise) have crossed the nation selling out venues and continue to generate a popular buzz based on enthusiastic word of mouth from people who have seen their live performances. The band's supporters have come to recognize that Strangefolk is committed to its music and to its ideals. The band joins its audiences each evening for some collective revelry.

The group was established in the fall of 1991 when University of Vermont students Reid Genauer and Jon Trafton, who had met through mutual friends, began to perform as an acoustic duo. By the following summer, the pair had resolved to expand their sound. They recruited fellow University of Vermont student Luke Smith to play drums and Trafton's hometown friend Erik Glockler to perform on bass. Trafton suggested the band's name, which he had culled from Jack London's novel *White Fang*. The word *strangefolk* also suggests the twin elements of the band: its folk roots and its corresponding penchant for exploring new spaces and territories.

Strangefolk's live shows manifest both the band's surging music and its affinity for collective, creative exploration. The group's set lists are designed to shift keys, vocal emphasis, tempo, and intent. Audience reaction will frequently fuel the band's efforts. Genauer notes, "For me, when I'm in an audience, half of what I feed off is the people around me and their reaction to the music, and it's the same for us when we're on stage. Seeing a crowd digging what we're putting out there gives us something to digest. It's a mutual feeding frenzy. So much of being in a traveling band is a gray wash on the road. What keeps us going is that interplay and the sense that our efforts are bearing fruit."

The band's compositions and performances also yield a collective ethos. Although some of its lyrics focus on social concerns and personal heartbreak, much of Strangefolk's music invites listeners to join in a reminiscence of glorious summer days sitting barefoot in the grass, celebrating life's wonders with friends. This kind of exultation has proven irresistible to the many fans who are flocking back to Strangefolk's shows with companions in tow.

DISCOGRAPHY

Lore (1996). The band's debut release presents its radiant vocals and lively interplay with clarity and conviction. "Sometimes" bounds out of the box in three-part harmony. "Lines and Circles" offers lustrous singing and swelling guitar. "Rather Go Fishing" features some quick-wristed guitar work. More serious expressions appear as well: "Alaska" may be one of the few songs ever to invoke Jimmy Carter and laud his creation of the National Arctic Refuge. Similarly, the imagery of "Poland" captures a poignant family history and subsequent introspection that ultimately gives way to an exuberant guitar display (which seems to exorcise through exercise).

Weightless in Water (1997). Once again, the band teams up with producer Dan Archer to create pleasing results. "Roads" benefits from Genauer's exuberant vocals and Trafton's mellifluous guitar phrases, and Smith and Glockler keep things shuffling. "Valhalla" is a second effort in this vein, built on wordplay and imagery. "Oxbow" emphasizes Strangefolk's use of dynamics, building to sweet harmonic elation. "Who I Am" provides some appealing funk. Guest picker Gordon Stone adds some colors to "Sad" with his yearning pedal steel guitar, and he vitalizes "Otis" with his rollicking banjo.

WEB SITE

www.strangefolk.com

STRING CHEESE INCIDENT

- ■ **KYLE HOLLINGSWORTH:** *keyboards, accordion*
- ■ **MICHAEL KANG:** *electric mandolin, electric violin*
- ■ **KEITH MOSELEY:** *electric bass*
- ■ **BILL NERSHI:** *acoustic guitar*
- ■ **MICHAEL TRAVIS:** *drums, percussion*

The members of String Cheese Incident are devout skiers. In fact, the group formed while its players were living and downhilling in Crested Butte, Colorado. This proves relevant as one could argue that the band's vocation is strongly influenced by its avocation: like the quintet's maneuvers on the slopes, its music is audacious and punctuated with free falls and hairpin turns. Above all, any String Cheese Incident performance offers an exhilarating run.

When the band formed in 1993, it dubbed itself the Blue Cheese String Band, reflecting a bluegrass focus. Acoustic guitarist Bill Nershi is a celebrated flat-picker on that circuit. Once the group started to rehearse and perform, however, it decided to expand its goals and change its moniker as well. Michael Kang, a classically trained violinist, is a revelation, particularly on electric mandolin. Although he is perfectly capable of tearing up a traditional bluegrass number, his mandolin is outfitted with tube screamers that enable him to explore and sustain notes. Percussionist Michael Travis's training in Cuban rhythms lends a Latin flair to the sound (indeed, it was only recently that he added a standard drum kit to his gear). Kyle Hollingsworth has gigged and recorded extensively as a jazz pianist. When Keith Moseley plays his electric bass, he expresses his devotion to bluegrass — although he reverently steps into Paul Chambers's loafers when the band covers a Miles Davis classic from *Kind of Blue.* Moseley elaborates: "It's been quite a challenge to pull off these songs with conviction. Anyone is allowed to bring anything to the table at any time. I was rooted in seventies rock, so I'm responsible for a number of those. We all spend a lot of time getting up to speed on what the others are interested in playing. But, then again, I couldn't imagine playing in a band where I wasn't challenged."

Recent standout appearances at the High Sierra Festival and the Telluride Bluegrass Festival have solidified String Cheese Incident's national reputation, and music fans on both coasts have become eager to see the group. In concert, the group's spellbinding jams emerge from its playful compositions or from a range of covers that includes selections from Tim O'Brien, Miles Davis, and the Allman Brothers Band. Says Moseley: "The set list is something we put a lot of time into. We'll often play four shows without any repeats. And every night we work in new segues, ideas, and jam structures. We view every night as a different incident." Many of the group's live gigs also demonstrate its efforts to initiate the revitalization of the hula hoop. Moseley explains, "We started out hooping just for fun. Now we see them as circular dance aids to get people up and moving if they need a little extra incentive. It's a multigenerational thing, just like our music." Due primarily to its improvisational gifts and evolving set lists, an increasing number of supporters is following the quintet from show to show, committed to the belief that the String Cheese Incident is one worth repeating.

DISCOGRAPHY

Born on the Wrong Planet (1996)

A String Cheese Incident (1997). This release presents the band live at Colorado's Fox Theater in February 1997. It is a standout offering that captures the musicians' individual talents and collective euphony. It is also quite fun — although this disc is comprised predominantly of original compositions, it may have the distinction of being the first live recording of a band covering both Vassar Clements and Aerosmith. The quintet transforms the opening number, Clements's "Lonesome Fiddle Blues," into ten minutes of charged improvisation. "Rhythm of the Road" uses Nershi's winsome melody as a point of departure. Kang's "Pirates," an extended instrumental, exudes a jazzier, Latin feel. The smooth vocals of "San Jose" are pleasing, as is the Aerosmith remonstrance to "Walk This Way."

'Round the Wheel (1998)

WEB SITE

www.stringcheeseincident.com

SUNFUR

- ■ **EMIL JAKOVCEVIC:** *electric and acoustic guitar, vocals*
- ■ **BILL LEWIS:** *bass*
- ■ **LU:** *drums and percussion, vocals*
- ■ **LUNA:** *vocals, acoustic guitar, percussion*
- ■ **DAHV STEWART:** *percussion*

Sunfur's percussionist and principal songwriter, Lu, describes the band's music as "a vehicle for the soul through rhythm." This characterization is quite apt, as Sunfur is a purveyor of dazzling, captivating polyrhythms. However, the group also likes to layer on denser textures. Guitarist Emil Jakovcevic produces sounds that not only manifest some Eastern influences but also throb with a harder edge reminiscent of Jimmy Page's early work with Led Zeppelin or David Navarro's performances with Jane's Addiction. Vocalist Luna introduces a similar sonic swagger. The results are hypnotic and often psychedelic.

The Bay Area group has acquired a dedicated following and a devout taping crew. It all began in 1994, when childhood friends Lu and Jakovcevic fused their energies. This collaboration soon yielded an array of songs that melded the pair's affinities for radiant percussion and assertive guitar tones. As the band coalesced, Luna appeared and imbued many of these songs with his own vigor. The group also has a spiritual side that is reflected in the lyrics to many of its songs, such as the plaintive "Gaia, Come Gaia." In describing the origins of the band's name, Lu characterizes the band's collective spirit, noting that, "in a visceral sense, it came from the energy of the sun, or the 'fur' of the sun. We as human beings also have that same energy to share, that positive energy that helps others grow."

DISCOGRAPHY

Comfort as One (1997). The band's engrossing aural tapestry is on display in this collection. The title track features some dexterous drum expressions, which buttress an Eastern vibe. By contrast,

"Crux" features Jakovcevic's edgier, bristling guitar. "Bees and Butterflies" pulses with a hypnotic élan, while "Higher than the Past" occasionally hints at vintage Zeppelin. Sunfur's players each erupt on the extended, cautionary "Gaia, Come Gaia."

WEB SITE

www.sunfur.com

TO THE MOON ALICE

- ■ **MIKE BENIGNO:** *drums*
- ■ **TIM GRAVELLE:** *bass*
- ■ **LESLIE MILLS:** *vocals*
- ■ **BRENT MORGAN:** *guitar*
- ■ **BRAD NAGLE:** *guitar*

To the Moon Alice emerged from the spectacular ambience of Yellowstone National Park. Itinerant troubadour Leslie Mills happened upon Brad Nagle and Brent Morgan while all three were working in the park. After playing together for only two weeks, an urgent, defining moment occurred: Mills was fired from her job and told to leave the park within eight hours. Nagle and Morgan decided to quit on the spot, and the three embarked together on a musical path. Recalls Mills: "I knew from the first day we played together that this is what I wanted to do. Write songs and sing 'em. I found my voice and my writing companions in one moment." They eventually ensconced themselves in Woodstock, New York, where they completed their lineup with drummer Mike Benigno and Nagle's childhood pal bassist Tim Gravelle.

The quintet is a vibrant live outfit that maintains an extensive touring schedule. Mills's strident vocals stand out, although they are well complemented by a tight rhythm section that drives the tunes forward. Morgan and Nagle supply a variety of textures while leading the band through delicate passages and funkier runs with some spacier expressions as well. To the Moon Alice's original compositions mesh evocative imagery with robust, engaging melodies; when performing live, the band also mixes in some choice covers — for instance, a spirited rendition of Jerry Garcia's "They Love Each Other."

Although the group's name directly invokes Ralph Kramden's familiar refrain from *The Honeymooners*, a more appropriate reference point is Alice of Wonderland fame. In fact, at the group's 1997 Halloween show and CD-release party at the Wetlands, all of the players costumed themselves as figures from the Lewis Carroll book. Like their fictional analogues, the members of To the Moon Alice present a kaleidoscope of sounds and images.

DISCOGRAPHY

3 Feet to Infinity (1997). This seven-song release offers five studio cuts and two live songs. "The Spider" immediately pulls the listener in with some sinewy guitar and Mills's expressive vocals. "Wind Chimes," a gentler number, is sweetened by guest John Popper's harmonica fills. "Get in the Van" affirms the band's ability to tell entrancing stories with hooks. "Lost," recorded at Woodstock's Tinker Street Café, mates fast-paced, melodic vocal phrasings with a liberating electric guitar solo.

WEB SITE

www.tothemoonalice.com

OMAR TORREZ BAND

- **DALE FANNING:** *drums*
- **GENE MATTHEWS:** *bass, vocals*
- **ARTURO RODRIGUEZ:** *percussion*
- **OMAR TORREZ:** *guitar, vocals*

The Omar Torrez Band currently galvanizes audiences with its fiery "afrocubanflamencofunk." The quartet spins out all of these influences while performing its zesty original compositions. Seattle guitarist Omar Torrez crafts these offerings and animates them through his exuberant guitar and vocals. His songwriting and flamboyant performance style testify to his ardor for such Spanish flamenco icons as Paco de Lucia and his affection for such rock and blues heroes as Jimi Hendrix — in fact, Torrez first came to the attention of many with his stirring performance at the National Jimi Hendrix Gibson Competition during the 1995 Bumbershoot Festival.

Torrez's quartet continues to win new admirers with its vigorous live shows, the catalyst of which is often Arturo Rodriguez's spirited congas and percussion. Drummer Dale Fanning of Living Daylights also appears with the Omar Torrez Band, lending his own signature kinetic display. Gene Matthews contributes a steady bass and backing vocals. Yet while the band creates spicy collective grooves, the focus of its shows is usually on Torrez, whose versatile performances are suffused with verve and passion.

DISCOGRAPHY

Omar Torrez Band (1997). The five songs on this release demonstrate the band's varied gifts. The opening, "Angel Fire," is laden with feisty, blues-tinged guitar riffs and insistent percussion. "Sangre Mia" is a bright flamenco composition. "Woke Up This Morning" captivates through Torrez's soulful vocals. The epic "Tribute" presents an expansive, incendiary display.

WEB SITE

www.elpopo.com

THE TRAGICALLY HIP

- **ROB BAKER:** *guitar*
- **GORDON DOWNIE:** *vocals*
- **JOHNNY FAY:** *drums*
- **PAUL LANGLOIS:** *guitar, vocals*
- **GORD SINCLAIR:** *bass, vocals*

Some Americans may be surprised to learn that Canada's most fervidly embraced touring jam band is The Tragically Hip. The group has endeared itself to legions of fans, many of whom follow it from show to show. The Tragically Hip may even be Canada's most zealously taped act: the World Wide Web contains a number of sites devoted to trading its shows.

The quintet unquestionably produces some stirring improvisational music. At times, it will create a traditional jam led by guitarist Rob Baker, who often injects some blues-based riffs into his free-wheeling expressions. Baker is ably supported by rhythm player Paul Langlois, who adds a number of intriguing accents. Bassist Gord Sinclair furnishes assertive splashes. Drummer Johnny Fay comments with his own thunderous vocabulary.

Yet The Tragically Hip's extemporizations differ from those of other jam bands due to the energetic contributions of front man Gord Downie. Often, while his bandmates are working up a furious groove behind him, Downie will riff with his vocal chords. He often directs the band's musical journey through his stream-of-consciousness commentary, replete with aphorisms and non sequiturs; at other times, he'll simply deliver a monologue on his view from the stage. The results can be surreal, entrancing, and sublime.

The quintet formed in Kingston, Ontario, in 1986. Finding itself part of a bar scene that was saturated with cover bands, the group elected to perform original material. Its name arose from a sketch in the Michael Nesmith video "Elephant Parts," which contains a sardonic description of the "tragically hip," those people afflicted with a need for only the trendiest of products. In order to build a catalog of songs, the Hip would meet and jam relentlessly. Now many of its new tunes are developed on stage, often during "New Orleans Is Sinking," which typically becomes the launching pad for musical exploration.

Since 1993, the group has hosted a touring summer festival, Another Roadside Attraction. This event travels across Canada, drawing together a number of other notable live acts (the band's perspective on this tour is captured in the 1994 film *Heksenketel*). The Tragically Hip has also animated a number of musical events and tours stateside. It has made multiple appearances on the HORDE tour (Blues Traveler, in turn, has participated in Another Roadside Attraction) and has played at events such as the High Sierra Music Festival.

DISCOGRAPHY

The Tragically Hip (1987)

Up to Here (1989)

Road Apples (1991)

Fully Completely (1992)

Day for Night (1994)

Trouble at the Henhouse (1996)

Live between Us (1997). This release supplies seventy minutes of live Hip recorded at Detroit's Cobo Arena on November 23, 1996. The band's unique live artistry is well represented. For instance, the pulsing opener, "Grace, Too," segues through Downie's vocal rap into the invigorating "Fully Completely." The disc also collects a number of longtime fan favorites, including the captivating "Spring-time in Vienna" and the throbbing "Twist My Arm." The band's distinctive collective jamming enlivens the blues-based "New Orleans Is Sinking."

Phantom Power (1998)

WEB SITE

www.thehip.com

DEREK TRUCKS BAND

- **BILL MCKAY:** *keyboard, piano, vocals*
- **YONRICO SCOTT:** *drums, percussion*
- **TODD SMALLIE:** *bass*
- **DEREK TRUCKS:** *guitar*

Derek Trucks's searing performances have recently earned the slide guitarist raves; Warren Haynes, for example, has described his play-ing as "scary." Trucks has lent his talents to the recording efforts of, among others, Junior Wells and the Fiji Mariners. He has joined a number of groups on stage, including the Allman Brothers Band and Widespread Panic. Moreover, Trucks is a member of the all-star lineup that comprises Frogwings. Also, he happens to be the nephew of Allman Brothers Band member Butch Trucks, but nepotism has noth-ing to do with his success, which instead has arisen from his musical dexterity (although, quite possibly, a little nepotism did help him to land the Frogwings gig).

To those who know only Trucks's slide guitar work with other performers, the music of the Derek Trucks Band will likely be a revelation. Bill McKay's keyboards provide a melodious counterpoint to Trucks's stinging guitar leads; McKay also adds occasional vocals to this outfit, which mainly performs instrumentals. The band also is quite effectively moored by Todd Smallie and Yonrico Scott. Additionally, while the DTB is certainly steeped in the blues (leading a number of critics to compare Trucks with his uncle's former bandmate Duane Allman), its members maintain an affinity for other genres as well. Thus, along with many original compositions, the band's explosive, exhausting performances include takes on Miles Davis ("So What"), Wayne Shorter ("Footprints"), and John Coltrane ("Mr. PC").

DISCOGRAPHY

The Derek Trucks Band (1997). Legendary producer John Synder (Ornette Coleman, James Cotton, Dizzy Gillespie, Etta James) helmed this effort, and he has done a fine job of capturing the many sides of the DTB. The release opens with Trucks on the sarod, a stringed instrument similar to the sitar. The band then moves through a number of originals, including the carefully sculpted "D Minor Blues," the all-out rave "#6 Dance," and "Egg 15," which provides the listener with a taste of each band member's considerable gifts. This recording also demonstrates the group's affinity for jazz — witness Trucks's transpositions on songs by horn greats Coltrane, Davis, and Shorter.

WEB SITE

www.derektrucks.com

TURTLE GROVE

- **MICHAEL BONNER:** *bass, vocals*
- **JIM "STONEY" KNIGHT:** *percussion*
- **GEOFF LEDOYEN:** *guitar, vocals*
- **JON SALTER:** *drums*
- **TONY SILBERT:** *piano, organ*
- **SCOTT STEPAKOFF:** *vocals, guitar*

Turtle Grove began its career as one of the many talented California bands working in the immense shadow cast by the Grateful Dead.

Founders Geoff LeDoyen and Scott Stepakoff were so enamored with the Grateful Dead that in 1994, when the pair formed a band called Groove Turtle, they sought to capture some of that illustrious outfit's spirit and energy. However, after playing together for a year, developing songs and a sound, the fledgling band's members realized that they had crafted their own musical space. Groove Turtle became Turtle Grove and began to draw in its own distinctive crowd of listeners.

The band is particularly proud of its song craft. Drummer Jon Salter affirms: "We try to move people through our jams and rhythms, but also through the songs themselves." Many compositions are brought to the group by lead singer Stepakoff, and then everyone collaborates on the arrangements. Stepakoff's vocalizations emote in accord with each tune's message and feel. The results have proven appealing – two of Turtle Grove's songs appear in the movie *Burn Hollywood Burn*.

Still, it is Turtle Grove's live performances that fuel the expansion of its reputation. Adds Salter: "With us, you get a different show every single time – but there's more to it. We can get weird on you, but there's a rock-solid core to what we're doing." Some of the group's improvisations emerge from the interplay of lead guitarist LeDoyen and rhythm player Stepakoff, and some are driven by the group's percussion section. Keyboardist Tony Silbert also weaves in a number of ideas. Salter emphasizes the sum of these contributions in assessing the Turtle Grove experience: "You'll get a lot of funky, crunchy, sticky grooves with a healthy balance of tasty songwriting."

DISCOGRAPHY

Tunnel (1997). This, the band's debut release, presents its compositions to good effect. The keyboards and drums are particularly well mixed, adding flavor without becoming obtrusive. "Sitting in the Desert," the disc's first song, is a subtle, folk-based offering sweetened with some cello. Other prominent cuts include the upbeat "Smell the Roses," the bluesier "Buckets," the driving "(Drinking in a) Striped Shirt," and the extended "Tunnel," which builds on the contributions of the band's drummers. The group's cover of Widespread Panic's "Porch Song" is an intriguing, well-executed selection that provides some lively harmonies.

WEB SITE

www.bomba.com/turtlegrove

ULU

- **LUCA BENEDETTI:** *guitar*
- **SCOTT CHASOLEN:** *keyboards*
- **AARON GARDNER:** *tenor saxophone, flute*
- **DAVID HOFFMAN:** *drums*
- **JUSTIN WALLACE:** *bass*

New York City's Ulu is yet another *Village Voice* success story. Keyboardist Scott Chasolen, drummer David Hoffman, and bassist Justin Wallace had been playing together as a rhythm section for a few years when, in 1996, they decided to take out a want ad for a guitarist in the *Voice*. The three hoped to extend the instrumental mélange of jazz and funk they had been creating. Hoffman jokes: "We were a rent-a-rhythm-section for a while. Our friends would hire us out for their parties. We were tight but didn't want to explore what Medeski, Martin and Wood were already doing so well. We decided to try something different." Their ad was answered by Berklee School of Music-trained guitarist Luca Benedetti, who came aboard and, in turn, recommended another Berklee alum, Aaron Gardner, who soon joined on tenor saxophone and flute. The band rehearsed and composed, emerging in 1997 to popular acclaim.

Ulu's music is a product of the individual proclivities of its players. Benedetti's pantheon of guitar heroes includes George Benson, Pat Martino, and Stevie Ray Vaughan. Chasolen is quite partial to the sounds of Herbie Hancock's Headhunters. The others enjoy an array of artists, among them James Brown and Miles Davis. Together, the members of Ulu work to apply the jazz-extemporization ethic to the band's deeply grooved offerings. Hoffman notes, "The heads of the songs tend to be somewhat intricate, but then we delve into a lot of organized improvisation. The songs take on new meaning each time out." He also sees Ulu's two predominant styles as existing harmoniously: "When I visualize it, I see the funk as linear and the jazz as curvier. With our music, the two are intertwined to make one shape."

UNCLE MINGO

- **BRYON MOORE:** *vocals, bass*
- **JASON MOORE:** *alto saxophone, keyboards, vocals*
- **JESSIE PRITCHARD:** *guitar*
- **ROBERT THORN:** *drums*

Uncle Mingo began its career on the festival circuit. Actually, the group created its own late-night, impromptu events, hauling a generator, some Chinese lanterns, and sundry beverages to empty fields a few miles outside Charleston, South Carolina, where its members attended college. The word spread, and crowds of people showed up to join the jamboree. To this day, Uncle Mingo strives to re-create the loose, party atmosphere of those early performances.

The band has long cited George Clinton and James Brown as two of its inspirations. The selection of these paragons bespeaks some central aspects of the Uncle Mingo experience. First, the band owes a musical allegiance to the world of funk, enthusiastically producing rubbery bass lines, reverberating guitar solos, and piercing saxophone trills. Second, like Brown, Uncle Mingo is committed to keeping its audiences involved and undulating by means of its stage presence, its banter, and — above all — its spirited original compositions. However, Uncle Mingo also baits its abundant hooks with some heavier sounds, and even a taste of hip-hop. Just for kicks, Jason Moore will also often embark on a wailing saxophone solo while jumping on a pogo stick.

Uncle Mingo suffered some difficult moments during the summer of 1997 when lead guitarist Scott "Mookie" Quattlebaum left: the band withdrew from the road to search for a replacement. Eventually, it tapped Jessie Pritchard, whose guitar work had animated the bluegrass-oriented Big Stoner Creek. Pritchard's deep musical vocabulary is now enriching Uncle Mingo. When the band recorded its second release, *Little Baby Brother*, at James Brown's Augusta, Georgia, studio, the Godfather of Soul poked his head through the door and called out, "I'll see you at the top." Given Uncle Mingo's penchant for exhaustive, exhausting live performances, Brown's prediction may well be realized.

DISCOGRAPHY

Fatty Mookie Mo' Booty (1993)

Little Baby Brother (1996)

Dancin' on the Moon (1997). This disc offers three studio cuts and seven live ones, all of which manifest the band's energetic, free-wheeling style. Among the studio selections are the uplifting, funky title track and the mellower, catchy "Pins and Needles." Of the live songs, "Aunt Buelah" proves particularly captivating with its thick grooves and saxophone salvos, while "Told You So" offers fierce bass lines along with guitar work that hints at the band's affinity for harder rock. The release concludes with a smile-inducing, raved-up cover of the "Jefferson's Theme (Movin' on Up)."

WEB SITE

www.unclemingo.com

VERTICAL HORIZON

- **SEAN HURLEY:** *bass*
- **KEITH KANE:** *vocals, acoustic guitar*
- **MATT SCANNELL:** *vocals, electric and acoustic guitar*
- **ED TOTH:** *drums*

Vertical Horizon began with Keith Kane and Matt Scannell, alone on stage, strumming their guitars and singing. The two had met at a college party in October of 1991 when they were both attending Georgetown University in Washington, DC. On that occasion, they had spontaneously performed together: Kane recalls, "He started playing Michael Hedges's version of 'Watchtower,' and I was really into that because I was in a Michael Hedges stage." Kane invited Scannell to join him for a weekly acoustic gig he had lined up, and the pair billed themselves as Vertical Horizon. Eight months later, when the duo was about to graduate, Kane and Scannell decided to record their music. Remarks Kane: "We did it just to have a memento of that time, something we could show our grandchildren." However, after they had released *There and Back Again* and begun selling it at their shows, a number of people embraced the band: the disc received many favorable reviews, the group Jackopierce took the duo under its wing, and clubs were eager to book the act. In 1994, Kane and Scannell reentered the studio to produce a richer-sounding album, drawing in a number of musicians, including Carter Beauford of the Dave Matthews Band. (Says Kane: "It was unbelievable working with him. We were such fans of his ability. And he showed up singing the tunes, it was exciting.") Soon afterward, the full electric version of Vertical Horizon made its debut.

The band now has plenty of supporters who are attracted to its ability to blend song craft with an affinity for improvisation. "At times," Kane notes, "it's definitely a free-for-all up there, but it's a structured improv — we don't want things to get too loose." The group opens a number of songs with Scannell taking the lead while Kane fills in the canvas on rhythm guitar. Kane heaps praise on Scannell, commenting: "In many ways, he's the musical director of the band. We all have an equal say, but he'll often take the reins, and he's made so many good decisions." Drummer Ed Toth, who has been with the group since 1996, and recent addition Sean Hurley, who plays bass, work within the parameters of each song while contributing their own accents. All of these elements, along with band members' general good nature and humor, combine to draw new fans into Vertical Horizon's orbit.

There and Back Again (1992)

Running on Ice (1995)

Live Stages (1997). This disc demonstrates how Vertical Horizon's original compositions are infused with fresh energy in the live setting. Scannell's warm vocals are showcased on the opener, "The Man Who Would Be Santa," while the spirited "Japan" is sung by Kane. The pair's harmonies predominate on songs such as "Falling Down." This disc also documents the band's ability to stretch things out: listen to the lively guitar of "Heart in Hand" and the more textured, atmospheric twelve minutes that comprise "Wash Away."

WEB SITE

www.verticalhorizon.com

VINYL

- **DANNY CAO:** *trumpet*
- **BILLY FRATES:** *guitar*
- **JONATHAN KORTY:** *keyboard, harmonica*
- **ANTONIO ONORATO:** *congas and timbales*
- **SEAN ONORATO:** *bongos*
- **ALEXIS RAZON:** *bass*
- **DOUG THOMAS:** *saxophone, flute*
- **GEOFF VAUGHAN:** *bass*

Since this California band's formation in 1995, it has swiftly distinguished itself in the Bay Area and beyond. While Vinyl originated during a series of Mill Valley garage jam sessions, it has long since moved on to sell-out headlining gigs at the Great American Music Hall and to perform on the main stage at the High Sierra Music Festival. Indeed, the octet's tantalizing grooves and volcanic improvisations are beginning to earn the group a national reputation as well.

Vinyl performs pulsing instrumentals that incorporate Latin percussion, jazz-flavored guitar, elastic bass lines, and percolating keyboards punctuated by splashy brass. As bassist Geoff Vaughan explains, "We take a lot of stuff and throw it in the pot. We write our songs by committee, and all of the stuff that we listen to has seeped its way into the writing process – the Meters, James Brown, seventies funk, old Latin stuff, reggae. We also pride ourselves on taking these influences in new directions by incorporating different genres within a tune."

The group developed organically. Marin County percussionists Antonio and Sean Onorato, drummer Alexis Razon, keyboardist Jonathan Korty, and Vaughan decided to get together, and Vinyl evolved out of their sessions. Recalls Vaughan: "We just set up a number of loose jams, and things started clicking. Along the way, we added another percussion player, and then we brought in the horns. We never really planned on being an instrumental band – it's just that the grooves that came out stood up without any need for vocals."

The band's moniker reflects its musical ethos. "A lot of us grew up in the eighties, when everything was synthesized," says Korty. "To us, what we're doing is a revival of real music, the way we feel it should be played." Vaughan adds, "We have an organic style rooted in the sounds of a few decades ago. We play on vintage instruments. That's where our name came from: it refers to older days when music was put down on vinyl." And Korty interjects, "a lot of us have some pretty sick record collections too."

DISCOGRAPHY

Vinyl (1997). This eponymous debut contains a number of majestic grooves. The opener, "Master Cylinder," begins with lush jazz tones, then kicks forward through lively percussion, guitar, and keyboards. The musical content of other tunes is well evoked by their song titles: "Funk in 5–4," "Pipe Bomb," and "Cowbell Funk." Finally, in "Mountain Roots," rock-steady bass is layered over ska-flavored explorations.

Live at Sweetwater (1998)

WEB SITE

www.vinylgroove.com

VIPERHOUSE

- ■ **BRIAN BOYES:** *trumpet*
- ■ **PHIL CARR:** *drums*
- ■ **MICHAEL CHORNEY:** *alto and baritone saxophone*
- ■ **P.J. DAVIDIAN:** *percussion*
- ■ **BRETT HUGHES:** *guitar*
- ■ **DAN MALLACH:** *trombone*
- ■ **ROB MORSE:** *acoustic and electric bass*
- ■ **RAY PACZKOWSKI:** *organ and piano*
- ■ **KAREN QUINN:** *violin*
- ■ **HELOISE WILLIAMS:** *lead vocals*

Vermont's ViperHouse is yet another band that quite masterfully leaps across several genres in a single bound. This ten-piece outfit gloriously mingles jazz, funk, and rock. The sultry-voiced Heloise Williams drops in and out of the mix, alternately guiding these efforts and yielding the floor to the other players. The group's live shows bring in an eclectic audience — people who want to stand up and express themselves physically, and those who prefer to sit back and contemplate the layers of sound. ViperHouse appeals to both sets of listeners because it produces sophisticated improvisations, yet this band can also work a groove.

During a trip to Europe in the spring of 1995, saxophonist Michael Chorney, fresh from a long stint in the So-Called Jazz Sextet, envisioned the instrumentation, the players, and the chemistry that would be needed to "bring jazz back to the dance hall." Returning to the United States, he assembled ViperHouse from the vast pool of musicians he had worked with over the years. His aim was to bring together performers of diverse ages and musical backgrounds to "produce vital, interesting music that one could dance to." Although Chorney's inspirations included Duke Ellington's orchestra and some early incarnations of Sun Ra's band, ViperHouse's sound remains rooted in the present, conscious of its funk, and even rock, predecessors. This is clearly demonstrated by the fact that, along with seven original compositions, the band's release *Shed* contains interpretations of songs by Duke Ellington ("Virgin Jungle"), Charles Mingus ("Pithycanthropus Erectus"), and Neil Young ("For the Turnstiles").

DISCOGRAPHY

ViperHouse (1996)

Ottawa (1997). This live set recorded at the Ottawa Jazz Festival opens with a cover of Jimmy McGriff's "Dig on It," then moves through a number of ViperHouse originals, including "In a Buffalo Bar" and "If It's Your Planet." The band then demonstrates its eclecticism, juxtaposing an agile take on Sly Stone's "You're the One" with Sun Ra's "A Call for All Demons."

Shed (1997). This disc offers seventy-one minutes of ViperHouse music. *Shed* presents seven original compositions that carry the group through soul, funk, big-band, and acid-jazz environments. Along with its intriguing covers of Ellington, Mingus, and Young, ViperHouse's own songs – such as "Give It Up," "Viperosity," and "Gettin' It" – embrace a number of moods, at times hypnotic, and at other times quite jarring, but in all instances complex and compelling.

WEB SITE

www.viperhouse.com

NATHAN WHITT AND CHIEF'S TALE

- ■ **ROB FUGATE:** *guitar, vocals*
- ■ **MIKE GERGEL:** *bass*
- ■ **BILL McCARTHY:** *drums, vocals*
- ■ **NATHAN WHITT:** *vocals, acoustic guitar*

For a number of years now, Nathan Whitt has lived a double life. By day, the mild-mannered Ohio resident leads individuals on canoe excursions. Many of his clients are none the wiser to the fact that by night their faithful guide fronts the band Chief's Tale. Admittedly, there is a bit of hyperbole here, and Whitt has less time now for his day job due to his expanding tour docket. Still, it is important to note that the singer takes much pleasure in America's natural environment. It is also crucial to emphasize that he is a passionate songwriter who performs his compositions in a rich tenor that some have likened to that of Chris Whitley.

Whitt's music takes on a new vigor when he performs with Chief's Tale. Rob Fugate plays rousing lead guitar and is a strong songwriter in his own right. Bassist Mike Gergel is an Ohio-based sound engineer and musician who has lent his talents to Ekoostik Hookah. Bill McCarthy is a spitfire on drums and contributes backing vocals. Together, these players have distinguished themselves by producing compelling improvisations that emerge from Whitt's compositions and build on them.

DISCOGRAPHY

Pictures of Memories (1995)

Night and Day (1997). This release presents an early incarnation of Whitt's band, but it is still a strong offering that showcases a number of compositions currently performed by Chief's Tale. Many of these songs, which draw on blues and a hint of country to produce a roots-rock feel, are elevated by Whitt's soulful vocals. Notable tracks include the entrancing "Shadow Jumping," the textured "You Won't Fall," and "Weatherman," which addresses environmental concerns.

THE WHY STORE

- **CHARLIE BUSHOR:** *drums, percussion*
- **GREG GARDNER:** *bass, vocals*
- **JEFF PEDERSEN:** *piano, keyboards*
- **CHRIS SHAFFER:** *vocals, guitar, mandolin*
- **MICHAEL DAVID SMITH:** *guitar, mandolin, lap steel*

At some level, any account of this band and its devotees reads like a Dr. Seuss story (albeit a Dr. Seuss story replete with growling vocals and demon riffs). The Why Store creates music for an ever-expanding army of Whomheads. These enthusiasts support the band by participating in the What Club. When questioned about their fealty, these fans respond, "Hey, we know Where it's at."

In response to all interrogatives, the Indiana band has been able to amass this legion of admirers on the strength of its euphonic compositions and combustive live gigs. Guitarist Michael David Smith and bassist Greg Gardner first came together in 1989 under the moniker Emerald City. Within two years, vocalist and second guitarist Chris Shaffer had joined the pair along with drummer Charlie Bushor, who was effectively lured away from his cover band P.S. Dump Your Boyfriend; keyboard player Jeff Pedersen was drawn into the fold a few years later. The group's name was derived from a condemned vintage-clothing shop that was located in Muncie, Indiana.

The Why Store distinguishes itself in the concert setting. Shaffer's commanding voice vigorously emotes his lyrics — critics have compared his vocals to those of, among others, Cat Stevens and Eddie Vedder. Smith complements him with a range of expressions, at times deftly strumming and at other times all-out shredding. In the latter instances, he is enthusiastically joined by Bushor, who has published a guide to thrash-metal drumming. Gardner is adept at negotiating the space around these players and grounding them according to the dictates of individual songs. Pedersen adds an alluring keyboard fundament. The resulting live shows present the Why Store's sonorous music with spirit and flair, transforming any Why Store performance into a Whomhead recruitment session.

DISCOGRAPHY

Welcome to the Why Store (1993)

Inside the Why Store (1994)

The Why Store (1996). This release introduced the nation to the Why Store. The band's songs were given a bit of studio sheen by producer Mike Wanchic, but the energy still comes through. "Broken Glass" is the hypnotic opener; in it, Bushor's steady drums and Smith's sinewy guitar phrasings throb behind Shaffer's compelling enunciations. "Nobody" and "So Sad to Leave It" have pleasing melodies and urgent lyrics. The band's live spirit shines through on the funky "Fade Away" and the fiery closer, "Lack of Water."

Two Beasts (1998)

WEB SITE

php.indiana.edu/~ceinfalt/whystore.htm

WIDESPREAD PANIC

- **JOHN BELL:** *vocals, guitar*
- **JOHN HERMANN:** *keyboards, vocals*
- **MICHAEL HOUSER:** *guitar, vocals*
- **TODD NANCE:** *drums*
- **DOMINGO ORTIZ:** *percussion, vocals*
- **DAVE SCHOOLS:** *bass, vocals*

On April 18, 1998, an event took place that awoke some individuals to a reality that had long been apparent to others. It became clear that many, many people dig the songs and sounds of Widespread Panic. On this date, the band decided to host a free concert to celebrate the release of its *Light Fuse Get Away* double CD. With the cooperation of the city of Atlanta, three downtown blocks near the University of Georgia (where the band had first come together) were cordoned off. As the day stretched on, more and more people arrived; additional blocks had to be closed to traffic. Eventually, thirteen city blocks were claimed, and one hundred thousand people made their way to downtown Atlanta to hear Widespread Panic perform two sets of music.

The band had formed nearly fifteen years earlier in calmer circumstances. In 1982, guitarists Michael Houser and John "J.B." Bell met while at the University of Georgia. The next fall, bassist and fellow student Dave Schools matriculated at the college and was introduced to Bell. The three musicians performed their first gig in 1985, dubbing themselves Widespread Panic after Houser's nickname (which had been Panic, but on one particularly frantic day he informed his friends that they should call him Widespread Panic instead). Some months afterward, the trio resolved to expand and drafted drummer Todd Nance. Percussionist Domingo Ortiz joined the group next, following a series of guest performances. This lineup remained in place until

1991, when Widespread Panic went into the studio to record an eponymous album. There it was joined by vaunted Dixie Dregs keyboard player T. Lavitz, who remained with the band after the sessions ended and performed with it on an as-available basis until 1992, when John "Jo Jo" Hermann came aboard.

Widespread Panic's sound reflects the varied predilections of its members. The sextet's original music draws on Delta blues, country, southern swamp boogie, and random, raucous rock. The group also performs covers ranging from Traffic's "Low Spark of High Heeled Boys" to Willie Dixon's "Weak Brain, Narrow Mind" to the Meters's "Cissy Strut." Of course, the presentation of any song varies from show to show, as the band rejoices in collaborative improvisation. Every band member contributes significant ideas to these jams, referencing the group's previous interactions, the specific requirements of the tune, and the feel of the moment to create robust and absorbing results.

Widespread Panic has rewarded its fans with some notable holiday performances. Halloween and New Year's Eve have become important dates on the tour docket for Spreadheads. At these shows, the group performs special songs (such as "Coconuts"), which it saves for the occasion. At the band's 1995 Halloween show, it offered a tribute to the departed Jerry Garcia, performing a tune that had long slipped out of its repertoire: "Cream Puff War" (one of the earliest Grateful Dead compositions, and one that the Dead itself had stopped playing in 1967). Widespread Panic holiday gigs also often include bonus acoustic sets as well as appearances by guest musicians (such as Vic Chesnutt, with whom the group recorded the release *Nine High a Pallet* under the collective moniker Brute). Widespread Panic will have trouble topping the hectic splendor of its *Light Fuse Get Away* concert, but the group's adventurous spirit keeps its fans returning, secure in the knowledge that, one day, it just might try.

DISCOGRAPHY

Space Wrangler (1990)

Widespread Panic (1991)

Everyday (1993)

Ain't Life Grand (1994)

Bombs and Butterflies (1996)

Light Fuse Get Away (1998). The title of this release is, literally, the directions found on a pack of firecrackers, and it becomes a suitable metaphor for the music contained within. Although the live tracks are culled from a number of shows given during 1997, the song sequences and the mixing of the crowd noise give the feel of a single concert. The release opens with the gentle introduction to "Porch," which swiftly gains momentum; a furious jam ensues and plows into "Disco." Another strong segue appears between the fine songs that follow, "Diner" and "Wondering." Branford Marsalis guests on an exhilarating "Picking Up the Pieces." The band's creative spirit is also manifested with a zesty cover of the Talking Heads's "Papa Legba." The group's percussionists put on an invigorating display in "Drums," which leads to a rousing closing run from "Gimme" to "Pigeons."

WEB SITE

www.widespreadpanic.com

THE WINEBOTTLES

- **STEVE HURLOCK:** *bass*
- **DOUG MURRAY:** *vocals, acoustic and electric guitar*
- **DARREN TAYLOR:** *guitar*
- **"YOUNG" SAM YOUNG:** *drums*

The Winebottles officially came together in 1990 while Doug Murray was a student at the University of Colorado, Boulder. Murray, who had played in a high school band with Darren Taylor and two other friends back home in Philadelphia, decided to reform the group and bring it out to Boulder. "We had played in high school," he recalls, "but we never figured out how to put together a full song until we were out in Colorado. At that time, we were hanging out with the members of the Samples. In fact, I learned everything about being a band by watching the Samples. They were the ones who inspired me to bring everyone out, and they were the ones who encouraged us to get out there on the road, doing the whole touring thing."

The band's exhaustive tour schedule garnered it national recognition; people who'd seen the Winebottles quickly spread the word about the group's hook-filled compositions and its enthusiastic live shows. Says Murray: "We didn't want to play covers, so we tried to fill a show, sometimes two sets, with our own music. And, particularly when we started, we really didn't have enough songs, so we'd take the ones we had and keep them going for a while." Positive audience response led to the band's inclusion on the *aware One* compilation, which won it additional exposure (the group later appeared on *aware Four* as well). The Winebottle's road dates consequently increased, triggering some personnel changes, although the band's core — made up of principal songwriters and guitarists Murray and Taylor —

remained intact. Just prior to a 1994 tour, the Winebottles actually hijacked drummer "Young" Sam Young, removing him from a high school class, and he has remained with the group ever since. Most recently, the band has fostered a relationship with Hollywood, supplying songs for films such as *Wide Awake*, *Chairman of the Board*, and *Thirty-Five Miles from Normal* (in which it performs). Murray sums up his experience with the Winebottles by remarking, "It's funny. When we got to Boulder, everyone out there was playing ten-minute songs. It wasn't until we left the area and started seeing other groups that I realized, 'Hey, I guess we're a jam band.'"

DISCOGRAPHY

Sober (1993)

Ride My Pony (1995)

Our Life Story (1997). This release focuses on the band's songs, a number of which have tight arrangements. Many of these compositions feature bright vocals, effects-laden guitars, and catchy melodies in the pop mold. Some notable efforts include "Different Light," "Boston Song," and "Up to Here." The disc closes with the pleasing, acoustic-driven "One like This."

WEB SITE

draper.runet.edu/~wbottles

YETI

- **TIM "T-BONE" BARNEY:** *bass*
- **MARK CAMPBELL:** *vocals, guitar*
- **MARK KAUFMAN:** *drums*
- **MICHAEL MYERS:** *tenor and alto saxophone, flute*

Much like its Tibetan namesake, San Francisco's Yeti stomps. The band presents an invigorating blend of funk and jazz, which at times trails into psychedelic realms. At any given show, the band tears into its extensive catalog of original songs and introduces a Yetified cover or two (including spirited versions of the Meters's "Look-a-Py-Py" and Miles Davis's "It's About That Time"). The band is building a steady stream of supporters; there have been Yeti sightings at venues all along the West Coast and a notable appearance at the High Sierra Music Festival.

The quartet benefits from the adroit contributions of each of its players. Although a number of Yeti's tunes are instrumentals, Mark Campbell provides some robust vocal leads. Campbell also produces an array of sounds from his guitar, which the southpaw plays upside down and strung for a righty. Michael Myers adds saxophone accents, which can be strident and frantic or soothing and melodic (on occasion, Myers even plays two saxes at once). The band's rhythm section is anchored by bass player Tim "T-Bone" Barney, who supplies some throbbing tones on his four-string. Drummer Mark Kaufman cushions the pocket and frequently furnishes some jazz fills. The band characterizes the sum of these efforts as its "big, hairy grooves."

DISCOGRAPHY

Down from the Mountain (1998)

WEB SITE

www.hooked.net/~michaell/yeti.htm

YOLK

- ■ **ANDREW BELLAVIA:** *tenor saxophone*
- ■ **BRIAN BURRELL:** *vocals, didgeridoo*
- ■ **DAVE FITZHUGH:** *guitar*
- ■ **JIM LOMONACO:** *bass*
- ■ **MATT MURPHY:** *drums*
- ■ **JEFF PETTIT:** *alto and soprano saxophone, percussion, flute*

Yolk is unquestionably a jam band, but the bristling grooves it creates are very in-your-face. This six-piece group from New York will sometimes present funk, rock, hard core, and ska within the context of a single song. Guitarist Dave Fitzhugh notes, "The band has changed a bit over the years. What happens now is everyone brings in whatever music they like and we put it together in our own style." Saxophonist Jeff Pettit adds, "We draw on everything from Sonny Rollins to Henry Rollins."

The band formed in 1992, bringing together players of diverse interests and backgrounds (some of whom were students at the State University of New York in Binghamton, some of whom were area residents). In describing the origins of the band's name, Pettit remarks, "It was the only one that everybody didn't hate"; and, Pettit adds, "We're more of a democracy than any other band I've seen." Yolk thrives through the varied voices of its players. Fitzhugh supplies some aggressive, searing guitar declarations. The group's two saxophone players, Andrew Bellavia and Pettit, are often shrill and raucous but can be subdued and harmonious as well. Jim Lomonaco contributes pulsing phrases on "low-vibration generators." Drummer Matt Murphy supplies frantic accents. Vocalist Brian Burrell will frequently draw these many elements together by acting as a rhyming emcee. Says Fitzhugh: "We go out there and give what we've got every single night. We hope to spread our messages. Even if we're just playing to a bar owner and his girlfriend – well, there's two people right there." Pettit concludes: "Because we play so many styles, I'm proud of the fact that we bring so many types of people together to see us, so many people together vibing in what we're doing." Indeed, band members explain that at Yolk shows the audience is made up of "hippies, punks, rave kids, long-hairs, dorky ska people, jazzers, and freaks."

DISCOGRAPHY

Yolk (1994)

Caution: Social Prescriptions May Cause Side Effects (1995)

Individually Twisted (1996). This release emphasizes Yolk's funkier side with a generous helping of hard core and a dash of ska. The band comes out blaring with "Infinity." "Into the Unknowns" follows, marked by metal guitar and strident brass. Then "Sofa Thought" provides a jazzy sax interlude before the harder "Urticaria." Another interesting offering is the intricate "Next Step for the Monkey," which in part has a Middle Eastern feel.

WEB SITE

www.zigmund.com/yolk

ZEN TRICKSTERS

- ■ **ROB BARRACO:** *keyboards, vocals*
- ■ **KLYPH BLACK:** *bass, vocals*
- ■ **JOE CHIRCO:** *drums*
- ■ **JEFF MATTSON:** *guitar, vocals*

New York's Zen Tricksters have never tried to hide their fondness for the music of the Grateful Dead. Lead guitarist Jeff Mattson certainly attended the meetings, with more than two hundred shows to his credit. Ever since he first started playing, Dead songs have been part of his musical repertoire. However, although Zen Tricksters continue to perform Dead covers with vigor and abandon, the band is particularly proud of its growing catalog of original material. In fact, since the release of *The Holy Fool* in late 1996, the group's growing repute may be attributed to the appeal of its own music.

Zen Tricksters continues to garner accolades for its flavorful extemporized jams. Notes keyboardist Rob Barraco: "We excel at group improvisation. In our case, there isn't just one guy soloing while the rest of the band supports him. The four of us could be a thousand miles apart and, at the drop of a hat, turn on a dime." The band's improvised journeys often yield creative segues. Both Mattson and Barraco, who have been playing together since 1989, when the band was known as the Volunteers, regularly introduce absorbing runs on their respective instruments. Bassist Klyph Black and drummer Joe Chirco actively provide a color balance. Reflecting on the group's endeavors, Barraco remarks: "When I was younger, I loved to see music that would take me to that special place. Now with the Dead gone and many of the players I love to see no longer with us, I have to rely on myself. And this band takes me there every night."

DISCOGRAPHY

The Holy Fool (1996). The band's gift for intercommunication is particularly evident on this release. It repeatedly locks in, from the thick grooves of "Lay down Your Love" to the lilting melody of "Shine Your Light." Other solid offerings include the sprightly "Arise" and the soulful "Drownin." Longtime fans will appreciate the return of former vocalist Jennifer Markard on "Homesick."

WEB SITE

zentricksters.com

ZERO

- **GREG ANTON:** *drums and percussion*
- **MARTIN FIERRO:** *saxophone, percussion*
- **STEVE KIMOCK:** *guitars*
- **JUDGE MURPHY:** *vocals*
- **CHIP ROLAND:** *keyboards*
- **BOBBY VEGA:** *bass*

Zero's musical lineage is rather extraordinary. Its current members have played with, among others, Etta James, John Lee Hooker, Sly and the Family Stone, and the Grateful Dead. Quicksilver Messenger Service guitarist John Cippolina performed with the group until his death in 1989. Pete Sears provided keyboards until he left to play with Hot Tuna. In short, Zero is ideally suited to be the subject of a musical version of the Kevin Bacon game (a.k.a. Six Degrees of Separation; see Appendix D for Zero Degrees of Separation). Zero fans, of course, find such trivia secondary to the band's seemingly unbounded gifts for collective improvisation.

Drummer Greg Anton and guitarist Steve Kimock formed Zero in 1984. Five years earlier, Anton had joined Keith and Donna Godchaux in Ghosts, which the couple had assembled after their departure from the Grateful Dead. In 1980, Ghosts retooled itself to become the Heart of Gold Band, adding a new guitarist of considerable repute named Steve Kimock. This outfit performed for a few years (despite being staggered by Keith Godchaux's fatal car crash). During this time, Anton and Kimock recognized their complementary styles and mutual penchant for creating ordered musical chaos. They would often rent studio space and work through some instrumentals they had crafted. Zero emerged from these sessions.

The group's lineup has evolved over the years. One longtime member is saxophonist Martin Fierro, who performed on the Grateful

Dead's 1973 horn tour in support of *Wake of the Flood* and later continued to play with Jerry Garcia. Fierro brings to the band a flair for jazz, an affinity for Latin percussion, and a spirit that defies convention. Bassist Bobby Vega, who appeared with Sly and the Family Stone at the age of sixteen, contributes his own estimable facilities in multiple musical genres. Another integral element is former Grateful Dead lyricist Robert Hunter. An old friend of Anton, Hunter encouraged the drummer to add a vocalist to the mix in 1991, pledging his own verse to the band. A search yielded San Francisco blues singer Judge Murphy, who now observes: "What can I say? I feel honored to sing Hunter material."

Zero is a band that should be experienced live. In this setting, the group sweeps the entire venue along on a mutual excursion. Keyboardist Chip Roland affirms the role the audience plays in this endeavor, insisting that without them "it would be like trying to cut your hair without a mirror." The band's shows are usually inaugurated by one player sounding a lone note or trill. The other performers reflect on that note and then begin to fill in the canvas. Typically, Zero presents a wide array of instrumental abstractions, which are considered and pared down. Then Murphy will step forward to interpret the lyrics that Hunter has gracefully crafted. Of course, between vocal numbers and even within songs, the band resumes its collaborative disquisitions. The result is a feast of ideas that nourishes both the performers and the audience — a banquet of Zero.

DISCOGRAPHY

Here Goes Nothin' (1987)

Nothin' Goes Here (1990)

Go Hear Nothin' (1991)

Chance in a Million (1995)

Zero (1997). The band recorded this disc live in the studio without any overdubs — a fact proclaimed in a wry liner note that labels this "innovative" recording technique "No Tools." However, quite possibly due, in part, to Hunter's contributions, Zero does not embark on any of the extended musical journeys that characterize its live shows. Nonetheless, the music does retain an organic feel. "Pits of Thunder" opens and features some of Vega's funky bass lines and a vibrant response from Fierro. "Spoken For" is a notable cut in which Murphy's powerful vocals are matched by Kimock's guitar, which bolsters the song's stately tone quite eloquently. Hunter's turns of phrase enrich a number of tracks, including "Possession," a poignant statement about mandatory sentencing laws. Kimock's ebullient performance in "Sun Sun Sun" also stands out, calling to mind Carlos Santana. The instrumental "Kissing the Boo Boo" closes the album in a spirited, cleansing manner.

ZOO PEOPLE

- **BRIAN CHAPMAN:** *vocals, electric and acoustic guitar*
- **JASON HANN:** *percussion, vocals*
- **ANDREW HARVEY:** *drums, vocals*
- **GREG HYATT:** *bass, vocals*
- **JOHN JAKUBEK:** *electric and acoustic guitar, mandolin, vocals*
- **JOHN NAU:** *keyboards, vocals*

Zoo People came together amid the visual splendor of Venice Beach, California. There drummer Andrew Harvey and keyboardist John Nau, who had been playing together since they were fourteen years old, initiated the jam sessions that led to the creation of the group. Nau had lent his talents to a number of projects and performers over the years, including Max Roach, Belinda Carlisle, Hootie and the Blowfish, and Ratt. He and Harvey recruited a number of similarly talented players to fill out the Zoo People roster. For instance, Brian Chapman, who assumed lead vocal duties, had recently finished a stint playing guitar with the band They Eat Their Own. John Jakubek joined the group to play guitar following the dissolution of his popular jam band, Jasmine Groove.

Zoo People's lineup has expanded to a sextet. This collection of players both collectively composes some melodious compositions and takes them to new heights in the concert setting. Guitarists Jakubek and Chapman often lay down dual leads in a manner reminis-cent of the Allman Brothers Band. Nau contributes animated expressions on keyboards. The band's sound is also animated by the dual attack of drummer Harvey and percussionist Jason Hann (who had performed with a range of jazz and African troupes before joining the group). Finally, Zoo People sweetens the pot with three- and four-part vocal harmonies. The group, which has earned invitations to perform on the HORDE tour and at the High Sierra Music Festival, is accompanied from gig to gig by a throng of tapers and a contingent of zealous fans who call themselves Zoopies.

DISCOGRAPHY

Zoo People (1994)

Sage (1997). Although the group doesn't exhibit the full force of its live vigor on this disc, Zoo People does present a number of the compositions that comprise the core of its concert presentations. "Lay Low" is rife with rich harmonies and possesses a gentle groove somewhat reminiscent of Steely Dan. The title track is a soaring instrumental. Other notable songs include "It's Alright to Be," which is enlivened by bright keyboards; "Wildflower"; and the rousing "Halfway Gone."

WEB SITE

bands.hive.net/zoopeople

ZUBA

- **MIKE CYKOSKI:** *bass, vocals*
- **WALLACE LESTER:** *drums*
- **LIZA O.:** *vocals, guitar*
- **MARK PAUPERAS:** *saxophone, keyboards*
- **BEN SENTERFIT:** *saxophone, vocals*

Zuba formed in Telluride, Colorado. Wallace Lester was waiting tables there, affably enduring the pejorative term that cooks often ascribe to restaurant staff: "zuba." When this group came together, Lester appropriated the term for its name. Over the years, the former zuba and his bandmates have released three discs, crisscrossed the United States on tour, and contributed original music to a number of films.

The year 1997 was a transitional one for the band. Zuba modified its lineup, welcoming new bassist Mike Cykoski (who replaced the venerable Sid Greenbud) and saxophonist Ben Senterfit (formerly of the popular Boulder group Chitlin). Despite these changes, the band maintained an active slate of live gigs, appearing on both coasts and playing nearly 150 shows. It did, however, spend most of July and August working in the new players, and it emerged revitalized, with a renewed commitment to its music, as evidenced by its kinetic live shows.

The band is comprised of five charismatic musicians working in concert. Liza O. fronts the group, supplying lead vocals and tearing things up on her Stratocaster. Mark Pauperas and Senterfit regularly interject dueling saxophones (actually, a third sax often enters the picture — Senterfit can play two at once). Pauperas also supplies keyboards on a number of tunes. Cykoski has proven that he possesses the chops to replace local hero Greenbud on bass. Veteran drummer Lester propels the band forward. The sounds Zuba produces often possess a funky bottom, but the band also creates some jazzier textures. In fact, although the group works up many thick, vigorous grooves, at times Liza O. will utilize her silken voice to present a more melodic, soulful offering. The band has also started adding three-part harmonies to many of its songs. The results have expanded Zuba's palette without detracting from its manic live presentation.

Zuba also has a burgeoning relationship with the film industry. Its music appears in Warren Miller's *Snowrider*, and it has recently contributed songs to two more films, *There's Something about Mary* and *Say You'll Be Mine*. However, Zuba's Hollywood apogee may have occurred when director Peter Farrelly spotted the band performing in an Aspen club and hired its members to appear as rednecks in his film *Kingpin*.

DISCOGRAPHY

Zuba (1993)
Live Soundboard '95 (1995)
New Cruelty (1996)

WEB SITE

www.zubalove.com

APPENDIX A

HOW TO TAPE AND TRADE LIVE SHOWS

Every group that appears in *Jam Bands* has been selected due to the energy, artistry, and creativity of its live performances. In fact, some of these groups have at times lamented the fact that their studio releases do not capture the vigor or intensity of their concerts. Many more have emphasized the role their audiences play as catalysts, contributing to peak performances. It is fortunate that such a high proportion of these bands' notable shows has been documented and is available to interested listeners. Every group in this book permits and promotes noncommercial taping. (It is important, however, to recognize that some bands' taping policies fluctuate. Additionally, certain venues do not permit audience recordings. One updated Internet source that reflects the current attitudes of jam bands is a list called "Bands That Allow Live Taping," which is sometimes posted to the newsgroup DAT-Heads and can be found at the site listed at the end of this appendix.)

Among the array of pleasures offered by the groups represented in *Jam Bands* is the chance to collect their live shows – both to reminisce about personal concert experiences and to sample other standout gigs. This essay will explore the principal ways of building a personal live-tape library. It will begin with an exploration of the issues involved in selecting a deck and microphones and then explore other ways of obtaining tapes, even if you decide not to purchase your own portable recording equipment.

First, though, it is crucial to stress that bands permit audience taping for private, noncommercial use only. One growing danger to the taping community has been the proliferation of unauthorized live CDs, which are occasionally sold at record stores. In recent years, groups such as the Dave Matthews Band and Widespread Panic have raised questions about the viability of live taping if these unsanctioned discs continue to appear. Moreover, both organizations have actively encouraged their fans to provide them with any information they may have about violations of taping guidelines. So, because such practices are potentially harmful to the future of live-concert taping, please make it a point to avoid buying unauthorized CDs, to refuse to lend your masters to anyone you think might use them to this end, and not to charge others for copies of your shows (aside from the cost of blank tapes and postage).

DAT VERSUS ANALOG

One initial decision you must reach is whether to start collecting in analog or digital. Each format offers its own distinct advantages. Although most people who have started collecting DATs (digital audio tapes) say they would never go back, there are still virtues to collecting analog tapes (which are the cassettes that currently fit your Walkman or car stereo).

The strongest point in favor of DAT is sound fidelity. The process that is used to store data onto a digital taping device creates crispness and clarity. Many recording-industry professionals record by means of this technology. Moreover, the music on compact discs is also stored digitally, so that the sound of many DAT recordings approaches that of CDs.

A second, related issue is that, unlike their analog counterparts, digital recordings receive no signal degradation from generation to generation. This alleviates a problem that sometimes occurs with analog tapes. For instance, if you begin with an analog source tape of a show and then copy it onto another cassette for a friend, who uses her copy to record the show for a third friend, who then uses his copy to dub for a fourth person, who spins it for someone else, then, by that fifth generation, some of the high frequencies are lost and replaced with hiss. (Some would say that significant losses occur sooner; it all depends on the quality of the equipment.) However, assuming that clean, properly maintained decks are used, digital copies do not suffer from the same problem.

Along these lines, there are a few procedures you should implement to ensure high-quality DAT copies. First, before you use a new digital tape, make sure you fast forward it all the way to the end and then rewind it. This unpacks the tape, releasing some tension, and it disperses any lubricant over the entire tape. A number of DAT copies have been ruined due to failure to employ this procedure, which is unnecessary for analogs. Also, in the case of DATs, it is wise to identify your shows with felt-tip markers rather than ballpoint pens or pencils, because graphite and ink particles could flake off and destroy the tape. Finally, it is important to clean your deck and take it in for regular maintenance (read your owner's manual for specific suggestions).

Recognize also that there is a small but vocal group of individuals who prefer the sound of analog equipment. Most of these individuals claim that analog tapes possess a warmth that is lacking in sterile, sanitized digital recordings. Another faction (represented by, most notably, Gordon Sharpless) asserts that, if you are running a superior set of mikes into a high-quality analog deck, any loss in fidelity that may occur will remain undetectable to the human ear, and that those who think otherwise are merely fooling themselves.

A less debatable point in favor of analog is expense. A low-end portable DAT recorder usually costs in the neighborhood of six to seven hundred dollars, with many priced at two or three times that amount. Furthermore, in order to enjoy this music at your leisure (and to spin tapes), a second home DAT is required. By contrast, the least expensive portable professional analog recorders are available for less than three hundred dollars, and many fine decks can be purchased for under eight hundred. Moreover, no additional devices are needed for home use, as most people already have analog cassette decks. Finally, individual digital audio tapes are often at least twice the cost of analogs.

Some people also prefer the convenience of analog cassettes. These tapes fit into devices they already own, such as Walkmans and car stereos, and there can be no more satisfying experience than getting into your car after a concert and replaying those riveting, explosive show highlights. Some digital aficionados resolve this issue by purchasing digital car decks (or adapters) and even digital Walkmans; others will instead spin analog tapes from their DAT masters.

Digital recorders offer another advantage for concert tapers: it's unnecessary to flip over a digital tape in the middle of a performance. Standard digital audio tapes (60-meter) last for two hours, while some (90-meter) run for three hours (although a number of DAT tapers prefer not to use the latter, as they are thinner and have been known to tear). By contrast, standard 90-minute analog tapes record only 45 minutes of music per side (the actual time is closer to 46), although many tapers use 100s (110s or any other long-running cassettes are discouraged for the same reason that digital tapers eschew 90-meter tapes). As a result, DAT tapers have the luxury of starting their decks at the beginning of a show and letting them run until the music stops. By contrast, analog tapers must crouch down at the 40-to-45-minute mark and flip over their tapes.

There is an art to flipping an analog tape. The idea is to do so without losing anything important, so ideally the goal is to flip between songs. The worst possible scenario is that you are forced to flip in the middle of some stunning improvisation. Not only will part of the jam be lost, but also, when you're listening to the tape later on and entering a trancelike state, everything will come to a crashing halt while the tape is turned over. So, when you're running an analog deck, there is the additional pressure of always having to watch the clock: if, for example, the band you're recording finishes a song at the 38-minute mark, you must decide whether to flip the tape or wait until the end of the next tune. It is for this reason that most analog tapers run 100-minute tapes – this affords them an additional window of five or six minutes within which to make such decisions.

PURCHASING MICROPHONES, PATCHING

One way to ensure that you receive high-quality live tapes is to buy your own mikes and use them (run them) at a show. The principal factor militating against such efforts is cost. A second consideration that also inhibits some individuals is the time and energy it takes to set up microphones properly at any given concert.

Purchasing microphones is a pricey venture for a number of reasons. First, a decent set of new mikes will typically cost a minimum of six hundred dollars, and prices escalate rapidly from there (although used sets can be purchased from a reputable dealer; a price report appears regularly on the DAT-Heads Web site). However, along with the microphone bodies and capsules you'll also need a pre-amp to regulate the incoming signals; this is often combined with a power supply. Additional costs include a microphone stand, a microphone mount (T-bar), cables, batteries, extra cables, extra batteries, duct tape, windscreens, umbrella, and a carrying case in which to store all of these items. There is also the cost of regular microphone maintenance.

As all of this suggests, running microphones is a labor-intensive endeavor. This is why you'll often see tapers lined up prior to the opening of the doors at a show: they want to ensure that their equipment is well situated and running properly. Troubleshooting can be particularly stressful, especially as the minutes click down to showtime and a signal still is not passing into your deck. It is a good idea to experience this situation before actually investing in mikes by borrowing or renting some equipment and recording some shows (many taper-friendly businesses are happy to rent so that potential purchasers can sample equipment).

Of course, another possibility is to rely on the generosity of those people who own microphones and are adept at running them to receive a line-out to your portable deck. Generally speaking, those people with mikes are willing to assist. The convention is to ask politely for a patch, or inquire whether you can have an analog (or digital) out. It's usually best to wait until the mike owner has finished setting up or is taking a break from doing so. Remember, though, that due to space limitations in many designated taping sections some of these people have already made commitments to their friends. Alternately, if a number of decks are linked together (daisy-chained), you can approach the taper at the end and ask that person for a patch (but again, remember that there may be prior commitments or space constraints).

Sometimes, a band will allow soundboard patches. In this case, one or two tapers receive direct feeds from the board, and everyone else chains out of those decks (and, as long as you are there well in advance of showtime, convention dictates that you should receive a patch). Don't forget, however, that DATs are usually given priority in line because there is no signal loss as they don't flip (a few analog decks, such as the Sony D-5, also allow a signal to be passed during a flip). If you have a deck at the end of a very long daisy-chain, it is vital that you do a level check before the show starts to ensure that you have a signal coming through and that your inputs are set to an appropriate spot.

Once someone agrees to supply you with a patch, all is well — provided you have the cords necessary to receive a signal. This is why you should come equipped with at least two cables that can emerge from your deck and enter either a 1/8-inch jack or dual RCA plugs (one cord and one adapter can accomplish this as well). Owners of DAT decks will want to invest in digital-to-digital plugs, although DATs can receive analog signals (and some people are content to accept these). Additionally, due to space constraints, it is often helpful to bring a longer cord that can extend a few feet in case you need to receive a patch and remain out of the way of other tapers.

Occasionally, because space is often at a premium in the tapers' section, someone who is running mikes may be happy to provide you with a patch but may prefer to run your deck for you. Some kind souls will even do your analog flips. If you find yourself in such a situation, express your profuse thanks and do not hesitate to buy this person a beverage. You could also volunteer to watch the decks and mikes for a few moments (before the show, during the set break, or even in midset).

In general, it is best to recall that courtesy begets courtesy. Everyone around you wants the same thing (crisp tapes), and most can appreciate such mutual sentiments. One final bit of advice: keep a checklist in your wallet so that before you head into a show you can pull it out and verify that you are properly equipped. Along with all of your recording devices, the list should include a watch (if you're running an analog deck, one with a timing function is helpful), a pen, and a small flashlight. Also, don't forget to place "ticket" on that list.

SETTING UP TRADES WITH TAPERS AT A SHOW

Another sure way to obtain high-quality, low-generation tapes is to solicit them from those who actually recorded a show. Many concertgoers pass by the tapers' section on their way out of a venue to discuss the possibility of acquiring a copy. However, it is important to recognize that those who ran decks are anxious to break down their equipment and head out (at times, venue security can be less than sympathetic to tapers' needs). So, in most cases, a frenzied grovel at a taper's feet will not elicit a positive response. Instead, try framing your request using one of the following methods.

One approach that many tapers find friendly is for spin solicitors to bring a self-addressed and stamped bubble mailer with some blanks to the show (bubble envelopes are suggested, as the paper-filled ones have been known to spring leaks, and the residue can get onto tapes and damage decks). The idea here is to ask the taper for a copy of the show and then simply hand over the envelope. However, it is important to recognize that many tapers have other obligations and may be on tour and unable to spin copies anytime soon. Incidentally, it is poor form to toss your envelope into the middle of the taper section in the hope that someone will take pity on you (a tactic attempted on a few occasions by one misguided individual). Keep in mind also that many digital tapers don't do a lot of analog spins, particularly for people they don't know, as it can be time consuming. (The flips require a bit more thought, because to do them perfectly you have to stop the DAT recorder, rewind the analog cassette to the starting point of the song that was cut off, hit record to fill the rest of the tape with silence, flip over the tape, find the appropriate space on the DAT tape, and commence recording again. Also, if it's a two-set show and the source is a 3-hour, 90-meter DAT, then you must ensure that the second set doesn't leak onto the first cassette or the same process must be repeated before inserting another analog tape to record the second set.)

A second possibility is to bring your tape list to a show to see if you can initiate a trade. People organize their lists in a variety of ways, but the generally accepted convention is to provide a series of information that includes the band, source, date, venue, grade, and tape length. For example:

moe.

1/21/97	Wetlands, NYC	I,II	190	DSBD2	A-
1/25/97	Iron Horse Music Hall, Northampton, MA	II	90	DAUD3	B+
4/3/97	Somerville Theater, Somerville, MA	I,II	180	AUD1	A-

In this hypothetical example of an analog trader's list, the band is moe., the first column gives the show date, and the second column identifies the venue. The next section specifies which sets the person owns (in the first and third examples, the trader has both sets; in the middle instance, only the second set). The number that follows indicates how many minutes of tape were needed to record the performance (the Wetlands show required both 90- and 100-minute tapes, while the other three sets required 90-minute ones). The letter D, which appears twice in the fifth column, indicates that the initial source was a DAT. The letters SBD identify the tape as coming from a soundboard, and AUD denotes that it was recorded through microphones (some traders will also list the brand of mike that was used, and some hardcores, particularly DAT traders, may identify the preamp as well). The last column grades the sound quality of the tape, and, given the prevalence of grade inflation in our society, it should not surprise you to learn that most any tape that has been given a grade lower than a B will likely contain much hiss and will be nearly unlistenable. Some traders will, however, include a guide at the top of the list that translates each grade (it is important to remember that this grade does not refer to the band's performance on a particular evening but only to the sound quality on the tape itself). When making a list, it is essential to include your name, address, phone number, and e-mail address (if you have one). Even if your list doesn't score you a trade on a given evening, it may help you to meet someone who'll turn out to be a future trading partner.

OTHER WAYS TO BUILD A TAPE COLLECTION (TREES AND TRADES)

You can build an entire live-tape library by trading. The advent of the Internet has facilitated building a collection. Several Web sites provide bulletin boards where people can post their tape lists. Interested parties surf past, view the current offerings, and e-mail trade requests. Of course, you can't become part of this process if you have nothing to trade. If this is your predicament, then start looking for tape trees and newbie offers.

Tape trees appear in many of the newsgroups that are devoted to particular bands. The idea is that someone seeds the tree with a high-quality source tape, and then a structure is created whereby other people (branches) spin a handful of copies for still others who do the same until everyone receives tapes (including leaves, who do not do any spinning). Tape trees have made it possible for hundreds of people to obtain copies of a show with no one receiving anything worse than a third-generation recording.

Another way to start a collection is by responding to newbie offers. These are made from time to time by those who have a cache of high-quality tapes and remember what it was like when they were starting out. These individuals will post a promise to spin copies for a predetermined number of people. Some offers may require a little creativity on the part of the respondent (such as answering a trivia question or telling an entertaining story), but just as often all that's necessary is a swift e-mail.

Once you've begun to build up a small collection of tapes, you can start communicating with others in the hope of establishing a trade. This can be done by responding to others' posts, by offering one of your own, or by contacting those individuals whose lists you have discovered on a Web site. In setting up a trade, be sure to take note of your prospective trading partner's full name and home telephone number in case a problem ensues. Before you enter into a trade, you may also want to establish the length of the turnaround so that you'll know when to send a friendly reminder to the other party. You'll also want to exchange specifics about the brands and lengths of tapes, whether to include the tape cases, and perhaps the types of decks used (dubbing decks that have two tape wells situated next to one another often yield lower-quality copies than tapes spun on two separate decks, and under no circumstances should you use high-speed dubbing, which is available on very few decks nowadays anyhow). For a long time, traders also had to resolve whether to keep or send "max points," which appear on Maxell tape labels, but at present the company seems to have suspended that program. It is also important to enter your trades in a logbook that lists all relevant information — from the name, address, and phone number of your trading partner to details of the shows to be exchanged (and remember not to store this information on your hard drive without backing it up).

If you do not have on-line access, you can still set up trades, as many people take out ads in magazines such as *An Honest Tune*, *Dupree's Diamond News*, *Hittin' the Note*, and *Relix*. You can use these resources to send your list to selected individuals and seek theirs in return, or you can take out an ad of your own. Then you can initiate trading relationships, keeping in mind all of the caveats, conventions, and concerns mentioned here. Finally, when your tapes do arrive, don't forget to pop the tabs so that you don't accidentally record over the show that you've been eagerly awaiting.

RESOURCES

- DAT-Heads Web site: www.eklektix.com/dat-heads/
- Bands that allow taping: www.enteract.com/~wagner/btat/
- Phish.Net Taping FAQ: www.phish.net/phishFAQ/tape-qs.html
- A vendor list appears at the DAT-Head site:
  www.eklektix.com/dat-heads/Vendors/
- However, some of the more widely used suppliers of tape and equipment include
  - Cassette House www.tape.com 1-800-321-5738
  - Hunts Wholesale 1-800-278-8273
  - Sonic Sense www.henge.com/~sncsns 303-698-1296
  - Terrapin Tapes www.ttapes.com 1-800-677-6850
- There are a number of trading sites that you should be able to find through searches or links at various bands' Web sites. One site that features many of the bands in this book is www.tapetrading.com
- An additional useful site where many band-related links may be found is www.ubl.com
- Of course, another fine source is the Jam Bands web site www.jambands.com

APPENDIX B

WETLANDS: TEN YEARS OF GROOVES

The Wetlands Preserve in New York City has long served as a nurturing environment and proving ground for many of the groups described in *Jam Bands*. The club's development actually parallels that of the evolving improvisational music scene chronicled in this book. However, Wetlands is much more than a music venue. It has striven to foster a sense of community by initiating friendships, creating alliances, and at times even shepherding the careers of particular acts. Just as importantly, the club maintains a commitment to environmental and social activism. Wetlands offers all of this *and* a VW bus in the main room as well.

Over the years, the club has hosted virtually every notable jam band performing today. In the first few years after its February 1989 opening, Wetlands hosted multiple performances by Aquarium Rescue Unit, Big Head Todd and the Monsters, Blues Traveler, Bela Fleck and the Flecktones, God Street Wine, Gov't Mule, the Dave Matthews Band, Phish, the Samples, the Spin Doctors, and Widespread Panic. Many of these bands often appeared on the same bill, since southern groups – such as Aquarium Rescue Unit, the Dave Matthews Band, and Widespread Panic – often gained their initial New York City exposure while opening for Manhattan denizens Blues Traveler. One interesting showcase bill from the mid-1990s included From Good Homes, Hootie and the Blowfish, the Dave Matthews Band, and Rusted Root. More recent headliners have included Agents of Good Roots, the Gibb Droll Band, Frogwings, Galactic, Leftover Salmon, moe., Moon Boot Lover, Ominous Seapods, Percy Hill, Strangefolk, and String Cheese Incident. Many individual performers have developed an abiding loyalty to the club: moe., for example, has performed at Wetlands under the pseudonym Monkeys on Ecstasy; and, in January of 1998, Blues Traveler commanded the stage, performing classics during a High Plains Drifter show at which the quartet also played with Chris Barron, Warren Haynes, Jono Manson, Noel Redding, and Eric Schenkman.

Wetlands has garnered its reputation with its history of notable performances and its vibe, both of which were lovingly, assiduously facilitated by founder Larry Bloch. The club's current talent buyer, Chris Zahn, recalls: "My first few moments in the Wetlands were a revelation. I had never walked into a nightclub before and seen people walking around barefoot." Reid Genauer of Strangefolk notes, "I think it's a landmark club in the country, a mecca. It's like a great band in that it's larger than itself, it's larger than its components." Lo Faber of God Street Wine remarks, "Once we started doing well there, it opened doors for us all over the country." Ominous Seapods bassist Tom Pirozzi adds, "The Wetlands has been the axis of the whole scene for the past several years. It has been the key venue. We can be in Montana or California, and we can say that we headlined at the Wetlands, and people are psyched about that."

One sentiment that many musicians and customers share is a sense of the affable, inviting atmosphere emanating from Wetlands. *Relix* publisher and performer Toni Brown reflects: "Back in 1987, I received my initial call from Larry, and from the moment I set foot in the club I knew that it would give us a place to call home." Blues Traveler mainstay Gina Z. remembers: "When Wetlands opened, I remember we said this was a big gift to New York City. It was a very exciting time, there were a lot of bands playing out. The moment we stepped inside we knew it was going to be a place for us. Half the friends and acquaintances I know I met at the end of the bar." Guitarist Chuck Garvey of moe. observes, "I've always felt that we were at home at Wetlands. We just played better at the club. It gets more out of us." Edwin Hurwitz, bass player for Skin and formerly of Shockra, adds, "That club gives everybody an oasis in New York City." Finally, current Wetlands owner Pete Shapiro, who was handed the reins by Bloch in April of 1997, asserts, "as the cyber age continues to evolve, I feel there is a greater need for a street-corner place to have human interaction and discourse. Wetlands presents an ideal atmosphere for that type of interaction."

From its inception, Wetlands has aspired to be more than a performance space. Larry Bloch's original vision was to create a club that not only presented music but also mobilized individuals to effect social and environmental change. "I knew I wanted to work in the environmental field," Bloch says, "but I didn't want to do it on the lobbying level. What I wanted to do was grow a place that people would enjoy but also would take a serious stance on a range of issues. I couldn't compare it to any other venture. So what I eventually decided to do was take raw industrial space and turn it into an inviting nightclub."

As soon as the club opened, Bloch slotted a weekly "eco-saloon." A series of working groups was created to focus on issues ranging from animal rights to human rights to land action. Bloch is particularly proud of Wetlands's efforts to protect rainforests. He notes, "The club alerted the *New York Times* that the paper was using forest wood. We started demonstrations, and eventually we sat down with the chairman of the board and convinced him not to renew his contract with the company supplying that paper. We've also become proxy shareholders in corporate meetings. Sometimes we've been lucky and walked in to find half a dozen multimillionaires in the room who are willing to listen to what we have to say rather than face negative publicity. That happened with the *Wall Street Journal*. There have been other strategies as well. We boycotted companies doing business in Burma, where a democratically elected government was taken out of power by a fascist regime." All in all, although Bloch perceives there is much work left to do, he is pleased with the club's impact. "Concertgoers walk out with knowledge even if they're not direct participants," he explains. "The bands take it away with them as well."

However, the Wetlands doesn't just preach – it abides by its own strict, environmentally sound regimen. Notes Toni Brown: "Larry had the environment in mind from the start. The only straws you could get there were paper. I don't know of anyone at any other club who was so completely concerned about all of it, from recycling bottles to the kind of soda it would serve." Similarly, the club is lit with low-wattage, energy-saving bulbs, it prohibits plastic cups, and it uses napkins and matches made of recycled paper. The toilets have been modified to flush with a minimum of water.

Even the club's moniker reflects these concerns. "The name just came to me," recalls Bloch, "and it seemed to sum up what we are doing. It clued people in to the fact that we were an environmental center. Also, a wetlands is a nurturing place for all sorts of creatures. It's also a pun that suggests the raucous nature of dancing and sweating." The latter point has led some people, following an evening of particularly unrestrained dancing, to dub the venue "Sweatglands."

John Dwork, publisher of *Dupree's Diamond News* and author of the *Deadhead's Taping Compendium*, suggests that "Wetlands Preserve is about setting a table for a meal and having it become a family meal. Something wonderful happens when you get together with your family and have a big meal. Although in this case the food is music, and there's no arguing with Aunt Edna. But, just as importantly, there is more to it than just eating good food with good friends; it is also about becoming educated about the real costs to society of what we are enjoying."

Bloch's ethos for the club extended far beyond environmental realms. He also made a number of very specific decisions in order to foster a feeling of community. Longtime employee Jake Szufarowski notes: "There were so many small decisions that Larry made. Unless you were to hear him explain why he did something a certain way, you might not understand it. But once he let you know, it made perfect sense." In fact, Bloch so effectively created a sense of community at Wetlands that Szufarowski has remained at the club even though he now runs his own record label, Which Records (www.whichsight.com). Bloch inspired Szufarowski to distribute candy to everyone who hands him money when he is working the door (says Szufarowski, "With a piece of candy and a smile, I think people are more likely to have a good time, particularly in New York City"). In concocting a convivial club atmosphere, Bloch payed close attention to details such as the color of lights in the room and the murals that adorn the walls (these are the work of artists Breck Morgan and Tim Vega; the latter has done quite a bit of design work for Blues Traveler).

One related aspect of Wetlands that sometimes surprises new-comers is the location of the stage. Bands perform at the far end of the upstairs room, and the stage does not face out into the room — it is oriented toward the opposite wall. Notes Bloch: "The stage was intentionally placed where it is. There are multiple ways of experiencing live music, and not everyone wants to experience it in the same way. No one ever said to me, 'I want to be in front of the band, and I can't be there.' If that was a critical aspect of their experience, then they'd find a way to do it. So people could be in other areas. They could even chill downstairs on the rug if they wanted. I thought that the stage location would reduce the ego of the club. The stage was never a high stage, because I didn't want the band so much bigger than the people." Shapiro adds, "I believe community is important. We don't always have the best sight lines, but we are a great place to go to a concert, a great place to hang out."

"I first heard of the club," reminisces Gibb Droll, "when the Spin Doctors released that live album they had recorded at the Wetlands [*Up for Grabs*, later rereleased with additional tracks as *Homebelly Groove*]. I had always assumed that it must be a big club. Then, a year or so later when we played there, I realized it is not an enormous room. But I've never been able to get as much energy from such a small group of people. I know some people think that it was some sort of mistake putting the stage where it is, but you really can't understand until you start playing there."

Bloch always had his patrons in mind when he was working on the design for the club. Observes Szufarowski: "Time and again, conventional business wisdom was thrown out the window for the benefit of the customer." Brown recalls, "He built a club for the fan. In fact, initially we asked him, 'Where's the dressing room?' He told us, 'When someone plays my club, there is no dressing room. Everyone's part of the audience.'" At first, bands were placed in a downstairs office, but this practice was later modified. Says God Street Wine's Faber:

"I think we contributed to why the dressing room is now in the kitchen and not the office, because there was one time when the place was really packed and we just couldn't get to the stage. I'll say this, though: we found our original management company while the dressing room was still in the office, because we rummaged around and flipped through some *Pollstars*."

Another important component has been the downstairs lounge, which is equipped with cozy couches and other comfortable furnishings. It often serves as a retreat, and recently, on some evenings, it has emerged as a second performance space. "When the club first opened," remembers Brown, "I actually gave Larry some pillows that my mother had made and told him to place them down there. Of course, when she came to the club, that was another story." Jeff Waful, host of the upcoming *Live from the Wetlands* radio show, remarks, "The downstairs is like having a band playing at a private party with all of the couches and the low lighting. It's an inviting atmosphere, a safe haven in a chaotic city."

Yet another aspect of the Wetlands experience came out of Bloch's decision to have his headliners perform two sets of music. Affirms Zahn: "Larry fought to the end with many acts to have them play two sets of music in one night." Bloch himself adds, "There's something extraordinarily magical about a band playing two sets. Many times a band is even better in the second set — it's looser once that first set is out of the way. But also, for audience members, the time spent interacting between sets is really a magical time. People are energized, and they are anticipating more of that wonderfulness. That element is lost when the headliner does one set. I think it's a less complete experience for the patrons."

Wetlands has also become known for its extended hours. Paul Parietti, publisher of *Fantastic Voyage System*, explains: "One great thing about the club is that they let the bands play. When I see music there, I walk out at a quarter after four in the morning." Faber interjects, "It's cool, because all of the other clubs were modeled after CBGB, where six bands play forty minutes apiece." Bloch affirms that Wetlands closes "whenever the event winds down. Some of my most memorable nights were hanging out with people until five fifteen in the morning. We wind down like a nightclub, not a concert hall." This philosophy certainly continues today. Waful recalls seeing Strangefolk at the club on New Year's Eve 1997. "The show had just ended. It was about seven o'clock in the morning. They handed out free bagels, which was great, and then one of the bouncers started to tell people to move out. As soon as that happened, Pete walked over, put his arm around him, and told him to let everyone hang out. A lot of places wouldn't care, they'd just want to get the people out, but Pete let people sit down, catch their breath, and chill."

Wetlands is also distinguished by the atmosphere created by the DJs who spin seven nights a week. "When I first came to the club, I admired that they had live DJs at all of the shows," comments Zahn; Szufarowski adds, "Most clubs just play tapes, which obviously is less expensive. You may not notice it, but a DJ can create a vibe and react to a mood. It's another of those little touches that Larry had – one of his philosophies that people might not notice." Jon Topper, manager of moe., remarks: "Larry really cared about the vibe in the club. A legendary story is that one morning he called the club after a show, and, instead of asking how much money they had taken in that night, his first question was, 'What music did the DJ play after the first set?'"

Bloch himself would often spin music on weekends, devoting quite a bit of energy to the endeavor. "I had the greatest fun DJing," he says. "I loved it. But within that context I loved to be thorough. I was DJing the way I managed and ran the club. DJing is an essential part of the evening; it's not just putting music in the background. It's part of the way an evening is programmed. My DJing was thoughtfully done with a passion that was shared by Chris and Walter [Durkacz, the original Wetlands talent buyer]. I worked from a series of principles. In particular, I didn't want to have a peak song and then cut it off in the middle."

Recalls Topper: "Those nights when Larry DJed, he was there in the morning getting his music together. There were certain rules. In particular, no one was supposed to go on until the music stopped. I can remember the first night that moe. played there. The four of them were just so nervous that they walked out there and plugged in while a song was playing and before the soundman was even in place. Larry turned to me with this look on his face, and I just crawled out of that DJ booth."

Another interesting Bloch DJ story involves the time Bob Dylan sat in the DJ booth watching his son Jakob perform with the Wallflowers. "It was their first New York City play," remembers Bloch. "Bob was hanging out in the DJ booth in a hooded sweatshirt while I was DJing. We had been instructed by Jacob not to play any of his father's music. Well, the Wallflowers left the stage, maybe there were a hundred people left in the club, and maybe the third or fourth song I played – which I thought was beautifully appropriate – was Joe Cocker and Leon Russell's cover of Dylan's "Girl from the North Country" from *Mad Dogs and Englishmen*. After thirty seconds, Jakob ran into the booth and confronted me. It was sad because I thought it was a sweet parallel."

Wetlands has also defined itself through its support of live concert taping. "The Wetlands was the only club I know of that was built with a taper's section in it," observes Gina Z. Says Bloch: "From the start, we did what we could to give everyone the opportunity to tape. We set aside a taping area on nights when it was needed. We also built a direct-taping mechanism into the club, which is a zone mix and doesn't capture the fullness of the room. If I was in the DJ booth and I wanted a copy of a show, I would tape it. Right now I have a bucketful of tapes, many of which are unlabeled."

And then there is the microbus. As soon as patrons walk into Wetlands, they notice the Volkswagen parked off to the right in the eco-center. Bloch recalls, "The earth station was an area in full public access where people could look at materials related to environmental and social justice. We concluded it would be nice to have a person in the area, and we decided to situate that person in a VW bus. There were only two years, 1966 and 1967, where the bus opened on the side. Eventually, we found the one we have now abandoned and rotting in a New Hampshire field. We sent it out to have it refurbished." Today the microbus serves as an information center and merchandise booth; it stocks a range of recordings made by the club's musical denizens.

Despite the club's current emphasis, on the Wetlands's opening night, in February of 1989, there was no live music. The first group to perform at the club, New Potato Caboose, appeared the next evening. Explains Bloch: "We didn't begin with a savvy talent-buying operation — we were going on the fly. What began was a mutually symbiotic thing whereby bands that played heard about us or we heard about them. It was not a conscious business plan."

Nonetheless, the club was soon fostering a thriving subculture, which gravitated toward some of the groups that had begun to perform there regularly. The band that really triggered this development was Blues Traveler. "Blues Traveler was the first group that took the scene to another level," maintains Bloch. "They were the first band to get the energy going in the club. They rocked your ass off all night long." Durkacz, who first booked the quartet, adds: "Somebody encouraged me to go to this restaurant, Papolini's, to check out Blues Traveler. There were only fifteen people there, but as soon as I saw them I knew this was going to be our house band." John Dwork contributes this recollection: "I remember seeing a Blues Traveler show where the band played for about five hours. Their final set just seemed to start and end with 'Gloria.' At five o'clock in the morning, they came out for a fourth encore and did their two-minute version of 'Johnny B. Goode.' Then they all just fell down on stage, and everyone in the club did the same. People all just collapsed onto one another on the dirty floor. It was postorgasmic. The band truly played until they dropped, and everyone dropped with them." Says Gina Z.: "In particular, I can recall two distinct evenings from that era. The first was the night that we sat Indian-style on the floor during a Blues Traveler show until four in the morning, and John had us all do a sing-along. I also remember that the first night when Blues Traveler was on Letterman,

Larry invited everyone down, and we all watched the show from the middle of the venue. It was a very exciting moment."

During these early years, Blues Traveler was often joined on bills and on stage by the Spin Doctors. Many evenings ended with the two bands locked in a jam, and Joan Osborne often entered the fray as well. "We accelerated the booking of Spin Doctors," comments Bloch, "because in talking with the patrons and watching the band ourselves we saw what they could be. I can remember one night, a benefit show, when they performed three sets. During that final set, they really cut loose. It was just transporting."

During its first few years, the club played host to a number of notable bands. In one two-year period, from 1989 to 1990, Phish performed at Wetlands every two or three months. "Maybe three weeks after we opened," recalls Durkacz, "someone said there was this band in town playing at a frat party that might be right for the club. I went and saw Phish for the first time. They just blew me away. They were hilarious. So we started booking them. I think that they hold the record for the most people we ever put in Wetlands. It was holiday time, and everyone was so uncomfortable that we realized that we couldn't allow so many people into the club." Says Bloch: "From the start, it was obvious that Phish had great musicians and was surrounded by people who knew how to put on a great show. Another thing that I remember was that they had a strong resistance to being described as psychedelic. On a certain level, I found them to be the most psychedelic band ever to play the club. I used to describe them as psychedelic, and they hated it."

Several other remarkable events took place during those first years. "Buddy Miles would get up on stage and entertain people before a show or between sets," says Bloch. "It probably happened half a dozen times." Recalls Zahn: "Greg Allman performed down here one night after an Allman Brothers Band show. He gave Larry his stars-and-stripes top hat, and it was hanging in Larry's office for many years." Dwork reflects, "I'm partial to a handful of events, but my happiest was a three-day event on the twenty-fifth anniversary of the Trips Festival. On that first night, Ken Babbs came by for the first public showing of the 1964 bus trip [a film depiction of the Merry Pranksters aboard Furthur, as documented in Tom Wolfe's *Electric Kool-Aid Acid Test*]." Faber adds, "We first played there in the summer of 1989, opening for Traveler, which was the only way we could get in there, because we were friends with Traveler. Then, between 1991 and 1993, those were our big years — it was our home venue." Edwin Hurwitz remarks, "My most vivid memory from the stage may be the night that we [Shockra] brought Jon Fishman in to do a reading from the *Book of Information* that we were given by Sun Ra. I think it was that same night that both Mike Gordon and I got chicken pox."

As many of its early regular acts began moving on to larger spaces, Wetlands welcomed a new generation of bands. For instance, the club has hosted a number of memorable moe. gigs over the years — although Zahn admits that the first time moe. manager Jon Topper called, "the only reason I took it was because I thought it was John Popper. I think I fell for that five or six times." Says Chuck Garvey: "The nights when we were recording *Loaf* were a lot of fun. I can remember that [fellow moe. guitarist] Al [Schnier] started freaking out when he found out that the place had sold out and there were people outside who couldn't get in. He said, 'Do you think we should go outside and say something?' I mean, we all couldn't believe it." Garvey also relishes the Monkeys on Ecstasy gigs, remarking, "It's fun for us and for people who are really fired up to see us to be able to stand so close you can spit on the band. I would kill to see a lot of groups where I could walk up to them, yank on their pants, and say, 'Hey, play this song.'"

Another interesting moe. show took place on the sixth anniversary of Wetlands. Bloch remembers, "moe. was great, and they were willing to work with us to create some ideas that were really unique." On this particular evening, the club advertised: "Dress as a flower or a bee and get in for free." Recollects Szufarowski: "Everyone who walked in was given a name tag with some crazy phrase on it, and during the set breaks some people were called onto the stage to perform in accordance with that phrase. But a lot of the action took place with the bees. We told the bees to go around and pollinate the flowers in between sets. There were head bees and worker bees. Before the third set, we told the head bees to round up the worker bees, who had to collect the flowers that they had pollinated. The idea was to see which group had pollinated the most flowers. Of course, we picked a queen bee as well, gave her a microphone, and told her to orchestrate all of this from the stage. We had prizes for the groups with the most flowers. But the motivation behind all of this was that Larry decided that this would be a good way to get people to talk to one another."

Another intriguing event occurred on the club's seventh anniversary: Alien Night, featuring the music of Moon Boot Lover. "Before their final set," explains Szufarowski, "the band was kidnapped by an alien who worked for the club. Larry was DJing, and he started playing this ambient, dark music, while everyone was told that the band would remain kidnapped until the audience produced enough love to set them free. And eventually love did indeed conquer all to release Moon Boot Lover."

Reid Genauer has some vivid recollections of Strangefolk's performances at the club. "We fought tooth and nail to get in there. We played a number of gigs in the city knowing we were building to the

Wetlands. It was a destination in itself. But there was one time in the beginning when a friend told us that we were booked there and we weren't sure. We didn't want to look bad, so we kept calling the club anonymously to try to confirm. Finally, twenty-four hours before the gig, we learned that we were indeed playing." A few years later, the band headlined a Wetlands New Year's Eve show that ended long after the sun had risen. Reflects Genauer: "It was surreal. Talk about energy and interaction. There was a quality of energy that we've never seen before. By the end of the evening, there was this blissful, lethargic hum emanating throughout the room."

Looking back over the bands that have appeared at Wetlands, Zahn observes, "I think you can see the various eras of the club through the jam bands. First, we had the Blues Traveler/Spin Doctors era. A lot of those people have moved on and drifted away. Phish created some quirky jazzbo jam rock bands. Nowadays, I see many more MMW-style bands that bring together cool boho jazz and psychedelic jam sensibilities. Many more bands are flirting with some weird ethnic sounds. Also, bluegrass is making a remarkable comeback."

However, Bloch also emphasizes that "while the jam-band scene was the first scene that developed from the club it was not the only scene. There have been less familiar ones." Certainly, over the years Wetlands has hosted many other acts, among them Pearl Jam, Rage against the Machine, Ani Defranco, Midnight Oil, Steel Pulse, Counting Crows, Jeff Buckley, Fishbone, Ween, Sublime, Everclear, Sick of It All, Ben Harper, Suzanne Vega, Spacehog, Burning Spear, KRS-1, Run DMC, Henry Rollins, Lee "Scratch" Perry, and Oasis (says Bloch, "[Oasis] had their first New York City play in the club, and I was there during soundcheck, and it was just horrible. They brought in their organization to overrule the house engineer, and something just went wrong. It sounded horrible, but everyone was afraid to say anything. So I went up to their manager, and I told him, 'Listen, my sound engineer can correct the problem in five minutes.' One of the Gallagher brothers — I don't know which one — saw what was going on and jumped off that stage and started getting hostile with me. Of course, in my absence the adjustment was made").

In 1996, rumors began to spread about the impending demise of Wetlands. This speculation was unfounded and often perpetuated with malicious intent. Bloch, however, had decided to phase himself out of the club and move to New England in order to spend more time with his son. "I was never going to shut the club down," he recalls. "It just took a while to find someone who would be committed to the environmental aspects." Zahn was shaken: "It frightened me. Larry said, 'I'm going to stay here as long as I can.' There was a target date, but we passed it. For the most part, two types of people approached him — those with a lot of money and no vision, and those with vision but no money. And there were a lot of people who wanted the public to think the club was done. Whenever I got on the phone, people said, 'I heard you are closing,' or, 'Aren't you closed yet?'" Szufarowski adds, "Larry was good at seeing through people, because a lot of phonies came by talking about the vibe, but you could see that all they really cared about was the money. I thought, 'No one is going to meet Larry's demands.'"

However, later that year someone finally did: Peter Shapiro, a young filmmaker whose fascination with the music and culture of the Grateful Dead led him to create *And Miles to Go: On Tour with the Grateful Dead* while he was still a student at Northwestern University. After this, he served as associate producer of the documentary *Tie-Died*, and he directed "A Conversation with Ken Kesey," a segment appearing at the end of that film. Shapiro went on to make *American Road*, which he screened at the Sundance Film Festival; this work features footage shot over a period of thirty days in all parts of the contiguous United States, and it sets the action to Phish's "You Enjoy Myself."

While showing his films at Pennsylvania's Bloomsburg University, Shapiro learned of Bloch's desire to sell Wetlands. Recalls Shapiro, "I approached Larry, and I said, 'I believe in the place, and I want to see what can be done.'" At last Bloch thought that he had found someone to whom he could entrust the club, so he worked at his end to make it a financially viable deal. But much more important to Bloch than the fiscal aspects of the negotiations was Shapiro's commitment to perpetuate the environmental mission of Wetlands. Says Bloch: "The contract contained good, strong, positive language, which we as friends acknowledge. It was too precious to ride on a handshake. Pete is licensed to use the name in New York and elsewhere if he wants, but in all instances he is under a strict contract to maintain responsibilities toward the environment."

Zahn observes, "Pete just brought in a refreshing nature that has inspired me to look at things in a new light. He hadn't even finalized the deal yet when he came into this show with a water sprayer and just walked around the club asking people if they wanted a spritz. At first I didn't really understand what he was doing. But eventually he had covered the club three times over personally spritzing people. It was brilliant. No other club has a personal water spritzer."

During Shapiro's tenure, Wetlands has witnessed a number of notable gigs as well as a few changes. "One big decision we made," explains Zahn, "was to commit to live performances in the downstairs lounge. So we bought new furniture and a tap system along with a new PA. Of course, we don't have music down there every night of the week — some nights we keep it as a getaway zone. Also, we don't like competing music, so when there is a break upstairs we start downstairs."

It is clear, however, that the essence of the club remains intact. "A lot of people grew up at Wetlands," says Zahn. "They're members. I've talked to so many people who had their first drink, their first psychedelic experience, their first any number of things at the club. Larry was my mentor, and he was certainly inspired by Bill Graham. No one ever convinced him that he couldn't do something, no matter how bizarre, embarrassing, or original it was. Now it's time for the new millennium to take this club to new, insane, bizarre, incredible heights." Shapiro notes: "At this point, the club has a life of its own. What I've tried to do is let it breathe. With the passing of Jerry Garcia, places like Wetlands are more important. Kids are still curious about the values of the sixties, and they want to experience live music. We're trying to follow Larry's lead. Any night of the week, even when the club is nowhere near sold out, there still can be magic created in this room that will just overwhelm you."

Wetlands Preserve is open seven nights a week at 161 Hudson Street, New York, NY 10013. The club is located three blocks south of Canal Street near the Holland Tunnel. The main phone number is (212) 966-4225. The environmental and social justice center can be reached at (212) 966-5244. You can access the Wetlands Web page at www.wetlands-preserve.org

Larry Bloch currently runs Save the Corporations from Themselves, an environmental center that sells environmentally sustainable goods. It is located at 169 Main Street, Brattleboro, VT 05301.

APPENDIX C

ADDITIONAL RESOURCES:
Magazines and Music

The Homegrown Music Network. Lee Crumpton formed the Homegrown Music Network in 1995 to help promote the rising jam-band scene. The network sells and distributes more than one hundred recordings of the groups mentioned in this book (the Homegrown Music Catalog contains twenty pages of offerings). Homegrown has its own Web site, where you can find music samples, tour dates, and other information. The site also supplies installments of Crumpton's *Home Grown Radio*, which features music and interviews. Crumpton has produced a number of compilation CDs to showcase particular bands. His initial offering, *Homegrown* (1995), includes songs by Ominous Seapods, the Gibb Droll Band, and Agents of Good Roots. *Home Grown 2: Smoking Jams* (1996) collects live tracks from, among others, Percy Hill, Grinch, Day by the River, and Schleigho, along with studio cuts from Strangefolk and Boud Deun. *Homegrown 3: Organic Grooves* (1998) supplies live Jiggle the Handle, Juggling Suns, and Ominous Seapods, as well as songs from Calobo, Disco Biscuits, Foxtrot Zulu, and Karmic. The Homegrown Music Network may be contacted at P.O. Box 635, Bell Arthur, NC 27811-0635 (1-800-6LE-EWAY). Its Web site is located at www.versanet.com/homegrown

AWARE. Chicago's AWARE records also focuses on a number of bands that appear in this book (although, to be fair to the label and its lineup, it also concentrates on many groups that produce well-crafted music but do not incorporate extensive improvisation into their live shows). The label was started by Gregg Latterman in 1993 when he produced a compilation disc, *AWARE*, that brought together songs from a number of bands, including Acoustic Junction, Everything, Jupiter Coyote, and the Winebottles. The disc was so well received that Latterman soon expanded his operations, eventually becoming a full-service label. He has also continued to make compilations, and his most recent effort, *AWARE 5*, includes Blue Dogs and the Pat McGee Band. Additionally, AWARE manages the HORDE tour CD store. In 1995, the label launched its own tour; participants include several of the bands that appear in this book: Blue Dogs, the Gibb Droll Band, and the Pat McGee Band. The label may be contacted at P.O. Box 803817, Chicago, IL 60680-3817 (1-800-AWARE65). Its Web site is located at www.awaremusic.com

Relix. *Relix* is the longest continuously published magazine devoted to jam bands. It was launched in 1973 with the exclusive purpose of examining the music of the Grateful Dead — in fact, its original title was *Dead Relix*. However, the magazine has long since expanded its coverage to include a full range of groups, from those dominating the national scene to those "Too New to Be Known." Eight issues of *Relix* appear annually, each of which typically exceeds eighty pages in length. The $34 subscription rate includes a free twenty-word tape-trade ad. The magazine may be contacted at P.O. Box 94, Brooklyn, NY 11229. Its Web site is located at www.relix.com

Dupree's Diamond News. This magazine has explored the joys and nuances of improvisational music since it first appeared in 1987. As its title suggests, the publication initially focused on the music of the Grateful Dead (the name is a play on the Dead song "Dupree's Diamond Blues"). However, this quarterly publication has long dedicated itself to exploring all "mind-expanding music and the culture that surrounds it." *Dupree's* supplies more than seventy pages of such exploration in most every issue. A year's subscription costs $16 and includes a twenty-five-word tape-trade ad. The editorial offices may be reached at P.O. Box 936, Northampton, MA 01061.

Hittin' the Note. This quarterly magazine was first published in 1992, and it focused entirely on the Allman Brothers Band. It still provides in-depth coverage of the Brothers, but it also considers other jam bands, particularly those that hail from the South. Recent issues have exceeded seventy pages in length. Subscriptions are $21 a year. More information (and a sample issue) may be found at the Allman Brothers Band Web site (www.allmanbrothersband.com). Address all inquiries or subscription requests to *Hittin' the Note*, Kid Glove Enterprises, 2305 Vineville Avenue, Macon, GA 31204.

An Honest Tune. This quarterly publication was established in 1997 to document the activities of Widespread Panic. It has since expanded its ambit to include additional coverage of the improvisational music scene with a distinctive southern flavor. A yearly subscription to *An Honest Tune*, which costs $25, also includes eight issues of the glossy *Lingering Lead* newsletter, which provides timely Panic information. The publication may be contacted at P.O. Box 781018, Orlando, FL 32878-1018. Its Web site is located at www.anhonesttune.com

Fantastic Voyage System. This magazine is the brainchild of Paul Parietti, who has been its publisher since 1995. Every two months, Parietti and a growing number of "Live Music Addicts" contribute commentary on the latest releases and concerts by those bands that inhabit the "groovyfunkgalaxy." *Fantastic Voyage System* defines groove music at its most expansive. A year's subscription costs $18. The magazine may be contacted at P.O. Box 6126, Hoboken, NJ 07030. Its Web site is located at tapetrading.com/fvs

Signal to Noise. This publication, which emerged in 1997 as *Soundboard*, is devoted to "improvised and experimental music." Much of its coverage is jazz-oriented, although each issue also includes articles on some of the bands listed in this book. A year's subscription is $12 and includes a free compilation CD of the music of groups such as the Jazz Mandolin Project, the Gordon Stone Trio, and ViperHouse. *Signal to Noise* may be contacted at 492 U.S. Route 2, Suite #1, South Hero, VT 05486. Its Web site is located at www.sover.net/~asp/signaltonoise

Jam Bands. A companion to this book, www.jambands.com is a monthly on-line magazine that offers in-depth articles, regular features, columns, tour dates, Web links, and much more.

APPENDIX D

ZERO DEGREES OF SEPARATION

Zero Degrees of Separation is based on the popular principle commonly referred to as "six degrees of separation." The idea is that any person can be linked to any other person in the world through their mutual associations with five other people. Three college students made quite a name for themselves when they popularized a version of this game that orbited around Kevin Bacon. Well, Kevin Bacon is certainly a fine actor who also performs music as one-half of the Bacon Brothers. Still, he is by no means the musical dynamo that Zero is (go back and check out that band's entry). Zero is not only renowned for its improvisational skills, but it is also — and more importantly for the purposes of this game — an outfit whose members have played with many other musicians, both on stage and in the studio. In short, Zero makes an excellent subject for this game, titled Zero Degrees of Separation.

The goal of the game is to connect the band Zero to other musical artists. You must do this by linking any Zero member with another performer while bearing in mind that legitimate associations only occur when the musicians have played on stage with one another or when they have appeared together on a studio recording. An association is not legitimate if one band has merely performed on the same bill as another band (unless, of course, members of one group have sat in with members of the other).

You can turn the game into a competition by seeing who can link one artist to the other with the fewest moves. The ideal number is zero, thus the name of the game. For instance, the link between the band Zero and the Grateful Dead can be established with zero moves because Zero's Steve Kimock first performed with Jerry Garcia and later with the Other Ones. Of course, not every band has played with a member of Zero, so some associations will require a few more moves.

Here are a few more examples of how the game works.

Medeski, Martin and Wood: (1) Pete Sears played with Zero; (2) Pete Sears played with Leftover Salmon on *Euphoria*; (3) Leftover Salmon played with John Medeski on *Euphoria*.

Phish: same as above; then add (4) John Medeski played with Trey Anastasio on *Surrender to the Air* or MMW jammed with Phish on October 14, 1995.

Meatloaf: (1) Steve Kimock played with Vince Welnick in *Missing Man Formation*; (2) Vince Welnick toured with Todd Rundgren's band; (3) Todd Rundgren played on Meatloaf's *Bat out of Hell*.

Try these associations yourself: the Slip (hint — Oteil Burbridge has played with the Slip); Strangefolk; Kevin Bacon (hint — Jon Bon Jovi appears on the Bacon Brothers release).

Zero Degrees of Separation can occupy time during set breaks, road trips, even when you're alone and trying to keep yourself entertained. The ultimate feat would be to link all of the bands in this book to Zero.

PHOTO CREDITS

The author and publisher gratefully acknowledge the photographers, bands, and management companies that provided photos for this book. All photographs are property of their copyright holders, and should not be reproduced in any form. A list of photographers follows:

AGENTS OF GOOD ROOTS, Dave Krieger; ALLMAN BROTHERS BAND, Kirk West; AQUARIUM RESCUE UNIT, Thomas G. Smith; BIG HEAD TODD AND THE MONSTERS, Thomas G. Smith; BLACK CROWES, Chris Patras; BLUE MIRACLE, Tiffany Hill; BLUES TRAVELER, Thomas G. Smith; BOUD DEUN, Rob Gassi; CALOBO, December Carson; CONEHEAD BUDDHA, Mike Mario; COOL WATER CANYON, Bryan Perraud; THE DISCO BIS-CUITS, Josh Altman; DONNA THE BUFFALO, Rob "Gumby" Hillard; SHEL-LEY DOTY, Misao Mizuno; GIBB DROLL BAND, Zane Nashed; FAT MAMA, Dara Blumenheim; FIGHTING GRAVITY, Danny Clinch; FIJI MARINERS, Zane Nashed; BELA FLECK AND THE FLECKTONES, Rob "Gumby" Hillard; FOOL'S PROGRESS, Tony Baker; FREDDY JONES BAND, Thomas G. Smith; FROGWINGS, Kirk West; FROM GOOD HOMES, Thomas G. Smith; G. LOVE AND SPECIAL SAUCE, J. Tayloe Emery; GALACTIC, Chris Patras; GILA MONSTERS, Katie Dalsemer; GOD STREET WINE, Thomas G. Smith; GOV'T. MULE, Zane Nashed; GRAN TORINO, Bob Bayne; GUS-TER, Liz Linder; HEAVY WEATHER, Eric Diedrich; HOMUNCULUS, Melissa Scheetz; HOT TUNA, J. Tayloe Emery; CHARLIE HUNTER AND POUND FOR POUND, Chris Patras; HYPNOTIC CLAMBAKE, Thomas G. Smith; INASENSE, Clark Jones; SHERRI JACKSON BAND, Chris Patras; JAZZ MANDOLIN PROJECT, Chris Patras; JIGGLE THE HANDLE, Laura Lakeway; JUGGLING SUNS, Les Kipple; LEFTOVER SALMON, Thomas G. Smith; DAVE MATTHEWS BAND, Thomas G. Smith; MAX CREEK, Thomas G. Smith; EDWIN McCAIN BAND, Chris Patras; PAT McGEE BAND, Cath-erine Williams; MEDESKI, MARTIN AND WOOD, Chris Patras; MERRY DANKSTERS, Carol A. Wade; MIGHTY PURPLE, Bette Allen; moe., Chris Patras; DAVID NELSON BAND, Lisa Law; NEW BROWN HAT, Thomas G. Smith; OMINOUS SEAPODS, Thomas G. Smith; PHISH, Thomas G. Smith; RATDOG, Chris Patras; MICHAEL RAY AND THE COSMIC KREWE, Zane Nashed; RUSTED ROOT, Thomas G. Smith; SANTANA, Thomas G. Smith; MERL SAUNDERS AND THE RAINFOREST BAND, Chris Patras; SCREAMIN' CHEETAH WHEELIES, Thomas G. Smith; SISTER HAZEL, Sam Erickson; SISTER 7, Karen Moskowitz; SOUP, Cara Markowitz; SOUR-WOOD HONEY, S. Murrie; STIR FRIED, Rita Weigand; STRANGEFOLK, Thomas G. Smith; STRING CHEESE INCIDENT, Rob "Gumby" Hillard; THE TRAGICALLY HIP, Clemens Rikken; DEREK TRUCKS BAND, Zane Nashed; ULU, Joshua Silk; VIPERHOUSE, Matt Sharpe; WIDESPREAD PANIC, Chris Patras; ZERO, Chris Patras.